Study Guide With Practice Tests

David Hoaas   Harold Christensen

PRINCIPLES OF
ECONOMICS

Karl E. Case

Wellesley College

Ray C. Fair

Yale University

Prentice Hall, Englewood Cliffs, NJ 07632

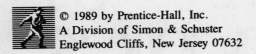 © 1989 by Prentice-Hall, Inc.
A Division of Simon & Schuster
Englewood Cliffs, New Jersey 07632

Printed in the United States of America

10 9 8 7 6 5 4 3 2

ISBN 0-13-223505-6

Prentice-Hall International (UK) Limited, *London*
Prentice-Hall of Australia Pty. Limited, *Sydney*
Prentice-Hall Canada Inc., *Toronto*
Prentice-Hall Hispanoamericana, S.A., *Mexico*
Prentice-Hall of India Private Limited, *New Delhi*
Prentice-Hall of Japan, Inc., *Tokyo*
Simon & Schuster Asia Pte. Ltd., *Singapore*
Editora Prentice-Hall do Brasil, Ltda., *Rio de Janeiro*

Contents

III. MACROECONOMICS

IV. INTERNATIONAL ECONOMICS

Foreword

This study guide is designed as a supplement to *Principles of Economics* by Chip Case and Ray Fair. It is important to emphasize that it is a supplement to the text and not a replacement for it. Students should not attempt to use this study guide in place of reading their textbook and attending class lectures. The instructor for the course in which this study guide is used can make suggestions as to the most effective way to use it.

Most students and instructors will admit that at first pass economics is a difficult subject. To learn the material presented takes time and patience. Experience has shown that an effective way to learn economics is to do economics. It is the purpose of this study guide to assist the student in doing economics. It will strive to accomplish this goal by providing the student with additional questions, problems and exercises that space limitations of the text do not allow.

For each chapter in the textbook there is a corresponding chapter in the study guide that reviews and tests upon the material presented in the text itself. Specifically each chapter of the study guide is divided into nine sections: 1) Learning Objectives, 2) Chapter Review, 3) Glossary, 4) Study Tips, 5) A Look Ahead, 6) Multiple-Choice Questions, 7) Analytic Exercises, 8) Essay Questions and 9) Answers. A brief comment on each of these sections will make their intent more apparent.

Learning Objectives: The first section of each chapter in this study guide provides an overview of the important ideas and issues discussed in the textbook. The student may want to survey this section of the study guide before reading each corresponding chapter in the textbook.

Chapter Review: This section provides a written summary of the important issues in the chapter. Due to the brevity of this section it must be re-emphasized that reading this section is not a substitute for reading the text. This section is a review for the student who has already read the appropriate chapter and wishes to refresh his or her memory concerning the key ideas.

Glossary: The discipline of economics has its own specific language. This section of the study guide helps the student learn the new terms and phases used in economics. This glossary should be used with the "Key Concepts" section found at the end of each chapter in the textbook. Not every "Key Concept" listed in the text is defined in this glossary, only some of the more important or often used terms are included.

Study Tips: This section presents study tips to make the student's study time more efficient. This section also points out common errors or potential sources of confusion that often arise in attempting to learn and remember important economic principles.

A Look Ahead: This section of the study guide has a two-fold purpose. Its first purpose is to relate the material presented in the specific chapter to the material presented in previous chapters. It describes how the new theory developed fits together with the material presented in the initial building of the economic model. Its second purpose is to foreshadow things to come. It describes where the material presented will again appear in later chapters. This will assist in understanding the relevance of the various models and diagrams developed.

Multiple-Choice Questions: This section of the study guide provides the first testing of the concepts learned in the relevant chapters. Each chapter will contain multiple choice questions which will test a student's knowledge of terms and concepts presented in the chapter. The level of difficulty of these questions should be comparable to what a student might find on an actual test for the course this text is being used for.

Analytic Exercises: The tools of mathematical analysis have become increasingly useful in the study of economics. This portion of the study guide contains exercises that often require the use of algebra or geometry to solve for a specific economic value. As the student will quickly learn, the use of graphs is one of the primary ways in which economists convey information.

Essay Questions: This section of the chapter differs from the previous section in that the answers to these exercises or questions cannot be quickly given by graphic or numerical analysis. There are problems that will require time and thought by the student to determine an answer. We suggest that the student write out answers to these problems and compare these answers with those of one's fellow students. In many cases these questions do not have one right or wrong answer.

Answers: This section will provide correct answers to the Multiple-Choice Questions as well as abbreviated answers to several of the Analytic Exercises. The students should consult this portion of the chapter only after they have attempted to work the questions and exercises.

Turn of the century economist Alfred Marshall has defined economics as, "a study of mankind in the ordinary business of life; it examines that part of individual and social action which is most closely connected with the attainment and with the use of the material requisites of well-being."[*] Marshall was quite right, we are all surrounded by economic occurrences. It is impossible to live in a capitalist economy and escape economic phenomenon. It is hoped that this study guide along with its parent text and classroom economics lectures will assist the student in better understand the workings of the economic system.

---

[*] Marshall, Alfred. *Principles of Economics*, ninth (variorum) edition. New York: The MacMillan Company, 1961, p. 1.

1
The Scope and Method of Economics

LEARNING OBJECTIVES

After you have studied this chapter in the textbook, attended class lectures over this material, and completed this study guide chapter you should be able to answer the following questions.

1. What is economics and why is it of interest to study?
2. What is the difference between microeconomics and macroeconomics and what areas are studied under each heading?
3. What is the distinction between positive and normative economics?
4. Why do economic theories and models require some abstraction from reality?
5. How does one graphically present material displayed in an economic schedule and how is the relation between two economic variables expressed?

CHAPTER REVIEW

This chapter begins the process of learning economics. Its purpose is to introduce the student to the meaning of economics as well as to define the scope of what economists study. Broadly speaking, economics is the study of how human beings and societies choose to use the scarce resources that nature and previous generations have provided. Economics asks the questions: what is produced, how is it produced, who gets it, why, is the result good or bad, can it be improved? In the industrialized world these questions are answered by the aid of the market mechanism. The purpose of this text is to analyze the market mechanism both at the level of individual economic units as well considering the simultaneous action of all economic units.

Two important concepts distinguish economics from other related fields. Whenever economists speak about the cost of an item or activity they are referring to the opportunity cost of that good or service.

1

Economists recognize that the full cost of making a specific choice includes what is given up by not making the next best alternative choice. The second key concept that distinguishes the economic way of thinking, from other ways of thinking, is its concern with marginalism. A concern with marginalism involves looking at the effects of extra units. For example the extra cost of producing another unit of output, the extra revenue from selling another unit of output, the extra amount of aggregate consumption that occurs when national income increases by one dollar. The extra amount of one variable that exists because of one more unit of another variable is the marginal of that variable.

For purposes of explanation the study of economics generally begins by separating the discipline into two halves. These two areas are called microeconomics and macroeconomics. Microeconomics is concerned with the activity of individual economics units, be they households, laborers, or firms. The other half of economics is called macroeconomics. Macroeconomics deals with aggregate economic activity or what is happening with the economy at the national level. Most students are familiar with the key variables in the macroeconomic economy simply by reading the daily newspaper. Macroeconomics concerns itself with topics such as inflation, unemployment and growth in the gross national product (GNP). Though the distinction presented here, as well as in many textbooks, makes the dividing line between the two subfields of economics very hard and fast, the distinction between microeconomics and macroeconomics is not that solid. Many macroeconomic events have microeconomic overtones and many microeconomic events have macroeconomic ramifications.

Economics attempts to be a positive science; that is, it attempts to present analysis of various situations in a value-free manner. The study of economics should describe what has happened or predict what will happen if a certain economic policy is undertaken. Economics attempts not to be a normative science; that is, economists are not to specify what ought to be. It is not the function of economics to prescribe what should be done.

To assist them, economists build models of particular economic theories. An economic theory is simply a statement of a certain relationship or relationships that exist between certain variables which have economic content. A formal statement, often in mathematical or graphical form, of any economic theory is referred to as a model. By nature an economic model is an abstraction from reality in that it ignores certain events. The abstractions, however, are necessary to determine the key elements which determine economic activity.

In building economic models economists often invoke the ceteris paribus assumption. This assumption involves holding certain variables constant while building an economic model. It does not mean that the variables are forgotten, only that they are not allowed to change in the initial building of the economic model.

Good economic theory is necessary so that good economic policy may be undertaken. Economic policy is the application of economic theories to the real world. When implementing economic policy one can measure the success of that policy on specific grounds. The objectives of economic policy fall under one of four headings: efficiency, equity, growth and stability. Which one of these objectives, or goals, is most important is a normative question.

GLOSSARY

ECONOMICS: The study of how human beings and societies choose to use the scarce resources that nature and previous generations have provided.

OPPORTUNITY COST: That which we forgo, or give up, when we make a choice or decision.

MICROECONOMICS: The branch of economics that deals with the functioning of individual industries and the behavior of individual decision-making units, that is, single businesses and households.

MACROECONOMICS: The branch of economics that examines the economic behavior of aggregates—income, employment, wages, taxes, output, prices, and so on—on a national scale.

POSITIVE ECONOMICS: An approach to economics that seeks to understand behavior and the operation of systems without making judgments. It describes what it is and how it works.

NORMATIVE ECONOMICS: An approach to economics that analyzes outcomes of economic behavior, evaluates them as good or bad, and may suggest improvements.

MODEL: The formal statement of a theory. Usually a mathematical statement, or series of such statements, of a relationship between two or more variables.

CETERIS PARIBUS: Literally, "all else being equal." Used to analyze the relationship between two variables while the values of other variables are held unchanged.

STUDY TIPS

1. At this point one should not become overwhelmed by the breath of economics. It is true that economics concerns itself with a wide range of diverse topics. It is also true, though, that a relatively small body of theory and a limited set of economic models explains very much.

2. The most important concept, and the one which will be seen over and over again, is the notion of opportunity cost. Opportunity cost plays a major role in both microeconomics and macroeconomics. The concept will be used repeatedly in this book, particularly in the first half of the book on microeconomics.

3. Since the primary model building tool of economists is graphic analysis, it is important that the student have a thorough understanding of the appendix to this chapter. The key concept here is the slope of a line or graph. As will be seen shortly the concept of marginalism and the slope of a line are very closely related.

A LOOK AHEAD

As has already been stated the concepts of marginalism and opportunity cost will be seen again very shortly. It can safely be said that most of the microeconomic section of this text can be traced back to marginalism or opportunity cost.

With respect to economic policy one will recall that an economic policy can be measured with respect to how it meets the criterion of being efficient, equitable, growth promoting or leading to stability. The student will notice how microeconomics versus macroeconomics considers one or more of these goals more important than another. Specifically the study of microeconomics is most concerned with the efficient allocation of resources. Macroeconomics is more concerned with stability and growth. Both subfields, however, often neglect a study of equity because it is a very normative area for economists to study.

MULTIPLE-CHOICE QUESTIONS

1. The statement that "Brand X is better than Brand Y," is an example of
   a. the ceteris paribus assumption.
   b. normative economics.
   c. positive economics.
   d. the market in action.
   e. equity.

2. Which of the following variables is not a concern of macroeconomics?
   a. The Consumer Price Index (CPI).
   b. Gross National Product (GNP).
   c. The rate of inflation.
   d. The rate of unemployment.
   e. The price of an individual movie ticket.

3. Which of the following expressions best describes the notion of opportunity cost?
   a. "A stitch in time saves nine."
   b. "A rolling stone gathers no moss."
   c. "There is no such thing as a free lunch."

d. "You can lead a horse to water but you can't make him drink."

e. "Red skies at night sailors delight, red skies in the morning sailors take warning."

4. What specialized field in economics studies the spatial arrangement of economic activity?

    a. Econometrics.

    b. Economic development.

    c. Industrial organization.

    d. Urban and regional economics.

    e. Public finance.

5. If an airline ticket from Atlanta to Washington D.C. costs $150 and an airline ticket from Atlanta to Washington D.C. to Boston costs $225, then the marginal cost of the flight from Washington D.C. to Boston is

    a. $150.

    b. $225.

    c. $50.

    d. 0.

    e. $75.

6. Which of the following is not an objective to measure economic policy against?

    a. Efficiency.

    b. Balanced Budget.

    c. Equity.

    d. Growth.

    e. Stability.

7. To conclude that what is true for a part is necessarily true for the whole is called

    a. the post hoc fallacy.

    b. ceteris paribus.

    c. the fallacy of composition.

    d. econometrics.

    e. correlation.

8. The change in a Y variable due to the change in an X variable is referred to as

    a. an average.

    b. slope.

    c. run over rise.

    d. calculus

    e. Murphy's law.

ANALYTIC EXERCISES

1. A positive relationship exists between two variables X and Y. That is, as X increases so does Y. Five combinations of X and Y exist as shown in the schedule below.

X	Y
1	4
2	6
3	8
4	10
5	12

a) Graphically show the relationship that exists for X and Y as specified in the schedule above.

b) What is the slope of the curve shown above between X = 3 and X = 4? What is the slope of the curve between X = 4 and X = 5?

2. An inverse relationship exists between two variables W and U. That is, as W increases U decreases. Five combinations of W and U exist as shown in the schedule below.

W	U
2	15
4	12
6	9
8	6
10	3

a) Graphically show the relationship that exists for W and U as shown in the schedule above.

b) What is the slope of the curve shown above between W = 4 and W = 6? What is the slope of the curve between W = 6 and W = 8?

3. For each of the following economic calculations specify whether it is a microeconomic or a macroeconomic concern.
   a) the determination of the price of a soft drink. *MICRO*
   b) the determination of the amount of investment in the entire economy. *MACRO*
   c) the level of unemployment. *MACRO*
   d) the determination of what job John R. Smith holds. *MICRO*
   e) the rate at which the economy grows. *MACRO*

ESSAY QUESTIONS

1. In our society single young adults date prior to becoming engaged or married. A typical date involves dinner, a movie, a sporting event or some other activity which may have to be paid for. Economists would argue that the cost of the date involves more than a financial transaction of paying for dinner and a movie. In terms of opportunity costs what is the full cost of going on a date?

2. What mistakes have been made in the following quotations?
   a) "I brushed my teeth prior to the last game the Boston Celtics lost. Since I want the Boston Celtics to win all the time I am never brushing my teeth again."
   b) "I have been feeling better since I began jogging two miles a day. Therefore if I jog 100 miles a day I will feel real good."

3. Economics attempts at all times to be a strictly positive science. Yet since it deals with human beings some would argue that normative components may enter into economics. What difficulties arise when a science such as economics becomes normative in nature?

ANSWERS

Multiple-Choice

1) b,	2) e,	3) c,	4) d,
5) e,	6) b,	7) c,	8) b.

Analytic Exercises

1) b. slope = 2 in both cases
2) b. slope = -3/2 in both cases
3)   a. microeconomic
     b. macroeconomic
     c. macroeconomic
     d. microeconomic
     e. macroeconomic

Scarcity and Choice: The Economic Problem

LEARNING OBJECTIVES

After you have studied this chapter in the textbook, attended class lectures over this material, and completed this study guide chapter you should be able to answer the following questions.

1. What is production and why does it take place?
2. What does it mean to say that goods are relatively scarce? Why don't we just say goods are scarce?
3. How does one measure the full or opportunity cost of any activity undertaken?
4. What is the production possibility frontier (ppf)?
5. Why is the production possibility frontier downward sloping and why does it have the particular shape that it does?
6. What is the law of diminishing returns and how is this law related to increasing opportunity costs?
7. What does it mean for a society to be inside of its production possibility frontier?
8. How does one solve the problem of determining what point along the production possibility frontier to produce?
9. What distinguishes a command economy from a laissez-faire market economy?

CHAPTER REVIEW

This chapter is really concerned with simply providing an extended definition of economics; economics studies the production process. Production involves transformimg resources into a form that meets consumers' desires and wishes. Once it has been decided what to produce, someone has to decide how to produce it and then who should receive the good once it has been produced. Analyzing this process is called economics.

As a group (or as is said in economics, in the aggregate) peoples' desires for goods and services are unlimited. The resources to produce these goods, however, are scarce. As such, resources are said to be relatively scarce. At full employment, to produce more of one good involves producing less of another good. Referring to the economic terminology that was learned in chapter 1, we say that there is an opportunity cost of producing any good. That opportunity cost is the benefit gained from the amount of another good that must be given up to produce more of the first good.

Economists use a graphic model to explain the notion of opportunity cost and relative scarcity. This model is called the production possibility frontier, or ppf for short. One example of this graphic model assumes we live in a world were only two goods are produced. These two goods may be consumption goods and capital goods. Furthermore, the model assumes that one resource is used to produce both goods. The frontier itself shows the maximum possible combination of the two goods that can be produced when society is fully employing all of its resources. Since the resources necessary to produce the two goods are relatively scarce, the ppf is downward sloping. The rate at which one good has to be given up to obtain more of a second good provides a measure of the opportunity cost of one good in terms of the other good. The special name given to this slope is the marginal rate of transformation (MRT). As additional units of one good are given up to get one more unit of the second good, the ppf generally becomes steeper and steeper. The opportunity cost of the second good will be rising with respect to the first good. This will occur because of diminishing returns to the factors or resources used to produce the two goods. Diminishing returns will be discussed in more depth later, but for now it is enough to understand that diminishing returns implies that the extra output produced by adding more of one factor to a given fixed factor will decline as the level of output increases.

When an economy is producing on its ppf, it is fully employing all of its resources. To produce a combination of goods outside of its current production possibility frontier an economy must experience economic growth. Economic growth involves obtaining more or better resources, through increases in technology. Economists are interested in more than just finding out when an economy is producing along its production possibility frontier. They are also interested in finding the specific point along the production possibility frontier where consumption and production take place for a particular society.

The point along an individual production possibility frontier which an economy wishes to be at is determined differently in different types of economies. In many countries it is determined by some central planning agency. This is the way in which many economic decisions are made in Soviet-Bloc countries. In other economies the decisions are made by the actions of laissez-faire free markets. In most economies, however, the method of economic decision making falls somewhere in between these two extremes. In the United States it falls closer to the market mechanism, yet the size of our government sector implies that a strong central authority is still directly or indirectly involved in many economic decisions. The book continues with a sorting out of how markets work and how government activity works to benefit market activity and how it works to hamper market activity.

GLOSSARY

PRODUCTION: The process by which resources are transformed into useful forms.

PRODUCTION POSSIBILITY FRONTIER: (PPF) A graph that shows all the combinations of goods and services that can be produced given the resources of a society and the existing state of technology.

MARGINAL RATE OF TRANSFORMATION: (MRT) The numerical value of the slope of the production possibilities function. The number of units of one kind of good you can get by giving up one unit of another kind of good.

LAW OF DIMINISHING RETURNS: The observation that when additional units of a variable input are added to fixed inputs after a certain point, the additional product of a unit of the added variable input declines.

COMMAND ECONOMY: An economy in which the state makes most economic decisions. That is, the central government decides what gets produced, when, and for whom.

LAISSEZ-FAIRE ECONOMY: Literally from the French: "allow them to do." An economy in which individual people and firms pursue their own self-interests without any interference or direction by government. The free market operates entirely without restraint.

CONSUMER SOVEREIGNTY: The idea that consumers ultimately dictate what will be produced (or not produced) by choosing what to purchase (and what not to purchase).

STUDY TIPS

1. This chapter introduces the first use of marginal analysis. The student must not become intimidated by the use of the term or phrase Marginal Rate of Transformation (MRT). This is simply the change in the amount of one good that must be made in order to obtain more of another good. If the concept of marginalism is learned in the early chapters of the text, the later chapters will be much easier.

2. Since resources are relatively scare, individuals cannot have as much of everything as they want. To get more of one good they must sacrifice units of another good. The benefit of alternative goods they must give up is the opportunity cost of the choice they made. It is essential to remember that in economics all costs are measured as opportunity costs.

A LOOK AHEAD

Economic models abstract from reality. They do this, however, to provide intuition as to how an economy operates. In later chapters we will discuss the formal models economists build to provide this intuition. Specifically, the presentation will center around how markets can answer or address the fundamental questions of economics. In the next chapter, however, slightly different concerns are addressed. The world that economics attempts to model is discussed in some detail. This discussion includes both the private (household and business) sector and the government sector.

MULTIPLE-CHOICE QUESTIONS

1. The process of transforming resources into useful products that consumers desire is called
   a. distribution.
   b. production.
   c. consumer sovereignty.
   d. macroeconomics.
   e. stability.

2. An economy that is producing inside of its production possibility frontier is said to be experiencing
   a. inflation.
   b. a recession.
   c. a deficit.
   d. unemployment.
   e. equilibrium.

3. The law of diminishing returns specifies that as more of a variable input is added to a fixed input the return to the variable input will eventually
   a. decline.
   b. increase at a decreasing rate.
   c. increase.
   d. remain constant.
   e. be negative.

4. The economy of the United States is most correctly described as
   a. a command economy.
   b. a laissez-faire, free-market economy.
   c. a mixed economy.
   d. a communist regime.
   e. a traditional economy.

5. The amount of one good forgone to receive more of another good is referred to as
   a. diminishing returns.
   b. the distribution of wealth.
   c. an opportunity cost.
   d. taxation.
   e. capitalism.

6. In order for an economy to produce at a point beyond its production possibility frontier, what has to happen in the economy?
   a. A recession.
   b. A zero percent rate of inflation.
   c. Central planning.
   d. Production.
   e. Economic Growth.

ANALYTIC EXERCISES

1. The law of diminishing returns and its analog increasing opportunity costs in production says that the production possibility curve will be convex or bowed out (the MRT will be increasing as one moves along the curve). Graphically present a production possibility curve that is linear (a straight line though downward-sloping). Do diminishing returns and increasing opportunity costs exist for this particular society?

2. Increases in technology will shift a production possibility frontier outward. In essence increases in technology will act just as an increase in resources, or what was called economic growth. Assume that the two goods produced by the society under consideration are capital goods and consumption goods. What would be the effect on the production possibility frontier if an increase in technology could only be used in the production of consumption goods? Of capital goods?

ESSAY QUESTIONS

1. Are things like pollution and crime relatively scarce? If they are not, why not?

2. If a student plays her stereo at the loudest volume possible in her dorm room, is the only opportunity cost of this activity the fact that later in life she will have to sacrifice good hearing?

3. Consider an economy that produces only capital goods and consumption goods. If that economy is fully employing its resources, it will be somewhere along the production possibility frontier, but we yet do not know exactly where. What type of economy would produce mostly consumption goods? What type of economy would produce mostly capital goods?

4. The United States economy is often referred to as a mixed economy; it has elements of both a command a and laissez-faire system. Consider the United States Postal Service, is it part of the command or Laissez-faire element of the United States economy?

ANSWERS

Multiple-Choice

1) b, 2) d, 3) a,
4) c, 5) c, 6) e.

Analytic Exercises

1) the economy is experiencing constant returns to the variable factor
2) the shift in the ppf will be skewed outward from the axis where the technology is effective

3

The Basic Structure of the U.S. Economy

LEARNING OBJECTIVES

After you have studied this chapter in the textbook, attended class lectures over this material, and completed this study guide chapter you should be able to answer the following questions.

1. What distinguishes the three forms of legal organization of business, proprietorship, partnership and corporations?
2. What is a perfectly competitive market?
3. What is a monopoly market?
4. What is a monopolistically competitive market?
5. What is an oligopolistic market?
6. How competitive is the United States economy and how has its competitive structure changed over time?
7. How large is the public sector and specifically what types of spending or production are carried out by the various levels of government?
8. In what ways do federal, state and local governments raise revenues?
9. [from the appendix] What is a balance sheet and what information does it convey about the financial condition of a firm?
10. [from the appendix] What is an income statement and what information does it convey about the financial condition of a firm?

CHAPTER REVIEW

This chapter describes the institutional structure of the United States economy in more detail. The U.S. economy is comprised of two major sectors: a private sector and a public sector. The private sector is made up of privately owned firms that exist to make a profit and of individual households. What defines the private sector is independent ownership and control of resources. The public sector is federal, state and local government.

In the private sector the majority of firms are organized to make a profit. In these profit maximizing firms organization takes place in one of three ways: by proprietorship, by partnership, or by means of a corporation. A proprietorship is a firm owned by one person. That person receives the profit for that firm, pays the taxes of the firm and assumes any debt liability of the firm. When two or more people agree to share responsibility for a business, they form a partnership. In a partnership there is no limit to the liability of the owners, as is true with the proprietorship. The difference is that each partner is jointly and separately liable for all the debts of the partnership. A corporation is a legal entity that exists separately from those who establish it and those who own it. When a corporation is formed, shares of stock are issued and either sold or assigned. A corporation is owned by its shareholders, who are in a sense partners in the success or failure of the firm. The liability of the shareholders, however, is limited to the amount they paid for the stock. If the company goes out of business or becomes bankrupt, the shareholders may lose what they have invested, but no more than that. The drawback to corporations is that the federal government and all but four states levy special taxes on corporations.

The term industry is used loosely to refer to groups of firms that produce the same or similar products. How firms within an industry behave depends on how that industry is organized. In the United States economists have categorized industries into four different types. At one end of the spectrum is the perfectly competitive industry in which many relatively small firms produce nearly identical products. In this form of industry no single firm has any control over prices. Price is determined by market forces and virtually unaffected by the decisions of any single firm.

At the other end of the spectrum is the monopoly, an industry in which only one firm produces a product for which there are no close substitutes. In this form of industry, subject to market constraints, the firm can set its price. In order for a monopoly to remain a monopoly, there must be some barrier to entry, some way to keep other firms from entering its market.

Somewhere between these two extremes, though falling closer to perfect competition, is the monopolistically competitive industry. A monopolistically competitive industry is one in which many firms compete for essentially the same customers, but each firm produces a slightly different or differentiated product. In monopolistically competitive industries there is both price and quality competition. Individual firms produce unique products and thus, despite their small size, exercise some control over price.

Finally, an industry in which there are only a small number of firms is called an oligopoly. In some oligopolies firms differentiate their products and in others they do not. Individual firms do exercise control over prices and generally behave strategically with respect to one another.

To understand the workings of any economic system, it is necessary to understand the role of the government in the private and public sectors. Government spending can be divided into three categories: purchases of goods and services, transfer payments to households and interest payments. Purchases of goods and services make up that portion of national output that the government actually uses or consumes directly. Transfer payments are cash payments made directly to households. Interest payments are also cash payments, but they are paid to those who own government bonds. Taken together, transfer payments and interest payments account for nearly the entire increase in government expenditure since 1960.

The government generates revenue through taxation to carry out spending. The largest single source of tax revenue is the individual income tax. An additional revenue source is social insurance taxes that are levied at a flat rate on wages and salaries up to a maximum amount. Corporate income taxes are levied on the profits of corporations only, not on the profits of other forms of business organization, such as proprietorships or partnerships. These three taxes are not the sole source of revenue for the government but they make up over 90 percent of the federal revenue total.

GLOSSARY

PROPRIETORSHIP: A form of business organization in which a person simply sets up to provide goods or services at a profit. In a proprietorship, the proprietor, or owner, is the firm. The assets and liabilities of the firm are the owner's assets and liabilities without limit.

PARTNERSHIP: A form of business organization in which there is more than one proprietor. The owners are responsible jointly and separately for the firm's obligations.

CORPORATION: A form of business organization resting on a legal charter that establishes the corporation as an entity separate from its owners. Owners hold shares and are liable for the firm's debts only up to the limit of their investment, or share in the firm.

PERFECT COMPETITION: An industry structure (or market organization) in which there are many firms, each relatively small for their industry, producing virtually identical products and in which no firm has any control over prices but takes price as given. In perfectly competitive industries, new competitors can freely enter and exit the market.

MONOPOLY: An industry structure (or market organization) in which there is only one large firm that produces a product for which there are no close substitutes. Monopolists can set prices although they are subject to some market discipline. For a monopoly to continue to exist something must prevent potential competitors from entering and competing for profits.

MONOPOLISTIC COMPETITION: The most common form of industry (market) structure in the United States. Characterized by a large number of firms, no one of which can influence market price by virtue of the size alone. Some degree of market power is achieved by firms producing differentiated products. New firms can exit such an industry with ease.

OLIGOPOLY: An industry structure (or market organization) with a small number of (usually) large firms producing products that range from highly differentiated (automobiles) to standardized (steel). One huge firm may dominate or a few large firms may share market power. Firm behavior in an oligopoly varies from monopolistic to highly competitive. In general, entry of new firms into an oligopolistic industry is difficult but possible.

GROSS NATIONAL PRODUCT (GNP): The total market value of all final goods and services produced within a given period by factors of production owned by the country's citizens.

GROSS DOMESTIC PRODUCT (GDP): The total market value of all final goods and services produced within a given period of time by factors of production located within the country regardless of who owns them.

BALANCE SHEET: An overall account of an organization's financial status, showing what it has, what it owes, and what it is worth at any given point in time.

INCOME STATEMENT: A statement of an organization's revenues and costs from its activities over an operation cycle, usually a year.

STUDY TIPS

1. The defining characteristics of proprietorships, partnerships and corporations are not grounded in economic theory but the legal system. Likewise the various types of industry structure, perfect competition, monopoly, monopolistic competition and oligopoly are not grounded in economic theory. What type of firm falls into each category is something that one will need to remember, as opposed to being able to derive the result from economic theory.

2. With respect to the macroeconomy one will also need to memorize the various forms of taxation and the relative importance of each form of taxation. On the spending side the exact amount of spending that takes place in the economy is an empirical question as opposed to one of economic theory.

A LOOK AHEAD

The topics from this chapter that will receive the most attention in later chapters are those dealing with industry or market structure. Specifically chapters 8, 9, 13 and 14 address various forms of market structure and the behavior of firms in those markets. Before that can be done, however, the most basic, yet possibly most useful, economic model must be built to study the economy. The first formalized model that this text will present is that concerned with what is called supply and demand analysis.

MULTIPLE-CHOICE QUESTIONS

1. The type of business organization with unlimited liability from debt for its owner(s) is
   a. partnership.
   b. corporation.
   c. proprietorship.
   d. both a and c.
   e. both b and c.

2. The soft drink market, which is characterized by many firms which produce a similar yet slightly differentiated product, is most likely in what type of market?
   a. Perfectly competitive.
   b. Monopolistically competitive.
   c. Oligopoly.
   d. Monopoly.
   e. Nationalized industry.

3. The form of federal taxation which raises the most revenue for the federal government is
   a. the state sales tax.
   b. social security taxes.
   c. the personal income tax.
   d. the corporate profit or income tax.
   e. inheritance taxes.

4. Since 1960 government expenditure has risen primarily because of an increase in
   a. transfer payments.
   b. interest payments.
   c. government purchase of goods and services.
   d. military expenditure.
   e. both a and b above.

5. The market for agricultural products is most likely in an industry which can be labeled as
   a. perfectly competitive.
   b. monopolistic.
   c. oligopolistic.
   d. monopolistically competitive.
   e. both b and d above.

6. A financial statement which takes a snapshot of a firm's economic status at a point in time is referred to as
   a. an income statement.
   b. an accounts receivable statement.

c. a balance sheet.
d. a cash flow statement.
e. a gross margin account.

ESSAY QUESTIONS

1. If shareholders in a corporation are limited in liability to the investment they make in the corporation, why don't husbands and wives pool their income and form a corporation?
2. A monopoly firm is a firm which has sole control of a product for which there are no close substitutes and there are strong barriers to entry into that industry. Provide an example of a monopoly firm. If an example cannot be found provide an example of a firm which is close to being a monopoly but not quite. Explain why the firm that is not quite a monopoly fails to be a monopoly.
3. The government sector purchases goods and services and as such can be thought of as a consumer. The government also provides services for other individuals which are purchased. This later function of the government gives it many characteristics of a firm. List several goods and services which the government provides for a price rather than through taxation.

ANSWERS

Multiple-Choice

1) d, 2) b, 3) c, 4) e,
5) a, 6) c.

Markets and Prices

4

LEARNING OBJECTIVES

After you have studied this chapter in the textbook, attended class lectures over this material, and completed this study guide chapter you should be able to answer the following questions.

1. What are the three basic economic questions that must be answered?
2. What distinguishes an input market from an output market?
3. How are a change in the quantity demanded and a shift in demand different?
4. What is the law of demand and why is it generally true?
5. What does the term "ceteris paribus" mean and how is it used in drawing a demand curve?
6. What is supply and what causes the supply curve to shift?
7. How does one obtain market demand and supply curves from individual demand and supply curves?
8. How do supply and demand interact to determine an equilibrium price and quantity?
9. In what instances does excess demand exist and in what instances does excess supply exist?
10. What shifts in supply and demand could cause either quantity sold or price to increase? To decrease?

CHAPTER REVIEW

All economies must solve the three basic economic problems of: what to produce, how to produce it, and for whom it shall be produced. This chapter builds a model which shows how these questions can be answered with the use of markets.

The amount of a good that a person wishes to consume is based on several factors: the income available to the consumer, the accumulated wealth of the individual, the price of the product, the prices of other products, tastes and preferences and the expectations of future events. It is often desirable to see how just one of these variables influences the amount of a good an individual wants to consume. To see this relationship economists invoke what they call the "ceteris paribus" condition which holds all but one of the variables (price) constant. The quantity demanded of a good is the amount of a product that a household would buy each period if it could buy all it wants at the current market price. If one is able to list the quantities demanded of a good, at all alternative prices, we refer to this as a demand schedule. A graphic presentation of this same information is called a demand curve. It will generally be found that demand curves slope downward to the right; an inverse relationship exists between quantity demanded and the price of the good.

If we have a change in one of the determinants of demand that was originally held ceteris paribus, the demand curve will shift. For example, when an individual has an increase in income, the demand curve for a good the individual has a preference for will shift outward. The reverse will occur for a decrease in income. Goods that exhibit this property are referred to as normal goods. For some goods an increase in income causes the demand curve for that good to shift inward, while a decrease in income causes the demand curve to shift outward. These goods are referred to as inferior goods.

A change in income is not the only variable that causes the demand curve for a good to shift. Changes in the price of a related good can also cause the demand curve for a good to shift. If an increase (decrease) in the price of good x causes an increase (decrease) in the demand for good y the goods are substitutes. Not all goods are substitutes, some goods are complements. Goods z and t are complements if an increase (decrease) in the price of z causes a decrease (increase) in the demand for good t such as cars and gasoline.

In a study of the economy we should not look at just individual demand curves for a good but the market demand curve for that good. The market demand curve for a good is found by the horizontal summation of all the individual demand curves for the particular good in question. It is found by considering how much each individual wants at alternative prices and summing those quantities.

How much an individual firm wishes to provide or supply for the market is based on many things: the price of the product, costs of production including resource prices and technology. In considering supply, economists generally also invoke the ceteris paribus assumption. They do this by initially considering the amount a firm provides, the quantity supplied, as a function of the price of the good. If one lists the various quantities supplied at alternative prices one has obtained a supply schedule. The graphic representation of a firm's supply schedule is known as a supply curve. Generally a supply curve will be positively sloped; a direct relationship will exist between the quantity supplied of a good and the price of that good. If one of the variables originally held constant changes, the supply curve will shift. An increase in production costs or resource prices will shift the supply curve inward. To obtain the market supply curve from individual supply curves also involves a horizontal summation of all firms' individual supply curves for a product.

One of the most important reasons to study supply and demand is to determine a point where the goals and wishes of firms equal the goals and wishes of consumers. This point is referred to as an equilibrium point for a market. This point can be found at a place where the quantity supplied of a good is equal to the quantity demanded of that good. Graphically this point is the point where the market supply curve intersects the market demand curve. Any shift in demand or supply will cause a change in the equilibrium price and quantity.

GLOSSARY

QUANTITY DEMANDED: The amount of a product that a household would buy in a given period if it could buy all it wanted at the current price.

DEMAND CURVE: A graph illustrating the data in a demand schedule--that is, how much households will buy of a good or service at different prices.

NORMAL GOOD: A good for which demand goes up when income is higher and for which demand goes down when income is lower.

INFERIOR GOOD: A good for which demand goes down when income goes up.

SUBSTITUTES: Goods for which an increase in the price of one increases the demand for the other.

COMPLEMENTS: Goods for which an increase in the price of one decreases the demand for the other.

SUPPLY CURVE: A graph illustrating the data in a supply schedule --that is, the quantity of a product that firms will supply at different prices.

EQUILIBRIUM: The condition in which the quantity supplied and quantity demanded are equal. The price at which this happens is the **equilibrium price**.

STUDY TIPS

1. One of the most important things to remember and one of the areas where mistakes are often made is in confusing changes in quantity demanded and shifts in the demand curve. A change in the quantity demanded comes about because of a change in the price of a good or refers to a movement along the demand curve. A shift in the demand curve is caused by a change in a variable originally held ceteris paribus. The variables that shift the demand curve are income, wealth, the price of related goods, expectations, tastes and preferences.

2. It is also important to remember the difference between a change in the quantity supplied and a change or shift in the supply curve. A change in the quantity supplied occurs because of a change in the price of the good in question. This constitutes a movement along a supply curve. A shift in supply occurs because of a change in a variable originally held ceteris paribus such as production costs, resource prices and technology.

3. Movements in supply and demand occur for different reasons. The factors that shift demand are different from the factors that shift supply. It is generally true that shifts in demand do not shift supply and vice versa.

4. It is better to think of graphic shifts in supply and demand as outward and inward movements or leftward and rightward as opposed to upward and downward. This is particularly true when one considers movements in the supply curve. Many students mistakenly say a leftward movement in supply is an increase in supply because it looks like the curve is moving upward. This, however, is incorrect. A leftward shift in supply is a decrease in supply. The same visual problem exists for increases in supply which are rightward movements in the supply curve.

A LOOK AHEAD

This chapter may well be the most important chapter in the study of microeconomics. This chapter has laid the groundwork for the supply and demand models which are so often used in economic analysis. This model will be built upon and expanded in the next few chapters. So far we have been discussing movements along and shifts in supply and demand curves. We have been doing this, however, only in terms of directions of change, (i.e., has quantity and/or price gone up or down?). In chapter five we begin to quantify those movements. We do this with a new concept called elasticity.

In chapters six, eight and nine we step directly behind the demand and supply curves developed in this chapter. Chapter five will explain how consumer preferences and satisfaction from a good determine consumers' willingness to pay for that good. Willingness to pay for a good constitutes demand for a good. Chapters eight and nine undertake a similar strain of analysis for the firm or supply side of the market. In these chapters costs of production and their determination of supply are considered.

In this chapter, and chapters five through nine, the markets under consideration have primarily been output markets. As we know there are also very active markets for resources which are called input markets. Chapters ten and eleven apply the supply and demand model developed in this chapter to the input markets of labor, capital and land.

MULTIPLE-CHOICE QUESTIONS

1. The law of supply states that:
   a. price and quantity supplied are inversely related.
   b. price and quantity supplied are positively (directly) related.
   c. the higher the price the smaller the quantity that will be sold.
   d. price and quantity demanded are positively (directly) related.
   e. the higher the price of a good the greater the shift in supply.

2. Equilibrium occurs in a market
   a. when the quantity supplied is its greatest amount over the quantity demanded.
   b. anytime a consumer is on the market demand curve.
   c. when the quantity supplied equals the quantity demanded.
   d. when the quantity demanded exceeds the quantity supplied by the greatest amount.
   e. when the price of the good is zero and unchanged.

3. Consider the market for agricultural products. If the price of fertilizer decreases, then one can expect
   a. the supply of agricultural products to increase.
   b. the supply of agricultural products to decrease.
   c. the demand for agricultural products to decrease.
   d. the demand for agricultural products to increase.
   e. the price of agricultural products to increase.

4. Which of the following events will not shift the demand curve for American automobiles?
   a. An increase in consumer income.
   b. A reduction in the price of steel used to produce American automobiles.
   c. A decrease in the price of Japanese automobiles.
   d. A reduction in the price of gasoline.
   e. All of the events listed will shift the demand for American automobiles.

5. Assume the demand for beer is downward sloping. An increase in price from $3 a six-pack to $4 a six-pack
   a. will cause the demand curve to shift inward.
   b. will cause a smaller quantity of beer to be demanded.
   c. will cause a larger quantity of beer to be demanded.
   d. could have been caused by a decrease in the quantity of beer supplied.
   e. will have no effect on the quantity of beer demanded.

6. When an economist states that the demand for a product has increased, he or she means that
   a. the demand curve for the product has shifted to the left.
   b. the price has increased and consumers will therefore purchase less of the product.
   c. the product is a normal good.
   d. consumers are willing and able to purchase more at any given price.
   e. the product has very few substitutes.

7. If the price of good w falls and the demand for good u falls as a result of this, then the two goods are most likely
   a. expensive.
   b. normal goods.

c. inferior goods.

d. substitutes.

e. complements.

8. Given a downward sloping demand curve and a positively sloped supply curve, what will happen to the market equilibrium price and quantity if the supply curve for the good in question shifts outward?

   a. Quantity will increase and price will increase.

   b. Quantity will decrease and price will decrease.

   c. Quantity will increase and price will decrease.

   d. Quantity will decrease and price will increase.

   e. The price of the good will fall to zero.

9. If excess demand for a product exists, then

   a. the supply curve will shift outward to meet that demand.

   b. the price of the good must fall.

   c. demand must shift inward to prevent inflation.

   d. equilibrium has been reached.

   e. the price of the good must rise.

10. The law of demand states that

   a. demand creates its own supply.

   b. a positive relationship exists between the quantity demanded of a good and its price.

   c. a direct relationship exists between the quantity supplied of a good and its price.

   d. the quantity demanded of a good will increase as the price of that good falls.

   e. the higher the price of a good the further the demand curve for that good will shift out.

ANALYTIC EXERCISES

1. The market supply and demand schedules for mango fruit are as follows:

Quantity Demanded	Price	Quantity Supplied
2	$8	14
4	$7	12
6	$6	10
8	$5	8
10	$4	6
12	$3	4
14	$2	2
16	$1	0

   a) What is the equilibrium price and quantity of mango fruit given the information presented above?

   b) Do both the law of demand and the law of supply hold for mango fruit?

   c) What situation exists at a price of $3? What will happen in this market if the price is $3?

2. Graph the market supply and demand curves for mango fruit according to the schedules given in problem one above. Be certain to clearly label where the market equilibrium price and quantity are.

3. Consider the two different mystery goods described below. Graphically show the two market equilibrium situations and described and attempt to give a real life example of each one of the goods.

   a) The market demand curve intersects the market supply curve along the horizontal quantity axis.

   b) The market demand curve intersects the market supply curve along the vertical price axis.

4. Assume the market for wing-back chairs can be represented by a downward sloping demand curve and a positively sloped supply curve. If there is a simultaneous increase in the demand and supply of wing-back chairs what will happen to the equilibrium price and quantity of wing-back chairs? Answer this question by graphically showing an initial equilibrium situation in the market followed by the increase in both the supply and demand for wing-back chairs. Does it at all matter that the magnitude of the shift in supply is relative to the shift in demand?

ESSAY QUESTIONS

1. Consider the market for illegal drugs. Using the supply and demand model developed in this chapter explain how the price of illegal drugs and the quantity of illegal drugs traded is determined. What things are originally held constant when deriving the demand curve for illegal drugs besides income and the price of related goods such as alcohol? What things are held constant when drawing the supply curve for illegal drugs besides the resource costs of producing the drugs? What would happen to the price of drugs and the amount of drug use that took place if tougher penalties were imposed only on the individuals found using illegal drugs? What would happen to the price and use of drugs if tougher penalties were imposed on only the sellers of illegal drugs? What would happen to the price and use of illegal drugs if stiffer penalties were imposed on both the consumers and sellers of illegal drugs? Would lowering the price of alcohol be an effective way to reduce the use of illegal drugs in this country? What does economic theory tell us concerning this matter?

2. The author of this study-guide lives in a city where the downtown business district still has parking meters. For twenty-five cents an individual can park in a parking space for one hour. The author recently had to go to the downtown branch of his bank to secure a loan for his new home. To undertake the paperwork for a loan takes approximately one hour. The author had several quarters in his pocket and was ready to pay for his hour of parking. Upon arriving in the downtown area the author could find absolutely no parking spots even though he was ready to pay for his parking time. What does economic theory tell us has happened in this situation and what is an economic solution to this parking problem?

3. The demand for labor can generally be considered to be downward sloping. Firms wish to demand more laborers at lower prices (wages). The supply of labor can generally be thought of as being positively sloped. Individuals will work more at a higher price (wage). The United States Congress has recently considered increasing the minimum wage. What will be the effect of a higher minimum wage if Congress ends up setting that wage above the equilibrium wage for labor? What will be the effect if Congress ends up setting the minimum wage below the equilibrium wage for labor?

4. Water is absolutely necessary for life though in most cases it can be had for a very low price. Diamonds on the other hand are not necessary for life. An individual can go an entire life without owning a diamond, but the same person can go only a few days without consuming water. Diamonds, however, are very high priced and only consumed in limited quantities. To many people this occurrence seems to present a paradox, something essential to life has a lower value than something nonessential to life. Using the economic theory presented in this chapter explain why this situation exists.

ANSWERS

Multiple-Choice

1) b,	2) c,	3) a,	4) b,
5) b,	6) d,	7) d,	8) c,
9) e,	10) d.		

Analytic Exercises

1) **a.** equilibrium price = $5; equilibrium quantity = 8
   b. both laws hold
   c. excess demand, the price must rise
3) **a.** this is a free good such as water
   b. the market for this good does not exist such as the market for home computers in 1950
4) the equilibrium quantity will rise no matter what the magnitude in the shift in supply and demand, but unless we know the relative magnitude in the shift of the two curves we do not know if the equilibrium price went up, down or stayed the same

Supply and Demand

5

LEARNING OBJECTIVES

After you have studied this chapter in the textbook, attended class lectures over this material, and completed this study guide chapter you should be able to answer the following questions.

1. How does market price serve as a rationing device for goods and services?
2. Who actually bears the burden of a tax such as an excise tax, the consumers of the product or the firms which produce the product?
3. How is price elasticity of demand calculated? What is indicated by the magnitude of the coefficient?
4. How can the concept of elasticity of demand be used to predict what will happen to total revenue when the price of a good changes?
5. What helps to determine a good's price elasticity of demand?
6. How is income elasticity measured and what information does its numerical value provide?
7. How is cross-price elasticity of demand calculated and what information does its numerical value and sign provide?
8. What is price elasticity of supply and what factors make supply more or less elastic?

CHAPTER REVIEW

The price system performs two important and closely related functions for society. First, it provides an automatic mechanism for distributing scarce goods and services; it serves as a rationing device for allocating goods and services whenever the quantity demanded exceeds the quantity supplied. Second, the price system ultimately determines how resources are allocated among producers and what the final mix of outputs will be.

The basic logic of supply and demand analysis can be used to show the incidence or burden of a tax. Most will agree that the person or institution that initially pays a tax does not necessarily bear its burden. When a tax is imposed, whether on consumers or producers, there is a difference between the price consumers pay and the price producers receive. The increase in price to consumers plus the decrease in return per unit to producers equals the total amount of tax per unit of product. Producers and consumers share the burden of the tax. Consumers pay part of the tax in the form of higher prices; producers pay the rest of the tax in the form of lower net receipts. The relative size of the consumers' versus the producers' burden depends upon the shape of the demand curve and the shape of the supply curve.

Economists are interested not only in the direction of change in one variable due to a change of another variable, but they are also interested in the magnitude of that change. Economists commonly measure responsiveness to price or income using the concept of elasticity. Elasticity is a general measure that can be used to quantify many different relationships. If some variable, A, changes in response to changes in another variable, B, the elasticity of A with respect to B is equal to the percent change in A divided by the percent change in B. In economics we are interested in several types of elasticities. In this chapter four will be defined and discussed: price elasticity of demand, income elasticity, cross-price elasticity and elasticity of supply.

The most often calculated elasticity is the price elasticity of demand. This measures the responsiveness of quantities demanded to price changes, ceteris paribus. Numerically it is calculated by dividing the percentage change in quantity demanded by the percentage change in price that took place. If the law of demand holds for the good under consideration, that number will always be negative since quantity demanded and price move in opposite directions along a demand curve. If elasticity of demand is calculated and numerically it falls between 0 and -1 one says demand is inelastic. If the elasticity coefficient is equal to -1 demand is said to be unitary elastic. If the elasticity of demand is less than -1 demand is termed elastic. Two special elasticities exist for extreme values of the elasticity coefficient. If the elasticity coefficient is equal to zero demand is perfectly inelastic. Vertical demand curves are perfectly inelastic. If the elasticity of demand is equal to negative infinity, meaning there is a infinite quantity change for any change in price, demand is called perfectly elastic. Demand curves that are horizontal are perfectly elastic.

Income and cross-price elasticity can be used to measure the magnitude of the shift in a demand curve. Income elasticity measures the magnitude and direction of a shift in the demand curve due to a change in income ceteris paribus. Numerically it is calculated by dividing the percentage change in quantity demanded by the percentage change in income which caused that shift. If the income elasticity coefficient is a positive number it is known that the good in question is a normal good. If the income elasticity coefficient is negative the good in question is an inferior good.

If the price of a related good changes we can use a cross-price elasticity measure to determine if that good is a complement or a substitute. Numerically the cross-price elasticity is calculated by dividing the percentage change in the quantity demanded of one good by a percentage change in the price of a related good. If this number is positive the two goods are known to be substitutes. Alternatively, if the number is negative the two goods are know to be complements.

The final elasticity to mention is the price elasticity of supply. This measures the responsiveness of quantities supplied to changes in the price of the good. As all the other elasticities have been calculated this is found by dividing the percentage change in quantity supplied by the percentage change in price which caused that change. A particularly important supply elasticity that will be discussed in later chapters is the elasticity of labor supply.

GLOSSARY

ELASTICITY: Responsiveness. Used to quantify the response in one variable when another variable changes. The elasticity of A with respect to B is the percentage change in A divided by the percentage change in B.

PRICE ELASTICITY OF DEMAND: The ratio of the percentage change in quantity demanded to the percentage change in price.

INCOME ELASTICITY OF DEMAND: Measures the responsiveness of quantity demanded to a change in income.

CROSS-PRICE ELASTICITY OF DEMAND: A measure of the response in demand for one good to a change in the price of another good.

INFERIOR GOOD: Goods for which income elasticity is negative.

NORMAL GOOD: Goods for which income elasticity is positive.

SUBSTITUTES: Goods that can serve as a replacement one for the other; when the price of one increases, demand for the other goes up.

COMPLEMENTS: Goods that "go together"; when the demand for one goes up, the demand for the other also goes up.

ELASTICITY OF LABOR SUPPLY: A measure of the response of labor supplied to a change in the price of labor. Can be positive or negative.

STUDY TIPS

1. Common sense tells us that the economic unit which initially pays a tax is not necessarily the economic unit that bears the burden of that tax. Common sense, however, also attempts to tell us that firms always shift the burden of a tax toward the consumers who purchase that good or the laborers which produce the good. This second situation is the one in which our common sense goes awry. When taxes are imposed, whether on consumers or the firm, the burden of that tax is generally shared between the consumers and the firm. It can be seen that it is a shared burden because consumers pay a higher price for the good and because firms receive a lower per unit return for the good.

2. Several different types of elasticities have been discussed in this chapter. Initially it appears as if there are several different formulas that one would have to remember if they are to calculate various elasticity coefficients. In reality there are not that many formulas to remember because all of the elasticity formulas are basically the same. They all deal with a percentage change in quantity due to a percentage change in some other variable. Each formula has quantity changes, expressed in percent terms, in the numerator of the fraction and some other variable in the denominator of the fraction. Price elasticity of demand divides by the percentage change in the price of the good. Income elasticity divides by the percentage change in income. Cross-price elasticity divides by a percentage change in the price of a related good. Finally, price elasticity of supply is calculated exactly like the price elasticity of demand with the exception that the price changes occurring are supply price changes and the quantity affected is quantity supplied.

3. Remember that when considering price elasticity of demand and what specific elasticity of demand exists, a comparison is made to the number -1. Whether the elasticity coefficient is greater than, less than or equal to -1 determines whether demand is inelastic, elastic or unitary elastic. When considering income elasticities or cross-price elasticities the comparison is made to the number 0. Being greater than or less than zero determines if the calculated elasticity is positive or negative. Being a positive or negative elasticity distinguishes that good between being a normal or inferior good, or it distinguishes it as being a substitute or a complement of another good.

4. One of the most useful pieces of information that knowledge of a good's price elasticity of demand can convey is information about changes in total revenues resulting from changes in the price of a good. Given different elasticity values, an increase or decrease in price can affect a firm's total revenues or consumers' total expenditures differently. Unless something is known about a good's price elasticity of demand, an a priori statement cannot be made about the change in total revenue that will occur from a price increase or a price decrease.

A LOOK AHEAD

In this chapter the movements discussed in the previous chapter have been quantified. Changes in quantity demanded or changes in quantity supplied have been measured by price elasticities of demand and price elasticities of supply respectively. The extent of shifts in demand curves is measured by income elasticity and cross-price elasticity.

In later chapters, when the discussion is turned to the firm side of the market, we will return to a discussion of how different price changes affect a firm's total revenue. As we know from this chapter the elasticity of demand that exists for a market determines the direction of change of total revenue when a price change occurs. What will be seen in future chapters is that the elasticity of demand that a firm confronts depends upon the competition it faces from other firms. The higher the level of competition in any industry, the higher the elasticity of demand faced by any one firm. This discussion falls under the topic of market structure. Look for the concept of elasticity to return particularly when the discussion in the text turns to that of imperfect competition.

MULTIPLE-CHOICE QUESTIONS

1. If a ten percent reduction in price leads to a twenty-five percent increase in quantity demanded, then demand is said to be
   a. unitary elastic.
   b. perfectly elastic.
   c. elastic.
   d. inelastic.
   e. perfectly inelastic.

2. If price rises along the inelastic portion of a demand curve, then total revenues will surely
   a. rise.
   b. remain unchanged.
   c. fall.
   d. equal zero.
   e. it is impossible to tell without knowing the magnitude of   the change in price.

3. If I spend my entire income on beer no matter what the price of beer, what is my price elasticity of demand for beer?
   a. Relatively inelastic.
   b. Perfectly inelastic.
   c. Unitary elastic.
   d. Some value between 0 and -1.
   e. Zero.

4. If a 34 percent increase in income leads to a 23 percent decrease in the quantity demanded of widgets, ceteris paribus, then widgets must be
   a. a substitute for another good.
   b. inelastic.
   c. an inferior good.
   d. a normal good.
   e. luxury items.

5. If an increase in the price of good w leads to a decrease in the demand for good x, then the cross-price elasticity between w and x must be
   a. negative.
   b. a number between 0 and -1.
   c. -1.
   d. positive.
   e. inelastic.

6. If the price elasticity of demand is equal to -1.5 and price decreases by 20 percent, then
    a. quantity demanded will increase by 30 percent.
    b. total revenue will decrease.
    c. quantity demanded will decrease by 30 percent.
    d. quantity demanded will increase by 3 percent.
    e. total revenue will remain unchanged.

7. A perfectly elastic demand curve has an elasticity coefficient
    a. greater than -1.
    b. less than -1.
    c. equal to -1.
    d. zero.
    e. infinity.

8. The demand for a product is elastic if total consumer expenditures
    a. rise more than price rises as a percentage.
    b. fall when price falls.
    c. fall when price rises.
    d. remain constant as price rises.
    e. remain constant as price falls.

9. A linear demand curve
    a. is unitary elastic at all points along the curve.
    b. is inelastic in the upper portions of the curve.
    c. is elastic in the lower portions of the curve.
    d. is always inelastic.
    e. is none of the above.

10. Assume the elasticity of demand is equal to -.20. Given a 10 percent increase in price, there will occur a
    a. 20 percent increase in the quantity demanded.
    b. 20 percent decrease in the quantity demanded.
    c. 2 percent increase in the quantity demanded.
    d. 2 percent decrease in the quantity demanded.
    e. .2 percent decrease in the quantity demanded.

11. An inferior good or service is any good or service for which
    a. an increase in price causes an increase in the quantity demanded.
    b. a decrease in price causes an increase in demand.
    c. an increase in income causes a decrease in demand.
    d. a decrease in income causes a decrease in demand.
    e. none of the above.

12. If the demand curve for pogo sticks is downward sloping and the supply curve is positively sloping, who will bear the burden of an excise tax placed on the production of pogo sticks?
    a. All consumers of pogo sticks.
    b. The producers of pogo sticks.
    c. The consumers who purchase pogo sticks prior to its price decline.
    d. Firms and consumers will share the burden.
    e. The federal government which collects the tax.

ANALYTIC EXERCISES

1. Suppose Morgan Mundane, the world's greatest prognosticator, made the two statements reproduced below. Please evaluate the validity of Morg's two remarks.
   a) "At a price of $1 my good friend Bob Ley will demand 10 widgets. Likewise, at a price of $2 Bob will demand 5 widgets. Therefore, holding all other things constant, I can safely say that Bob has unitary (-1) price elasticity of demand."
   b) "Furthermore, if I hold the price of widgets constant at $1 and give Bob $10 more income he will increase his demand for widgets from 10 units to 20 units. That leads me directly to the conclusion that Bob's income elasticity of demand is equal to (1) as well."

2. Assume the market for sweatshirts embossed with your favorite sorority's initials can be depicted by a normally shaped supply curve and a perfectly inelastic demand curve. Show and explain who (the firm or the sorority sisters) would bear the burden of an excise tax if it were imposed on the firms that produce these sweatshirts.

3. The demand for tobacco from West Virginia can be characterized by a downward sloping linear demand curve. At a price of $8 the quantity demanded of tobacco will be 10 thousand pounds. If the price falls to $7 the quantity demanded of tobacco will rise to 20 thousand pounds. Between a price of $8 and a price of $7, what is the price elasticity of demand for tobacco? Will the price elasticity of demand always be this value?

4. If there is a single "all-important" commodity that absorbs all of an individual's income, what is its price elasticity of demand? What is its income elasticity of demand?

ESSAY QUESTIONS

1. Returning to the tobacco example from problem 3 above, near the end of the nineteenth century Ian Webb, a Welsh emigrant peasant farmer, formulated the law: "An early winter in West Virginia, by wiping out much of the tobacco crop, will certainly decrease the revenues of tobacco growers." Is farmer Webb's statement true or false, and why?

2. The textbook discusses two types of general elasticity measurements, point elasticity and arc elasticity. What is meant by each one of these terms and when is it appropriate to use an arc elasticity measurement and when is it appropriate to use a point elasticity measurement?

3. The Justice Department of the United States Government at times has brought legal action against firms which attempted to monopolize a particular industry. Monopoly status in an industry implies that one firm has sole control of an industry for which there are no close substitute goods. Describe a way in which the concept of cross-price elasticity could be used to determine if a firm had monopoly control of a market.

4. Explain why the elasticity of demand for goods tends to increase over time. Namely, why is the author of this study-guide very unresponsive to price when he is buying a new shirt on a business trip (since the airline lost his luggage) yet during the summer when he is restocking his wardrobe for the fall semester he is very responsive to price?

5. Explain why an elasticity of demand measure is needed. Why can responsiveness to price changes not be simply measured using the slope of the demand curve for a particular good?

ANSWERS

Multiple-Choice

1) c,   2) a,   3) c,   4) c,

5) a,   6) a,   7) e,   8) c,
9) e,   10) d,   11) c,   12) d.

Analytic Exercises

1) **a.** true
   b. uncertain, since the initial income level is unknown
2) the sorority sisters will bear the entire burden
3) -5
4) price elasticity of demand = -1; income elasticity of demand = 1

6

Household Behavior and Consumer Choice

LEARNING OBJECTIVES

After you have studied this chapter in the textbook, attended class lectures over this material, and completed this study guide chapter you should be able to answer the following questions.

1. What are the three basic decisions that every household must make?
2. What constraints do consumers face when they purchase goods and services?
3. Why do economists focus on marginal utility rather than total utility?
4. What is the law of diminishing marginal utility and why do economists generally believe that it exists for all goods and services purchased?
5. How can income be allocated between the consumption of various goods in a way that will maximize a consumer's satisfaction or utility?
6. Why do economists argue that in general demand curves are downward sloping?
7. What is consumer surplus and how does diminishing marginal utility lead to its existence?
8. How do individuals decide how much labor to supply and how much leisure to consume? In what instances will the supply of labor curve be backward bending (i.e., less labor will be supplied at a higher wage)?
9. [from the appendix] What is an indifference curve and what determines its slope?
10. [from the appendix] How can indifference curves and budget constraints be used to determine how consumers should allocate their income, between the consumption of various goods, in order to maximize their utility?

CHAPTER REVIEW

This chapter deals with households and the choices they make in both output markets and input markets. Every household must make three basic decisions: how much of each output to demand, how much labor to supply, and how much to spend today versus how much to save for the future.

When deciding how much of each good to consume a household or individual is faced with a budget constraint. This budget constraint specifies all the affordable combinations of goods and services that a consumer has the ability to purchase. The budget constraint is determined by an individual's income, wealth and the fixed prices for goods and services purchased. Though a consumer is faced with constraints, his or her ultimate choices are governed by their individual preferences and tastes. A good or service will be purchased by an individual if that good or service provides satisfaction. Economists have a very special term for satisfaction, they call it utility. More importantly one should consider the marginal utility derived from the consumption of a good or service. Marginal utility represents the extra satisfaction obtained from consuming one more unit of a particular good. For most goods the law of diminishing marginal utility is expected to hold. Simply stated, this specifies that the extra satisfaction obtained from the consumption of additional units of a good will decline.

Given a fixed budget constraint and two goods with diminishing marginal utility, one can determine the combination or bundle of those two goods that an individual should consume to maximize his or her utility. The point of utility maximization occurs where the marginal utility per dollar (MU_x/P_x) for each good is equal and the consumer has spent his or her entire income. If the consumer's income or the price of one of the goods changes, the consumer will have to reallocate his or her income to find a new point of utility maximization.

Given that diminishing marginal utility exists for most goods (along with certain other properties), it can be argued that demand curves are downward sloping. If the extra satisfaction from consuming extra units of a good declines, the price that people are willing to pay for additional units of that good consumed will also decline. Specifically, an inverse relationship will exist between price and the quantity demanded of a good (the law of demand).

It is usually the case that a consumer pays the same price for each and every unit of a good, though that consumer would be willing to pay more for the first few units consumed. Because of this pricing strategy an individual is said to have a willingness to pay for that good above and beyond what that consumer actually has to pay for a good. The amount by which this willingness to pay exceeds what is actually charged for a good is termed consumer surplus. Graphically it can be represented as the area below the demand curve and above the price of the good.

Individuals must also make decisions in input markets: they must decide how much to work or how much labor to supply. This choice, however, is very much like the choice made in output markets. The choice to work involves choosing between two goods, leisure and labor (labor generates income to purchase all other goods and services). Solving the utility maximization problem in the labor/leisure market, where the constraints are a fixed number of hours in a day or week, can show how a labor supply curve may be derived. A labor supply curve shows the quantity of labor supplied as a function of the wage rate. The shape of the labor supply curve depends on how households react to changes in the wage rate. In some instances portions of the labor supply curve may have a negative slope or be backward bending.

Households must make two other decisions: they must decide how much of present income to save for future spending and they must decide how much future income they will borrow to finance current consumption. In market economies these decisions are made in capital markets. Interest rates are what determine the rate at which trade-offs can be made between present consumption and future consumption. Higher interest rates mean that we sacrifice more future consumption when we spend today because any additional present consumption must be financed either by borrowing or by saving less. Higher interest rates tend to encourage saving and discourage borrowing. Lower interest rates do the opposite.

GLOSSARY

BUDGET CONSTRAINT: The limits imposed on household choices by income, wealth, and product prices. A line which separates those bundles of goods that are available to a household from those that are not.

UTILITY: The basis of choice. The satisfaction, or reward, a product yields. The intangible "worth" we find in things that enables us to compare and rank unlike things.

DIMINISHING MARGINAL UTILITY: The decrease in satisfaction found in a single unit of a product as more and more of it is consumed.

INCOME EFFECT: A measure of the proportionate change in consumption of a good due to a given proportionate improvement (reduction) in well-being caused by a price decrease (increase).

SUBSTITUTION EFFECT: An increase (decrease) in the consumption of a good due to a fall (rise) in its relative price.

CONSUMER SURPLUS: The difference between the maximum amount a person is willing to pay for a good and its current market price.

INTEREST RATE: The "price" that borrowers pay to lenders for the use of money; it provides a link between the money market and the goods market.

MARGINAL RATE OF SUBSTITUTION: The rate at which a person is willing to substitute X for Y. More formally, the ratio of the marginal utility derived from consuming good X to the marginal utility derived from good Y.

STUDY TIPS

1. The most essential concept in this chapter is that of marginal utility. One should remember that decisions are made at the margin, not on average and not by looking at total utilities. If the student understands the concept of marginal analysis it will simplify the learning of the material in the next few chapters. Marginal always refers to the extra amount of one variable that results from an extra amount of some other variable. Those students who have had a course in calculus will notice that calculating a marginal is the same as taking a first derivative.

2. The most important concept to remember in this chapter is referred to as the equimarginal condition. This condition determines the point of utility maximization for a consumer consuming two goods such as x and y. If consumers have spent all of their income they are in equilibrium when:

$$MU_x/P_x = MU_y/P_y$$

3. In words the condition stated above means the extra satisfaction obtained from spending the last dollar of income on x is just equal to the extra satisfaction obtained by spending the last dollar of income on good y. If this were not an equality, but an inequality, consumption of the good with a higher marginal utility per dollar should increase and consumption of the good with the lower marginal utility per dollar should decrease.

4. When studying labor supply you are really studying the demand for a good. That good is leisure. Since leisure is generally considered to be a normal good a higher wage will lead to a higher income which implies, according to the income effect, more leisure will be demanded. More leisure being demanded is the same as less labor being supplied.

A LOOK AHEAD

The next few chapters will be leaving the consumer or demand side of the market and be concentrating on the supply or firm side of the market. If the student understands the concept of marginal utility the next few chapters will be easier because these chapters also deal with marginals, though not marginal utility. Mathematically the concept of marginals is the same no matter what marginal variable is considered.

Firms base their decisions, on the production side, on marginal products of factors and the marginal cost of producing output. On the revenue side they base their decisions on the marginal revenue of output sold. As will be seen marginal analysis can be used to show the specific price and quantity that a firm, no matter what type of firm, wishes to produce at. In a market economy most firms decide to produce the level of output which maximizes that firm's profits.

MULTIPLE-CHOICE QUESTIONS

1. Suppose you conclude that you can increase your level of satisfaction by eating more yogurt and fewer burritos, then for you the marginal utility of the last dollar spent on yogurt is
   a. more than the marginal utility of the last dollar spent on burritos.
   b. less than the marginal utility of the last dollar spent on burritos.
   c. zero.
   d. positive and equal to the marginal utility of the last dollar spent on burritos.
   e. negative and equal to the marginal utility of the last dollar spent on burritos.

2. Suppose pizzas are free. Pizzas will then be consumed up until
   a. the total utility of pizzas becomes zero.
   b. the marginal utility of pizzas is maximized.
   c. the marginal utility of pizzas is minimized.
   d. the marginal utility of pizzas is zero.
   e. marginal utility is the same for all goods that are substitutes for pizza.

3. Stevey Student with a fixed budget constraint is purchasing two goods, x and y. In order to maximize his utility, he should purchase an amount of x and y such that
   a. the marginal utility of good x equals the marginal utility of good y.
   b. the marginal utility of both goods is equal to zero.
   c. the marginal utility of x divided by the price of x is equal to the marginal utility of y divided by the price of y.
   d. the marginal utility of both goods is maximized.
   e. he consumes only x and no y or only y and no x.

4. Marginal utility
   a. must always be positive.
   b. equals zero in all cases.
   c. is the additional utility derived from consuming an additional unit of a good.
   d. is equal to total utility divided by quantity consumed.
   e. all of the above.

5. When the price of a good falls, more of it is purchased because the good is *relatively cheaper*. This phenomenon is called
   a. the income effect.
   b. the Giffen effect.
   c. the law of one price.
   d. the substitution effect.
   e. the paradox of value.

6. In order for an individual's supply of labor curve to be backward bending
   a. the substitution effect of a wage change must be greater than and in the opposite direction from the income effect of that wage change.
   b. the substitution effect of the wage change must be in the same direction as the income effect of that wage change.
   c. the income effect of a wage change must be greater than and in the opposite direction from the substitution effect of that wage change.

d. leisure must be an inferior good.

e. workers must be irrational.

7. Which of the following is not responsible for determining whether the demand curve for a good is downward sloping?

   a. The income effect.

   b. The substitution effect.

   c. The price of related goods such as substitutes and complements.

   d. The law of diminishing marginal utility.

   e. All of the above are responsible for determining the slope of the demand curve.

8. If the demand curve for a good is downward sloping, what happens to the amount of consumer surplus as the price of the good falls?

   a. It increases.

   b. It decreases.

   c. Nothing happens.

   d. The change is indeterminant.

   e. It depends upon the elasticity of demand for the good.

ANALYTIC EXERCISES

1. Suppose Opus consumes only two goods, Anchovies (A) and Herring (H). Furthermore assume Opus has $15 dollars of income to spend, where the price of Anchovies is $2 and the price of Herring is $3. If Opus' marginal utility schedules are:

MU_A	$Q_{A,H}$	MU_H
10	1	18
8	2	12
6	3	9
5	4	6
3	5	3

   a) How many units of Anchovies and Herring should Opus purchase to maximize his satisfaction?

   b) How much total utility does Opus receive from the bundle selected above?

   c) How many units of both goods would be purchased if Opus' income and the prices of both goods doubled?

2. **a)** In terms of money, define the concept of consumer surplus and explain what causes consumer surplus to rise.

   b) Graphically show the consumer surplus for a linear demand curve and explain how it can be measured.

   c) Along a perfectly elastic demand curve does any consumer surplus exist?

3. Suppose nationally known radio personality Garrison Keilor consumes only Powdermilk Biscuits (PB) and beer from the Sidetrack Tap (B). The total utility Garrison receives from consuming these two goods is shown in the schedule below. Garrison makes $5.50 every week, working for National Public Radio (NPR), which he spends on the two goods. The price of one of those delicious Powdermilk Biscuits is 50 cents and the price of a cold frosty beer at the Sidetrack Tap is one dollar.

TU_{PM}	$Q_{PM,B}$	TU_B
6	1	8
11	2	14
15	3	18
18	4	20
20	5	20
21	6	18

a) How many Powdermilk Biscuits and beers from the Sidetrack Tap should Garrison consume in order to maximize his satisfaction?

b) How much total utility does Mr. Keilor receive from this combination of goods?

c) If NPR gives Garrison a 50 cent a week raise to increase his income to $6.00, how many units of both goods will he consume?

4. Assume John Hoaas has a choice of consuming Lutefisk (a delicious tasting preserved fish that Norwegians and gourmets eat during the holidays) or meatloaf. Under what circumstances will John specialize (eat only) in the consumption of Lutefisk?

5. [from the appendix] Consider the three sets of indifference curves described below. In each case a diminishing marginal rate of substitution does not exist for the two goods under consideration. For each of the situations describe the relationship that exists between x and y and the nature of preferences as we move along each indifference curve and as we move to higher indifference curves.

a) The indifference curves are vertical lines.

b) The indifference curves are horizontal lines.

c) The indifference curves form right angles.

ESSAY QUESTIONS

1. a) What constraints or limitations does a consumer face in seeking to maximize the total utility from his or her expenditure?

b) Express mathematically the condition for consumer equilibrium.

c) Explain the meaning of your answer to part (b) above.

2. Individuals can be thought to receive utility from income. This can either be directly or indirectly since income can be used to purchase goods that provide utility. In either case one can consider the marginal utility of income. This would be the extra satisfaction one obtains from having one more dollar of income. It is not unrealistic to believe that diminishing marginal utility, as for most goods, would exist for income. An extra dollar of income means more to a street person than to a millionaire.

   With this in mind, assume that you are a social planner whose only purpose is to maximize society's total utility through redistributing income with taxes and transfer payments. Further assume that there are only two classes of people in the world, the rich and the poor. How should income be redistributed between the rich and the poor to maximize an economy's satisfaction?

3. Some goods may have negative marginal utilities. What does it mean for a good to have a negative marginal utility? In voluntary exchange would a consumer ever knowingly purchase a good with a negative marginal utility to him or her? What would be an example of a good with negative marginal utility?

4. As the text argues, some individuals may have a backward bending supply of labor curve. At higher wage rates the quantity of labor they supply may actually fall. As was explained, a change in the wage rate causes the occurrence of both an income and a substitution effect. Generally

these effects work opposite of each other. Who is more likely to have a backward bending supply of labor curve, a street vendor with an income of a few thousand dollars a year or a neuro-surgeon with an income of several hundred thousand dollars a year?

5. Utility is not a measurable quantity though we discuss it as if it were in this chapter. This is done to obtain an intuitive understanding of the process of consumer choice. In place of utility, what is an alternative comparative measure of different individuals' satisfaction from goods and services?

ANSWERS

Multiple-Choice

1) a,   2) d,   3) c,   4) c,
5) d,   6) c,   7) c,   8) a.

Analytic Exercises

1) **a.** Anchovies = 3 units; Herring = 3 units
   b. 63 units of utility
   c. the same as in part a
2) **a.** willingness to pay above and beyond what is actually paid
   c. no
3) **a.** Biscuits = 5 units
      Beers = 3 units
   b. 38 units of utility
   c. one more biscuit since that is the only affordable good and it has positive marginal utility.
4) The marginal utility per dollar spent on Lutefisk is always greater than the marginal utility per dollar spent on meatloaf.
5) **a.** only good x increases utility, more of good y does not increase utility
   b. only good y increases utility, more of good x does not increase utility
   c. x and y must be consumed in fixed proportions to increase utility

The Firm: Organization, Profits and Production

7

LEARNING OBJECTIVES

After you have studied this chapter in the textbook, attended class lectures over this material, and completed this study guide chapter you should be able to answer the following questions.

1. What is a firm and what motivates it?
2. What does it mean to say the products of a perfectly competitive industry are homogeneous?
3. What is the distinction that exists between the short-run and the long-run for a firm?
4. How are a firm's profits determined?
5. What is a normal rate of return, or normal profit, and why is it included as part of total cost?
6. What is a production function?
7. How is marginal product calculated and how does it differ from average product?
8. What is the law of diminishing returns and why is it expected to hold for most firms in the short-run?

CHAPTER REVIEW

This chapter turns the discussion to the supply side of the market. Business firms purchase inputs in order to produce and sell outputs. They demand factors of production in input markets and they supply goods and services to output markets. A firm will come into existence whenever someone or some group of people decides to produce a good or service to meet a perceived demand. In most cases firms exist to make a profit. They engage in production because they can sell their product for more than it costs to produce it.

The simplest type of firm to analyze is one that exists in a perfectly competitive industry. As one will recall from chapter 3, the most important characteristic of a perfectly competitive industry is that no single firm has any control over prices. This characteristic follows from two important assumptions concerning perfectly competitive markets. First, a competitive industry is composed of many firms, each small relative to the size of the industry. Second, every firm in a perfectly competitive industry produces exactly the same product; the output of one firm cannot be distinguished from the output of the others. In perfect competition it is assumed that new firms can and do have free entry to and exit from the industry. The assumption of free entry implies that if firms in an industry are earning excessively high profits, new firms that seek to do the same thing are likely to spring up.

Firms in competitive industries must make several decisions in an attempt to reach their primary objective. Firms must decide: how much output to supply, how to produce that output, and how much of each input to demand. The answers to these questions will lead a firm to its primary objective of maximum profits. Profit is the difference between total revenues and total costs. Total revenue is equal to the number of units produced and sold times the price received per unit. Total costs include a normal return or normal profit for the owner of the firm and the opportunity cost of each factor of production.

A normal rate of profit, or return, is the rate that is just sufficient to keep owners or investors interested in the firm. When a firm earns positive economic profits, it is earning profit at a rate more than sufficient to retain the interest of investors. Economic profits are likely to attract new firms into an industry and cause existing firms to expand. When a firm suffers negative economic profits, that is, when it incurs economic losses, it is earning at a rate below that required to keep investors happy. Some firms may exit the industry; others will contract in size.

When considering firm behavior it is important to specify a time element in which the firm makes decisions. Time, however, in economics is not discrete or absolute. In economics a distinction is made between the short-run and the long-run. The short-run is defined as that period during which existing firms have some fixed factor of production; that is, the time period during which some factor locks them into their current scale of operations. New firms cannot enter an industry and existing firms cannot exit in the short-run. Firms may curtail operations, but they are still locked into some costs, even though they may be in the process of going out of business. In the long-run there are no fixed factors of production. Firms can plan for any output level they find desirable. New firms can start up operations, and existing firms can go out of business.

When a firm's relationship between inputs and outputs is expressed mathematically, it is called a production function. The item of interest when considering production functions is the marginal product of a factor. The marginal product is the additional output that is produced by hiring an additional unit of input, holding all other inputs constant. When one examines production functions he will notice an interesting phenomenon, that being the law of diminishing returns. The law of diminishing returns states that after a certain point, when additional units of a variable input are added to fixed inputs, the marginal product of the variable input declines. Note that what is being considered here is the marginal product of a factor and not its average product. Average product is the average amount produced by each unit of a variable factor. Average product follows marginal product, but it does not change as quickly. If marginal product is above average, the average rises; if marginal product is below average, the average falls. The point at which the average product reaches its maximum, the marginal product is equal to it.

GLOSSARY

FIRM: A person or group that transforms inputs or resources into an output. The primary producing units in a market economy.

REVENUE: Receipts from the sale of a product. P x Q.

NORMAL RATE OF RETURN, OR PROFIT: A rate of profit that is just sufficient to keep owners and investors satisfied; for relatively risk-free firms it should be the same as the interest rate on fixed-rate corporate bonds or on risk-free government bonds.

SHORT-RUN: The period of time for which two conditions hold; the firm is operating under a fixed scale (fixed factor) of production and firms can neither enter nor exit an industry.

LONG-RUN: That period of time for which there are no fixed factors of production. Firms can increase or decrease scale of operation and new firms can enter and existing firms can exit the industry.

PRODUCTION FUNCTION: The relationship between output and inputs--that is, how much output can be produced given a variety of combinations of capital and labor and other inputs.

MARGINAL PRODUCT: The additional output produced with the addition of one additional unit of input ceteris paribus.

LAW OF DIMINISHING RETURNS: The observation that when additional units of a variable input are added to fixed inputs after a certain point, the additional product of a unit of the added variable input declines.

STUDY TIPS

1. It is important to remember that the distinction between the short-run and the long-run is not measured by the passage of time but by the variability of factors. In calendar time the short-run may last only a matter of days for a street vendor but for an automobile production factory it may be a matter of years. The short-run long-run relationship is different for different firms. Furthermore, when answering an economic question one most know whether the period under consideration is the short-run or the long-run. In economic decision-making the short-run and long-run solution to problems may differ.

2. As has been stressed, the important thing to remember in economics is that decisions are made on the margin or through the use of marginal analysis. In this chapter the appropriate area of interest is a firm's marginal product. The marginal product of a variable factor is the *extra* amount of output which that factor produces, holding all other factors constant.

3. One must remember the relationship that exists between a factor's marginal product and that same factor's average product. When the average product is rising the marginal product of that factor is greater than the average product. When a factor's average product is falling its marginal product is less than the average product. When the average product has reached its maximum it is equal to the marginal product.

A LOOK AHEAD

The discussion of perfectly competitive firms will be carried on in the next few chapters. Specifically a formal economic model of how perfectly competitive firms choose the level of output they wish to produce, both in the short and long-run, will be developed. The analysis will continue to use marginal techniques to solve the economic problems presented. New marginal concepts will be introduced. Included will be a discussion of marginal revenue, which is the change in total revenue due to the sale of one more unit of output. Marginal cost will also be discussed. Marginal cost is the change in total cost due to the production of an additional unit of output.

MULTIPLE-CHOICE QUESTIONS

1. If four workers produce 44 units of output and five workers produce 50 units of output, the marginal product of the fifth worker is
   a. 11 units of output.
   b. 10 units of output.
   c. 50 units of output.
   d. 6 units of output.
   e. between 4 and 5 units of output.

2. The short-run is a period of time
   a. less than six months.
   b. when all factors are variable.

    c. the firm can exit the industry.

    d. less than one year.

    e. the firm has at least one fixed factor.

3. A return on investment just sufficient to keep the owners of a business content to stay in that business is called

    a. normal profit.

    b. fair price.

    c. total cost.

    d. total product.

    e. marginal product.

4. For a perfectly competitive industry, which of the following is *not* true?

    a. The products produced are homogeneous.

    b. No firm has control of the price of the good.

    c. There are strong barriers to entering the industry.

    d. Firms can easily exit and enter the industry.

    e. Firms earn a normal rate of return or profit.

5. An example of a very simple Cobb-Douglas production function is

    a. $Q = K$

    b. $Q = (LK)1/2$

    c. $Q = L/K$

    d. $L = L + K$

    e. $Q = L + 3K$

6. The law of diminishing returns states that as more of a variable factor is added to the production process, the extra output produced by that factor will

    a. increase.

    b. increase at an increasing rate.

    c. decline.

    d. be equal to the average product.

    e. be zero at all levels of production.

7. The goal or objective of all firms is to

    a. maximize output.

    b. maximize costs.

    c. maximize the marginal product of labor.

    d. minimize the marginal product of capital.

    e. maximize profits.

8. The demand curve that a perfectly competitive firm perceives it faces is

    a. perfectly inelastic.

    b. downward sloping if the law of demand holds.

    c. vertical.

    d. perfectly elastic.

    e. nonexistent.

ANALYTIC EXERCISES

1. Various amounts of labor can be used to produce widgets as shown by the total product schedule for widgets below.

Quantity of Labor	Total Product of Widgets Produced
0	0
1	10
2	22
3	30
4	36
5	40
6	42
7	42
8	40

   a. Calculate the marginal and average product of labor for the production of widgets.
   b. Does the law of diminishing returns hold for labor in the production of widgets?

2. A firm's total revenue is found by multiplying the number of units sold times the price of the good sold. Given that a perfectly competitive firm can sell every unit of its good at the market price, what is the perfectly competitive firm's marginal revenue? Remember marginal revenue is the extra revenue brought in by selling one more unit of the good.

3. The average weight of 5 people who are carrying on a conversation is 150 pounds. Into the room walks Richard "the Refrigerator" Perry (dry weight 325 pounds) who wishes to join the conversation. What is the marginal weight of Mr. Perry? What has his marginal weight done to the average weight of the people holding the conversation?

ESSAY QUESTIONS

1. In calendar time, how long would the transformation from the short-run to the long-run be for a street vendor selling hot-dogs? For a gasoline station how long would the transition take? For an automobile manufacturer, how long would it take to move from the short-run to the long-run?
2. Perfectly competitive industries have many strict defining characteristics. As such, there are very few examples of perfectly competitive industries. If this is true, why does this book take several chapters to study them and why do economists even study them?
3. It was stated that owners of firms must earn at least a normal rate of return, or profit, to keep them interested in staying in a particular business. If they earn positive profits others want to enter the industry and if they earn negative profit some owners will leave the industry or contract the size of their firm. Explain how profit should actually be thought of as an opportunity cost of the owner of a business. What is true about profits relative to owners' opportunity costs when either positive or negative economic profits exist?

ANSWERS

Multiple-Choice

1) d,	2) e,	3) a,	4) c,
5) b,	6) c,	7) e,	8) d.

Analytic Exercises

1) **b.** the law of diminishing returns holds
2) marginal revenue = price
3) marginal weight = 325
   average weight increases, average weight = approx. 179

The Firm: Short Run Costs and Competitive Output Decisions

8

LEARNING OBJECTIVES

After you have studied this chapter in the textbook, attended class lectures over this material, and completed this study guide chapter you should be able to answer the following questions.

1. What is the difference between a short-run fixed cost and a short-run variable cost of production?
2. How does one calculate average fixed cost, average variable cost and average total cost in the short-run?
3. What is marginal cost and how is it calculated?
4. What relationship exists between marginal cost, average variable cost and average total cost?
5. How does the law of diminishing returns affect the shape of the marginal cost curve?
6. What is marginal revenue? How is marginal revenue related to price, for a perfectly competitive firm?
7. How does one determine the short-run supply curve for a perfectly competitive firm?

CHAPTER REVIEW

This chapter focuses on the activities of perfectly competitive firms in the short-run. The goal of a perfectly competitive firm is to maximize its total profits, the difference between total revenues and total costs. Since to measure profits, one must measure costs and revenues, some care must be taken in explaining the concept of both these quantities in the short-run.

Since in the short-run a firm has at least one fixed factor of production, there exists what are called fixed costs. These are the costs of the factor that cannot be changed in the short-run and, as such, are constant. These costs do not vary with output even if the firm stops production or shuts down. Often the fixed costs of production are associated with the capital stock of a firm, though they can be associated with any factor whose cost does not vary with output.

Fixed costs are not the only type of costs; there are also variable costs. As their name implies these costs vary with output in the short-run. Specifically, variable costs will increase as the level of output increases, though they will not always increase at the same rate. Variable costs are most often associated with the use of variable amounts of labor in the production process.

By adding total fixed costs and total variable costs one obtains total costs in the short-run. Total costs are not the only type of costs that economists consider. Economists also are interested in average costs. Specifically, one can calculate three types of average cost: average fixed cost, average variable cost and average total cost. Each of these is simply the respective total cost divided by the quantity of output produced. Average fixed cost is total fixed cost divided by the level of output produced. Since total fixed cost is constant in the short-run, average fixed cost declines continuously as the level of output increases. Average variable cost is total variable cost divided by the quantity of output produced. Average variable cost will initially decline, but after a point it will begin to rise. Graphically, the average variable cost curve is U-shaped. The final type of average cost to consider is average total cost. Average total cost is total cost divided by the level of output produced or the sum of average fixed cost and average variable cost. Since the average variable cost curve is U-shaped the average total cost curve will also be U-shaped.

The most important cost concept for purposes of economic analysis is marginal cost. Marginal costs exist because of variable costs. Marginal costs are changes in either total variable costs or total costs due to a change in the level of output produced. Marginal cost is the cost of producing one more unit of output. Given that the law of diminishing returns generally holds in the short-run, a firm's short-run marginal cost may initially decline, but after a point the marginal cost of producing additional units of output will rise. Marginal costs are important in determining a firm's average cost of production. If marginal costs are less than average total costs, then average total cost will be declining. If marginal costs are greater than average total costs' then average total costs will be rising. This implies than when average total costs (or average variable costs) are at a minimum, marginal costs will be equal to average cost.

On the other side of the picture one most consider a firm's total revenue. Total revenue is the price of the product times the number of units sold. Since the firm under consideration in this chapter is a perfectly competitive firm, the price of the product sold will always be taken as a given by the firm. This implies is that the firm's marginal revenue is equal to the price of the good. Marginal revenue is the additional revenue obtained by selling one more unit of output. Since the firm always receives the market price for selling another unit this is the firm's marginal revenue. Graphically the firm's marginal revenue curve is the perfectly elastic demand curve which is established at the market price.

Using marginal revenue and marginal cost, one can determine a firm's profit maximizing level of output. Profit maximization occurs where marginal revenue is equal to marginal cost. What this equality implies is that the extra cost of producing an extra unit of output is just equal to the extra revenue from selling that unit of output. If production were increased or decreased the firm's profit would decline. Since the perfectly competitive firm has marginal revenue equal to the price of the good, one could also say the profit maximization rule could also be stated as price should equal marginal cost.

GLOSSARY

FIXED COSTS: Any cost that a firm bears in the short-run that does not depend on the level of output. These costs are incurred even if the firm is producing nothing. There are no fixed costs in the long run.

VARIABLE COSTS: Any cost that a firm bears as a result of production and which depends on the level of production chosen.

TOTAL COSTS: The sum of total fixed and total variable costs.

AVERAGE FIXED COST: Total fixed cost divided by the number of units of output; a per unit cost measure.

MARGINAL COST: An increase in total cost that results from producing one additional unit of output; a per unit cost measure.

AVERAGE VARIABLE COST: Total variable cost divided by the number of units of outputs, a per unit cost measure.

AVERAGE TOTAL COST: Total cost divided by the number of units of outputs, a per unit measure.

MARGINAL REVENUE: The additional revenue that a firm would earn by raising its level of output by one unit.

STUDY TIPS

1. The important point to remember in this chapter is that economic activity is taking place in the short-run. The factor which is fixed has a cost attached to it, but that cost does not vary with output. Because fixed cost does not change it should not be considered when making economic decisions. In the short-run fixed costs do not matter. What does matter is marginal costs. Microeconomic decisions are made on the margin.
2. Because the perfectly competitive firm is a price taker, the marginal revenue it receives from selling an additional unit is equal to the price of the good. This situation is true for the perfectly competitive firm, but it is not true for every type of firm, as later chapters will show.
3. Possibly the most important condition to remember from this chapter is the condition for profit maximization. Profit maximization occurs when the marginal revenue from selling an additional unit of a good is just equal to the marginal cost of producing that unit of the good. One will see in later chapters that though the marginal revenue received by firms is not always equal to the price of the good, the MC = MR condition will still produce the point of profit maximization.

A LOOK AHEAD

In the next two chapters the discussion stays with that of perfect competition. Chapter Nine, however, leaves the short-run and considers how a perfectly competitive firm makes decisions in the long-run. Chapter Ten moves away from the output market and considers how decisions are made by firms in the market for factors of production or input markets.

Once these chapters have thoroughly developed the theory of perfect competition other types of markets are considered. In most markets approached in one's everyday activity some type of imperfect competition exists. It is the purpose of later chapters to compare various types of markets which are not perfectly competitive to those markets which are.

MULTIPLE-CHOICE QUESTIONS

1. The profit maximizing rule for a perfectly competitive firm is to produce where
   a. ATC = P
   b. ATC = MC
   c. MC = MR
   d. AFC = 0
   e. AVC = AFC

2. If a perfectly competitive firm is producing at a point where marginal cost exceeds marginal revenue the firm should
   a. reduce output.
   b. curtail operations.
   c. charge a higher price.
   d. increase output.
   e. charge a lower price.

3. If average variable cost is increasing then marginal cost must be
   a. constant.
   b. equal to it.
   c. decreasing.
   d. increasing.
   e. unresponsive to the law of diminishing returns.

4. Marginal revenue is equal to
   a. total revenue divided by the quantity of output.
   b. the extra revenue from selling an additional unit of output.
   c. the extra profit from selling one additional unit of output.
   d. the change in total revenue due to a change in the quantity of output.
   e. both b. and d. above.

5. The type of cost which does not vary with output is referred to as
   a. variable cost.
   b. labor cost.
   c. marginal cost.
   d. total cost.
   e. fixed cost.

6. Average total cost is the summation of
   a. marginal cost and marginal revenue.
   b. average fixed cost and average variable cost.
   c. average variable cost and marginal cost.
   d. price and marginal cost.
   e. none of the above.

7. If short-run total costs of producing 25 units is $50 and the short-run total cost of producing 26 units is $55, then the marginal cost of the 26th unit is
   a. $2.
   b. $55.
   c. $50.
   d. $5.
   e. 0.

8. As output increases, average fixed costs will
   a. never change.
   b. increase.
   c. be constant.
   d. decline.
   e. approach average total cost.

ANALYTIC EXERCISES

1. The incomplete table shown below lists the total fixed cost, the total variable costs and the total cost of producing a certain good. Complete the table from the given information.

Quantity	Total Fixed Cost	Total Variable Cost	Total Cost
1	100		150
2		——	170
3	100	80	——
4	——	100	——
5	100	140	——
6	100		300
7	——	——	400

2. Suppose a firm's short-run total cost of production can be expressed as a simple linear function of the quantity it produces. Specifically, consider the firm with the total cost function:

$$TC = 125 + 8Q$$

where,

   TC = total cost

   Q = quantity of output produced.

   a) What is the numerical value of this firm's fixed costs?
   b) What is the marginal cost of the tenth unit of output?
   c. What is the marginal cost of the twentieth unit of output?
   d) Does this firm experience diminishing returns?

3. Graphically show the average and marginal cost and average and marginal revenue curves for a perfectly competitive firm that maximized profits. Indicate the profit maximizing level of output. Show on this same graph any profits that the firm is making.

4. When developing and graphically displaying a firm's total and average cost curves, factor prices such as wages were held constant. When wages change the cost curves shift. Graphically show the effect on the average and total curves of a firm for which the wage rage increases.

ESSAY QUESTIONS

1. Explain why a firm which produces at a point where its marginal cost of production equals its marginal revenue, will maximize its profits.

2. Some individuals argue that not all firms are profit maximizers. If a firm were not a profit maximizer it would not necessarily produce the level of output where marginal revenue equals marginal cost. If a firm is not a profit maximizer what other possible goal or objective could it have (list several)? Given a goal other than profit maximization, is there a condition, such as MC = MR, which will tell the firm what quantity of output to produce?

3. At many colleges and universities students have the option of dropping a class during the first few weeks of the semester. In terms of fixed and variable costs what things should a student consider when making the decision to drop a class? What things should the student not consider? If the student has already worked very hard in the class for the first few weeks should that influence the student's decision?

4. A perfectly competitive firm always receives the market price for its good and therefore has marginal revenue which is equal to the price of the good. If a firm had to lower its price to sell more units of its product how would that affect its marginal revenue, from selling additional units of output?

ANSWERS

Multiple-Choice

1) c, 2) a, 3) d, 4) e,
5) e, 6) b, 7) d, 8) d.

Analytic Exercises

1)

Q	TFC	TVC	TC
1	100	50	150
2	100	70	170
3	100	80	180
4	100	100	200
5	100	140	240
6	100	200	300
7	100	300	400

2) **a.** fixed cost = 125
   b. marginal cost = 8
   c. marginal cost = 8
   d. the law of diminishing returns does not hold

3) The area below the price line and above the relevant point on the ATC, times the quantity produced

4) the curves would shift upward for an increase in the wage

The Firm: Costs and Competitive Supply in the Long Run

LEARNING OBJECTIVES

After you have studied this chapter in the textbook, attended class lectures over this material, and completed this study guide chapter you should be able to answer the following questions.

1. What distinguishes the long-run from the short-run?
2. What does it mean for a firm to be making an above normal rate of return?
3. In what situations is a firm incurring economic losses?
4. When should a firm earning losses in the short-run shut down and when should it stay in business?
5. What distinguishes economies of scale from diseconomies of scale?
6. What causes the existence of external economies and diseconomies of scale?
7. What conditions have to be met for a perfectly competitive firm to be in long-run equilibrium?
8. How does one define the long-run industry supply curve?

CHAPTER REVIEW

In the short-run, one of three profit situations can exist for a perfectly competitive firm. First the firm may be making a normal rate of return or normal profit. In this situation profits are just sufficient to cover the opportunity costs of the investors. The investors are earning a return just equal to the riskless return they could earn elsewhere.

The second possible situation would be for the firm to be earning a positive return or what are called economic profits. In this situation the investors in firms are earning a return that more than covers their opportunity cost of being in this industry. In this situation there is an incentive for other firms to enter the industry or for existing firms to expand. In a short-run situation, however, neither of these actions can occur.

55

The third and final situation is for the firm to be earning negative profits, that is, economic losses. In the short-run the firm cannot exit the industry, it can however, shut down operations. If the firm shuts down operations, its losses do not go to zero. The firm still has to pay its fixed costs even if it produces nothing (if it shuts down). Therefore, the firm stays in business if the losses it incurs from producing are less than its fixed costs. In other words if a firm is covering its variable costs (its costs of producing a positive level of output) it should stay in business in the short-run. This will occur anytime the price received (the marginal revenue) by the firm is above the minimum point on the average variable cost curve. That point on the curve is called the shut-down point.

This chapter specifically concerns itself with the long-run. As one will recall, the long-run is a situation in which a firm, in this case a perfectly competitive firm, has no fixed factors of production and firms are free to enter and exit the industry. Because all factors are variable, a firm's costs can change because of a change in the firm's scale of production or plant size. In some circumstances a firm's average costs fall as its scale of operation increases; this is referred to as increasing returns to scale or economies of scale. A firm is experiencing economies of scale if its long-run average cost curve is declining. In other instances a firm will experience higher average costs as its scale of operation increases; this is referred to as decreasing returns to scale or diseconomies of scale. A firm that is experiencing diseconomies of scale will have a long-run average cost curve that is positively sloped. Finally, in some situations a firm's average cost of production will not change as its scale of production changes, this is referred to as constant returns to scale. A firm experiencing constant returns to scale has a horizontal long-run average cost curve.

Increasing, decreasing and constant returns to scale all have to do with things internal to the firm and, as such, deal with movements along a long-run average cost curve. External economies of scale shift a firm's long-run average cost curve downward, that is, lower its average costs. External diseconomies of scale shift a firm's long-run average cost curve upward or increase its long-run average cost.

Since in the long-run firms can exist and enter a perfectly competitive industry, the industry will expand anytime that economic profits exist and contract any time excess losses exist. The perfectly competitive industry will only be in a state of equilibrium when all firms in the industry are earning a normal profit. When this occurs the firm's price will be equal to its short-run marginal costs, its short-run average costs and its long-run average costs. When this occurs there is no further incentive for firms to exit or enter the industry.

GLOSSARY

SHUT-DOWN POINT: The lowest point on the average variable cost curve. When price falls below AVC, and total revenue is insufficient to cover variable costs, the firm will shut down and bear losses equal to fixed costs.

EXTERNAL ECONOMIES AND DISECONOMIES OF SCALE: If industry growth results in a decrease of long-run average costs, that means there are external economies of scale; if industry growth results in an increase of long-run average costs, that means there are external diseconomies of scale.

CONSTANT RETURNS TO SCALE: When an increase in scale of production has no effect on average costs per unit produced.

LONG-RUN COMPETITIVE EQUILIBRIUM: When P = SRMC = SRAC = LRAC and economic profits are zero.

STUDY TIPS

1. The student should not be discouraged by the fact that this chapter was more vague than the previous chapters. The change in costs due to an increase in the scale of operation or an increase in industry size is an extremely complex process to analyze. The goal of firms, however, is still to maximize their profits. This goal is met where price (which is the same as marginal revenue for the perfectly competitive firm) is equal to the marginal cost of production. This is the same profit maximization condition that was developed in the previous chapter.

2. One will note that in long-run equilibrium the perfectly competitive firm is driven to a point where long-run average costs are minimized. It is not the goal of this firm to minimize its costs, it just so happens that the perfectly competitive firm maximizes its profits at a point of minimum costs in the long-run because exit and entry are free in this type of market. Economic profits call forth entry by other firms and losses cause some firms to leave the industry. The perfectly competitive industry is only in a state of equilibrium when there is no incentive for exit or enter. This occurs when all firms are just earning a normal rate of return or profit.

A LOOK AHEAD

The next three chapters continue the discussion of perfect competition but in a slightly different sense. Chapters 10 and 11 consider the market for inputs, or factors of production. As one will remember from the early chapters of the book, the factors of production of interest here can generally be grouped into the categories of labor, capital and land. Each of these factors will be considered in some detail.

The discussion so far has also considered what is happening with one firm or one industry at a time. The world is seldom so simple. As is true most of the time, the prices and quantities of goods and services are all changing at the same time. The way one should study this simultaneous change, across several markets, is with a general equilibrium model. Chapter 12 introduces the student to this topic.

MULTIPLE-CHOICE QUESTIONS

1. The shut-down point for a perfectly competitive firm can be found at the lowest point on the
   a. marginal cost curve.
   b. marginal revenue curve.
   c. average total cost curve.
   d. average variable cost curve.
   e. total variable cost curve.

2. A perfectly competitive firm incurring losses in the short-run should stay in business if it is covering its
   a. fixed costs.
   b. total costs.
   c. normal profit.
   d. overhead costs.
   e. variable costs.

3. The number of fixed factors a firm has in the long-run is
   a. one.
   b. at least one.
   c. none.
   d. two or more.
   e. indeterminate.

4. If a firm doubles its inputs and its output more than doubles, production for this firm is said to exhibit
   a. constant returns to scale.
   b. decreasing returns to scale.
   c. increasing returns to scale.
   d. diseconomies of scale.
   e. external economies of scale.

5. In a constant cost industry the long-run industry supply curve will be
   a. horizontal.
   b. the marginal cost curve above the shut-down point.
   c. above the lowest point on the average variable cost curve.
   d. vertical.
   e. none of the above.

6. An increase in the wage rate due to the expansion of a perfectly competitive industry can best be described as
   a. a diseconomy of scale.
   b. an external diseconomy of scale.
   c. bad luck.
   d. an external economy of scale.
   e. decreasing returns to scale.

7. Which of the following equalities does not hold in long-run equilibrium for a perfectly competitive market?
   a. P = LRAC
   b. P = SRMC
   c. SRMC = SRAC
   d. SRMC = LRAC
   e. they all hold true.

8. In a perfectly competitive industry, in the long-run, what will happen if the price of the product sold exceeds the average cost of producing the good?
   a. Other firms will enter the industry.
   b. Firms will be earning economic profits.
   c. Some firms may exit the industry.
   d. Firms will earn a normal rate of return.
   e. Both a. and b. above.

ANALYTIC EXERCISES

1. An increasing cost industry is one in which costs increase as more firms enter the market. Expansion of the industry drives up the average cost of production. What happens in an increasing cost industry as firms leave the market; as the industry contracts? Graphically show an industry and firm, in an increasing cost industry, as firms leave the market. Is the long-run industry supply curve still positively sloped?

2. Does the production function Q = 3L + 2K, exhibit: constant returns to scale, decreasing returns to scale, or increasing returns to scale? (Hint: increase labor and capital by some fixed proportion and explain what happens to output).

ESSAY QUESTIONS

1. If one were to consider actual business corporations, what type of industry would be most common: an increasing cost industry, a decreasing cost industry or a constant cost industry?

2. If attending college can be considered the production of a good (knowledge), what distinguishes the short-run from the long-run. Namely, which costs are short-run fixed costs and which are long-run variable costs?

3. Are there any industries that can be perceived to be currently earning positive economic profits? Can one predict that other firms will enter these markets and compete excess profits away? What could possibly keep other firms from entering these markets?

ANSWERS

Multiple-Choice

1) d,	2) e,	3) c,	4) c,
5) a,	6) b,	7) e,	8) e.

Analytic Exercises

1) the long-run average cost curve will shift down and the long-run industry supply curve will be positively sloped
2) constant returns to scale

10

The Firm: Demand in Competitive Input Markets

LEARNING OBJECTIVES

After you have studied this chapter in the textbook, attended class lectures over this material, and completed this study guide chapter you should be able to answer the following questions.

1. Why are input demand curves referred to as derived demand curves?
2. How is the input demand curve determined for a firm using one variable factor?
3. How is the input demand curve determined for a firm using two or more variable factors?
4. What is a factor's marginal revenue product (MRP)?
5. What is the factor substitution effect of an input price change?
6. What is the output effect of an input price change?
7. What affects the extent to which factors are substitutes for or complements to one another?

CHAPTER REVIEW

The discussion in this chapter turns to the other side of the decision-making process for firms, how many units of input factors should be employed. The demand for an input is referred to as a derived demand. The demand for an input is derived from the demand for the output good produced. Demand exists for inputs because they produce some good or service that others are willing to purchase.

The simplest input demand curve is one for a firm that only employs one variable factor of production. What a firm is willing to pay for an extra unit of a factor of production is equal to the amount of money that factor brings into the firm. This can be called that factor's marginal revenue product (MRP). A factor's marginal revenue product is found by multiplying the marginal product of that factor times the price of the good sold (one will remember in perfectly competitive markets the price of the good sold and the marginal revenue of that good are the same). The MRP is the demand curve for the particular factor under consideration. To find the quantity of variable factors the firm wishes to hire, one should find the point at which the given market wage is equal to the marginal revenue product of the input.

Determining a firm's optimal input hire, when it has more than one factor, is slightly more difficult. It is made more difficult because as the price of any one factor changes, there is both an output and substitution effect due to that factor price change. The substitution effect says that more (less) of the factor whose price fell (increased) will be purchased by the firm. The output effect says that more (less) of all factors will be purchased by the firm when the price of any one factor decreases (increases). Since the degree of substitutability and complementarity changes with different types of production processes, this is a problem for which a general solution of how a certain price change affects a factor's demand, cannot be immediately given.

The thing that can be said in general, however, is that factors should be hired up to the point where the marginal product per dollar spent on that factor is equal for all factors. If labor and capital are the only two factors used, the equilibrium condition may be stated as MPl/Pl = MPk/Pk. If this equality does not hold, money should be allocated to the input factor which has the higher marginal product per dollar. Doing this will raise the marginal product per dollar of the factor substituted away from and decrease it for the factor substituted toward. This reallocation should continue until once again the equality holds between the marginal products per dollar for all factors.

GLOSSARY

COMPLEMENTARY INPUTS: Factors of production are used together to enhance each other.
SUBSTITUTABLE INPUTS: Factors of production are used in place of one another.
MARGINAL REVENUE PRODUCT (MRP): The additional revenue earned by the use of one additional unit of input, ceteris paribus.

STUDY TIPS

1. The process of making economic decisions in factor markets is exactly the same process that is used in output markets. As the student should be well aware by now, decisions are made on the margin. The optimal amount of a factor to hire is the amount where the marginal revenue product of that factor equals the market price which must be paid for that factor.

2. Equating the MRPL = wage is exactly the same as equating P = MC. Maximization in the input market leads to the same conclusions as maximization in the output markets.

3. When considering a firm or a production process that uses more than one factor of production it becomes more difficult to specify the factor demand curves. It becomes more difficult to specify the demand curves for the factors because the factors can be both complements and substitutes for each other.

4. The condition that determines a point of production equilibrium is an equamarginal condition just as the condition that specifies equilibrium in the consumer choice analysis discussed in earlier chapters.

A LOOK AHEAD

The conceptual material developed in this chapter primarily corresponds to the factor of labor. The conceptual material, however, can be extended to deal with other types of factors such as capital and land. Capital and land have some very special properties, however, that should be studied separately. Land is an immobile factor, it must be used where it is. Capital is a factor that is somewhat durable. Therefore a particular machine or piece of equipment is not used up in the production process. Only a part of that machine is used up or depreciated. Capital equipment can be used over time which means one has to consider its present or discounted value in different time periods. It is the purpose of the next chapter to address these issues.

MULTIPLE-CHOICE QUESTIONS

1. The marginal revenue product for a factor is calculated by
   a. MRP = P x MC
   b. MRP = P x MP
   c. MRP = P x AP
   d. MRP = MC
   e. MRP = MC x MP

2. If the price of an input rises, the factor substitution effect says
   a. more of all factors will be demanded.
   b. more of the factor whose price increased will be demanded.
   c. less of the factor whose price increased will be demanded.
   d. the output of the firm will fall.
   e. the price of the output good must increase.

3. If the price of an input rises, the output effect says
   a. fewer of all factors will be demanded.
   b. more of all factors will be demanded.
   c. the price of the output good must increase.
   d. more of the factor whose price increased will be demanded.
   e. output can not change.

4. If the marginal product of capital per dollar spent on capital is greater than the marginal product of labor per dollar spent on labor, the firm should
   a. shut down in the short-run.
   b. increase the price of capital.
   c. use more labor.
   d. use more capital and less labor.
   e. use capital until it has a zero marginal product.

5. If the marginal product of the fourth worker is 12 units of output and the price of the output is $2, what wage is a firm willing to pay the fourth worker?
   a. $2.
   b. $12.
   c. $6.
   d. $14.
   e. $24.

6. If a firm produces output with one variable input, an increase in the price of the output good will
   a. cause a reduction in the demand for the input.
   b. cause the input demand curve to shift outward.
   c. will cause the factor substitution effect to be larger than the output effect.
   d. will cause the output effect to be larger than the factor substitution effect.
   e. reduce the price of the factor input.

ANALYTIC EXERCISES

1. The total product of labor schedule for the production of widgets is shown below. The selling price of a widget is $4 and constant. Derive the demand for labor schedule from this information. If the wage rate is $16, how many units of labor will be hired?

TP_L	Q_L
0	0
12	1
22	2
30	3
36	4
40	5
42	6

2. Variable factors such as labor are hired until the marginal revenue product of the last unit of labor hired is equal to the wage rate. If the law of diminishing returns holds, the demand for labor will be downward sloping or the marginal revenue product falls with the successive hiring of more units of labor. This implies that all but the last worker has a marginal revenue product greater than the wage paid for that factor. What this is saying is that the initial workers hired bring more revenue into the firm than they are paid (a cost to the firm). What happens to the extra revenue that they bring into the firm, above and beyond what they are paid? (A graphic presentation of these results may be of assistance in answering this question).

ESSAY QUESTIONS

1. In many production processes land is a variable factor. How can the marginal product of land be measured?
2. Think of the production of several different goods and services which are purchased and consumed every day. In which of these production processes are labor and capital substitute factors? In which of these production processes are labor and capital complementary factors?
3. How does the elasticity of demand for a good sold in the output market affect the elasticity of demand for the inputs which produce that output?

ANSWERS

Multiple-Choice

1) b,   2) c,   3) a,   4) d,
5) e,   6) b.

Analytic Exercises

1) 5 workers
2) it pays the other factors of production

Capital Markets and Land Markets

11

LEARNING OBJECTIVES

After you have studied this chapter in the textbook, attended class lectures over this material, and completed this study guide chapter you should be able to answer the following questions.

1. What is capital and what distinguishes it from other factors of production?
2. How do the flows of investment and depreciation affect the stock of capital?
3. How do household savings get transferred into productive investment projects?
4. What incentive is there for an entrepreneur to supply financial capital?
5. How is the present discounted value of an asset determined?
6. How is the market price of a capital asset determined?
7. What is land and what distinguishes it from other factors of production?

CHAPTER REVIEW

Households do provide the financial resources necessary for firms to produce capital assets, though the process by which this occurs is more complex than the supply of labor. The financial capital market is the mechanism of stock markets, banks, venture capital funds, and brokerage houses that help facilitate this process.

Capital goods are those goods produced by the economic system itself, which are used as inputs to produce other goods and services in the future. These capital goods can be classified into two categories, tangible capital and intangible capital. Tangible capital is the form of physical capital that most people are familiar with. It includes nonresidential structures (factories and office buildings), durable equipment (machines), residential structures (homes), and inventories (both inputs and outputs). The other form of capital is less familiar, intangible capital. Intangible capital is comprised of nonphysical capital such as goodwill or brand loyalty that may come from advertising. It also includes increased productivity that comes from training laborers. This is often referred to as human capital.

Both of these forms of capital must be measured indirectly because capital comes in so many forms. The measure of a firm's capital stock is the current market value of its plant, equipment, inventories, and intangible assets. It is referred to as a stock of capital because it is measured at a point in time. When one wishes to consider how the stock of capital changes over time one is interested in a flow variable. There are two flow variables which can affect the stock of capital. These variables are investment and depreciation. Investment is a flow that increases the stock of capital. Depreciation is the decline in the economic value of an asset over time.

Interest and profit are the income flows that are paid to the owners of capital to get them to supply capital. Interest and profit provide the incentive to postpone gratification or consumption of a certain unit of capital. Interest and profit also serve as rewards for innovation and risk taking. A potential investor will evaluate the expected flow of future productive services that an investment project will yield. Once expectations of future events have been formed firms must quantify the perceived dollar and cents value of the benefits of a project versus its cost. This is referred to as the rate of return on the investment project. This rate of return must be compared to the cost of providing capital or investment. This cost is known as interest. Interest is the fee that a borrower pays to a lender for the use of her or his money. Only those investment projects in the economy that are expected to yield a rate of return higher than the market interest rate will be funded. The lower the interest rate the larger the number of investment projects that will be funded.

One way of thinking about interest is to say that it allows us to buy and sell claims to future dollars. The current or present price of a future dollar is not simply a dollar. A dollar sometime in the future has a discounted value to us today. The present discounted value of a dollar received one year in the future is one dollar divided by one plus the interest rate. It is the amount that one would have to put aside now if he or she wanted to end up with one dollar a year from now. If one wishes to find the present discounted value of a dollar received two years in the future they simply divide by one plus the interest rate a second time.

Investment should be undertaken if the present value of an expected stream of earnings, from an investment, exceeds the cost of the investment. If the present value of an expected stream of earnings falls short of the cost, then the financial market can generate the same stream for less money, and the investment should not be undertaken. The market price of an asset is generally driven to the present discounted value of the stream of earnings that the asset is expected to produce, over time, for the owner.

The market for land is yet another market that is related to the market for the factors labor and capital, but it is slightly different. The price of land is said to be demand determined because it is fixed in supply. The return to any factor of production in fixed supply is called a pure rent. Any given site has a number of different alternative uses, and so, as with any other factor in a market setting, it will presumably go to the potential user who is willing to pay the most for it. The value of land to a potential user may be derived from the characteristics of the land itself or from its location. The process of land allocation is no different from the process of labor or capital allocation, except that its supply is perfectly inelastic.

GLOSSARY

CAPITAL: Anything that is produced by the economic system which is used subsequently as an input in the production of future goods and services.

INTANGIBLE CAPITAL: Invisible, nonmaterial things that contribute to the output of future goods and services, such as reputation and good will.

INVESTMENT: Purchase by firms of the new buildings, equipment, and inventories that add to their capital stock.

DEPRECIATION: The decline in economic value of an asset that occurs over time.

INTEREST: The price of money, usually figured as a percentage of the principal borrowed (the interest rate); the fee paid by a borrower to a lender over time.

FINANCIAL CAPITAL MARKET: A set of institutions that together channel household savings into productive capital investment projects by firms.

PRESENT DISCOUNTED VALUE: The present discounted value of R dollars to be paid t years in the future is the amount you need to put aside today, at current interest rates, to insure that you end up with R dollars t years from now. It is the current market value of a contract to deliver R dollars in t years.

PURE RENT: The return to any factor of production that is in fixed supply.

STUDY TIPS

1. The study capital, as a factor of production, is more difficult than a study of labor, as a factor of production, because capital is such a heterogeneous factor. Because of this heterogeneity capital is measured by its dollar value as opposed to a unit measurement. One must always keep in mind, however, that capital should be thought of as a physical factor of production and not merely a monetary unit of account.

2. When considering the market for financial capital one may think of a simple supply and demand market for funds. The supply price of financial capital is referred to as the interest rate. The rate of return is the demand price that investors are willing to pay for borrowed funds.

3. One should not be overwhelmed by the calculation of present discounted values. The present discounted value of any dollar amount can be calculated by dividing the given amount of money, or the value of the asset, by one plus the interest rate raised to the power of how many years in the future the asset will be received. If the asset will be received in five years the discount or divisor factor is one plus the interest rate raised to the fifth power.

A LOOK AHEAD

The implicit assumption made in this chapter and the last is that the factor markets under consideration were perfectly competitive. Of course this will not always be the case. In some instances the purchasers of factors of production will have some type of market power or be able to influence the price of factors. This is a situation which will be discussed in greater detail at the end of chapter 13. At other times the suppliers of factors of production may have some degree of market power, an example of this would be the existence of a strong labor union. Labor unions are discussed specifically in chapter 19.

The discussion of land and land uses has been very brief in this chapter. There is much, however, that the science of economics can say about the use of land and the location of economic activity. In fact an entire subfield of economics is devoted to the study of land use questions. This is the subfield of urban and regional economics. Chapter 20 applies the microeconomic models developed in earlier chapters to the study of urban and regional economics.

MULTIPLE-CHOICE QUESTIONS

1. The present discounted value of one dollar received one year from now, when the interest rate is ten percent, is approximately
   a. $0.91.
   b. $1.10.
   c. $0.10.
   d. $0.09.
   e. 10%.

2. If the interest rate falls, the present discounted value of any future asset will
   a. remain the same.
   b. decrease.

    c. increase.

    d. decline.

    e. become negative.

3. The supply of land is generally assumed to be

    a. unitary elastic.

    b. perfectly elastic.

    c. relatively inelastic.

    d. relatively elastic.

    e. perfectly inelastic.

4. A reduction in the value of capital stock over time is referred to as

    a. investment.

    b. depreciation.

    c. acclamation.

    d. inflation.

    e. diminishing returns.

5. Which of the following factors could be expected to earn pure rent?

    a. The leading pass receiver in the National Football League (NFL).

    b. The best vineyard in Napa Valley, California.

    c. A rare painting by a now deceased artist.

    d. none of the above.

    e. all of the above.

6. More and more investment projects will be funded up until the point where

    a. the interest rate is its greatest amount over the expected rate of return.

    b. the expected rate of return is zero.

    c. the interest rate and the expected rate of return are equal.

    d. diminishing returns to capital set in.

    e. the amount of capital and labor used is equal.

ANALYTIC EXERCISES

1. What is the present discounted value of $500 received at the end of each of the next three years, if the interest rate is 10%? What happens if the interest rate falls to 5%?

2. If the rate of interest is 8% and the rate of inflation, or price increase, is 11%, what is the real rate of interest? If one owns a bond paying this rate of interest, what is happening to the real value of this individual's asset?

ESSAY QUESTIONS

1. Explain why the interest rate can be thought of as the opportunity cost of borrowed funds or financial capital.

2. Why is future consumption worth less than present consumption? Or in other words, why must assets received in the future be discounted?

3. If travel to other planets was readily available at low cost, how would this affect the pure rent that currently accrues to the factor of production land?

4. If a firm had a negative expected rate of return on an investment project, what would that actually mean?

5. What human capital skills are acquired in attending college? What human capital skills are acquired outside of the classroom when one attends college?

ANSWERS

Multiple-Choice

1) a,	**2)** c,	**3)** e,
4) b,	**5)** e,	**6)** c.

Analytic Exercises

1) present discounted value = $1243.43
present discounted value = $1361.62

2) real rate = - 3%
real value of asset is declining

12

General Equilibrium, the Efficiency of Competition, and Sources of Market Failure

LEARNING OBJECTIVES

After you have studied this chapter in the textbook, attended class lectures over this material, and completed this study guide chapter you should be able to answer the following questions.

1. What is general equilibrium analysis and how does it differ from partial equilibrium analysis?
2. Why is a perfectly competitive market said to be allocatively efficient?
3. How does a perfectly competitive market differ from the real world?
4. What are imperfectly competitive markets?
5. What is a public or social good?
6. What causes an externality to arise?
7. What is the effect on a market when imperfect information exists?

CHAPTER REVIEW

To this point in the text equilibrium conditions in individual markets for individual goods have been examined. This process of examining the equilibrium conditions in individual markets is called partial equilibrium analysis. In partial equilibrium analysis exogenous economic activity disturbs the equilibrium situation in the market under consideration. What is forgotten is that when an event changes the equilibrium condition in one market, it may disturb many other markets as well. The ultimate impact of any event depends upon how all markets adjust. Partial equilibrium analysis, which looks at adjustments in one market in isolation, may be misleading.

What is needed is a general equilibrium analysis of the economy. A general equilibrium exists when all markets in an economy are in simultaneous equilibrium. General equilibrium analysis considers the effect of exogenous economic activity on all markets at the same time.

In economics there is a widely accepted definition of allocative efficiency. This definition was first developed by the Italian economist Vilfredo Pareto in the nineteenth century. A change is said to be efficient if it at least potentially makes some members of society better off without making other members of society worse off. An efficient, or Pareto optimal, system is one in which no such changes are possible.

The competitive mechanism discussed in the earlier chapters of this text leads to an efficient allocation of resources. In this system no changes are possible that will make some people better off without making others worse off. This is true because of three conditions that exist within this system: 1) resources are allocated among firms efficiently, 2) final products are distributed among households so that transferring them between households won't improve well-being, and 3) the system is producing the things that people want.

In the real world the conditions for perfect competition cannot always be met or market failure occurs. Some firms have control over price and their potential competition, this is referred to as imperfect competition. The result of imperfect competition is an inefficient allocation of resources. There are several types of imperfectly competitive markets. What they all have in common, however, is that in these markets too little output is produced at too high a price, relative to perfect competition.

Private producers do not find it in their best interest to produce everything that members of society want. There is a group of goods known as public or social goods that will be underproduced or not produced at all in a laissez-faire market economy. Public goods or services are goods and services that bestow collective benefits on society. The difficulty with a public good is that in general everyone gets to consume it, whether they pay for it or not. Once the good is produced, no one can be excluded from enjoying its benefits. An unregulated system will not produce everything that all members of a society want.

Another problem with a competitive market is the existence of external costs and benefits. An externality is some cost or benefit imposed on an individual, or group, that is external to a market transaction. Externalities are a problem in the efficient allocation of resources if decision makers do not take them into account. The market mechanism provides no incentives for decision makers to consider external effects, both positive and negative.

The final source of market failure is imperfect information on the part of buyers and sellers. The premise that markets work efficiently rests heavily on the assumption that consumers and producers have full knowledge of product characteristics, available prices and so forth. The absence of full information can lead to transactions that do not promote allocative efficiency. Because of these four situations an efficient allocation of resources cannot always be reached by the operation of the market mechanism, there is a potential role for the government to intervene in the market process.

GLOSSARY

EFFICIENCY: When applied to economics, the condition in which the system is producing what people want at the least cost. More formally, a condition in which no one can be made better off without making someone else worse off.

PARETO EFFICIENCY: A condition in which no change is possible that will make some member of society better off without making some other member of society worse off.

PUBLIC GOODS: Goods or services that bestow collective benefits on members of society; they are, in a sense, collectively consumed. Generally, since benefits are collective, one cannot be excluded from enjoying them once they are produced. The classic example is national defense.

EXTERNALITY: A cost or benefit resulting from some activity or transaction that is imposed or bestowed upon parties external to the activity or transaction. Sometimes called spillovers or third-party effects. Often externalities are in the form of public goods, falling collectively on many people.

STUDY TIPS

1. One should not be concerned that a formal mathematical or graphic model has not been presented dealing with general equilibrium analysis. The mathematical rigor of this type of model is beyond the scope of this book and beyond the scope of an introductory class in economics. What is important to remember from this chapter is that partial equilibrium analysis may lead to different answers to economic questions than general equilibrium analysis.

2. The other important point to remember is that perfectly competitive markets lead to allocative efficiency. Since these markets are allocatively efficient all other types of markets are compared to perfectly competitive markets. In other words, perfectly competitive markets will serve as the benchmark to which imperfectly competitive markets will be compared in later chapters.

A LOOK AHEAD

The function of this chapter has been to provide a transitional step in the study of microeconomics. The previous eleven chapters have considered the best of all worlds in economics, the perfectly competitive laissez-faire world. A point of allocative efficiency, however, cannot always be reached when the conditions of perfect competition can not be reached. The existence of imperfect competition, public goods, externalities and imperfect information means that points other than Pareto optimal points must be considered in the real world. It is the intent of the next few chapters to analyze some of these concerns in more detail. Specifically, chapters 13, 14 and 15 consider the possibility of imperfect competition. Chapter 16 considers the existence of public goods and externalities. An entire subfield of economics is devoted to the study of the topics in Chapter 16, that subfield is called public finance. Each of these chapters, though, draws upon the student's understanding of the perfectly competitive model. The presentation in these chapters compares how each of these situations differs from that of perfect competition.

MULTIPLE-CHOICE QUESTIONS

1. Market failures may occur for all of the following except
   a. perfect competition does not exist.
   b. externalities exist.
   c. information available to sellers and buyers is perfect.
   d. social benefits and social costs are present.
   e. public goods are not produced by the private sector.

2. Pollution is an excellent example of
   a. an externality.
   b. a public good.
   c. imperfect competition.
   d. imperfect information.
   e. Pareto Optimality.

3. If one analyzes the market for hamburgers, holding everything constant in the market for French fries, they are using
   a. general equilibrium analysis.
   b. mathematical economics.
   c. the post hoc, ergo proctor hoc assumption.
   d. partial equilibrium analysis.
   e. the sum of the parts reasoning.

4. Which of the following statements is true?
   a. When one person consumes a public good or service, there is less available for others to consume.
   b. Because it is difficult to establish a market price for public goods it is not easy to determine how many units of the good should be produced to achieve allocative efficiency.
   c. Private firms find it easy to earn excess profits by producing public goods.
   d. There is no easy way to exclude an individual from consuming a private good once it has been produced.
   e. Public goods are those goods and services produced by the government.

5. An industry comprising a relatively small number of firms, each with some price setting power, is
   a. a monopoly.
   b. a perfectly competitive market.
   c. a monopolistically competitive market.
   d. an oligopoly.
   e. a trigonometry.

ESSAY QUESTIONS

1. Public goods are those goods which can be simultaneously consumed by many individuals and no one can be excluded from consuming once the good has been produced. Are radio and television signals public goods? If they are not, why are they not? If they are, why are they?
2. From the point of view of efficiency, perfectly competitive markets are very good, they are after all allocatively efficient. If one is primarily concerned about equity, are perfectly competitive markets still the preferred type of market structure?
3. If one were to analyze the decision to attend college, in a general equilibrium framework, they would have to consider many factors in making the decision. It would be impossible to list all of these factors. What, however, are the five most important factors or other markets that would have to be considered?

ANSWERS

Multiple-Choice

1) c,   2) a,   3) d,
4) b,   5) d.

Imperfect Competition: Monopoly Markets

13

LEARNING OJBJECTIVES

After you have studied this chapter in the textbook, attended class lectures over this material, and completed this study guide chapter you should be able to answer the following questions.

1. What is a monopoly and what has to exist for a monopolist to maintain its market power?
2. What are the various barriers to entry that may be present for a monopolist?
3. Why is price considered a fourth decision variable for a monopolist?
4. How is the market demand curve related to a monopolist's demand curve?
5. Why is marginal revenue less than price in a monopoly market?
6. How should a monopolist determine the profit maximizing level of output to produce?
7. What is the social cost of a monopoly?
8. What are the proposed remedies to deal with a monopoly situation?
9. What is a natural monopoly and what problems are encountered when attempts are made to regulate natural monopolies?
10. How does imperfect competition in factor markets affect the optimal number of inputs to hire?

CHAPTER REVIEW

A monopoly is the existence of a sole firm in an industry, which has complete market power in that there are no close substitutes for the product that the monopoly firm produces. It is very difficult for other firms to enter the monopoly industry, even when the existence of excess profits says there is an incentive for entry by other firms. For a firm to keep its monopoly position, or its complete market power, it must have strong barriers to entry. Entry barriers are obstacles or institutions which keep other firms out of a particular industry.

Barriers to entry can take on several forms. Two examples are a government franchise which gives the sole right to service a market to one firm, and patents which give one firm the exclusive right to produce a good in a certain manner.

Even though a monopoly firm has sole control of a market it cannot sell whatever quantity it wants at whatever price it wants, it must respond to market conditions. Since it is the only firm in the market, the demand curve it faces is the downward-sloping market demand curve. Because the firm charges the same price for every unit of its product (it does not price discriminate) it must lower its price on all units sold when it wishes to sell more units. Since the firm lowers its price on all units sold, the extra revenue brought into the firm from selling another unit is less than the price of selling another unit. The extra revenue from selling another unit is called marginal revenue. For a monopolist, the marginal revenue from selling an extra unit of a good is less than the price of that good.

The monopolist functions as a profit maximizing firm; it will continue to produce output as long as the extra revenue from selling another unit of output is greater than the extra cost of producing it, this will always increase profits. In other words, the monopolist will produce up until the point where marginal revenue equals marginal cost. The monopolist charges a price, read off the demand curve at the profit maximizing level of output, which is higher than marginal revenue and higher than marginal cost. If price is higher than average cost the firm will be making excess profits. In the long-run this would call forth entry on the part of other firms. If the monopolist has strong barriers to entry these other firms can be kept out of the market and the monopolist can maintain its excess profit position.

In terms of efficiency one can see that a monopolist is not efficient. The monopoly firm produces too little output at too high a price. From the cost stand point, the monopolist does not always minimize its average costs. Not producing at the minimum point on the average cost curve implies that the firm is inefficient. Likewise, the firm will not produce the exact combination of output that consumers desire, because it does not produce where price equals marginal cost. This second condition further implies that the monopoly firm is inefficient.

There is one situation in which a single firm servicing an industry is desirable. This is the case of a natural monopoly. A natural monopoly is a firm that has an average cost curve that is always downward sloping. This type of firm always has lower average costs or scale economies from producing a larger level of output. To capture these scale economies, and to pass the cost savings on to society, the firm needs to have a large share of the market or optimally it should be the only firm in the market. It may be the case that the government needs to regulate that the firm be the only firm in the market. In return for the right to be the only firm in the market, the government, or regulating agency, may exert some control over the the price and output which the firm chooses to produce. The typical point at which regulation will occur is a point at which the firm is making a normal profit. At this point the firm's price should be regulated to be equal to its average cost of production.

Imperfect competition can also occur in factor, or input, markets. The extreme case of imperfect competition in factor markets is the case of a monopsony. A monopsony exists when there is only one purchaser of an input factor, such as labor. A monopsonist does not face a perfectly elastic supply of labor curve. It faces the positively sloped market supply of labor curve. To hire more workers the monopsonist must increase the wage paid to all workers. Since the wage increases for all workers, the extra cost of hiring an extra worker is greater than the wage paid that worker. The extra cost of hiring an extra laborer is referred to as the marginal factor cost of that worker, which rises faster than the supply of labor curve. The monopsonist firm will continue to hire workers up until the marginal factor cost of another worker is just equal to the marginal revenue product of that worker.

GLOSSARY

PURE MONOPOLY: An industry with a single firm that produces a product for which there are no close substitutes and in which significant barriers prevent other firms from entering to compete away profits.

BARRIERS TO ENTRY: Those factors that prevent new firms from entering an industry in which economic profits are being earned.

MARGINAL REVENUE: The additional revenue that a firm would earn by raising its level of output by one unit.

NATURAL MONOPOLY: An industry which realizes such large economies of scale in producing its product that single-firm production of that good or service is most efficient. An industry with a continuously declining average cost curve.

MONOPSONY: A market in which there is only one buyer for a good or service.

MARGINAL FACTOR COST (MFC): The cost of hiring (or buying) one additional unit of labor (or other input).

STUDY TIPS

1. Even though it is said that a monopoly firm has complete control of a market, that firm can not charge whatever price it wants for whatever quantity it wishes. The monopoly firm must respond to market conditions. The market conditions are represented by a downward-sloping market demand curve.

2. A monopolist is a profit maximizer and follows the profit maximizing rule presented in earlier chapters. Profit maximization occurs at the level of output where marginal revenue equals marginal cost. At this level of output the price is set at peoples' maximum willingness to pay for this quantity, as shown by the demand curve.

3. A monopoly firm can be inefficient on two accounts. First it can be considered inefficient because it generally will not minimize its average cost of production. Second, it may be considered inefficient because it does not produce the level of output people desire; it does not produce at a point where price is equal to marginal cost.

4. The one situation in which a single firm would be preferred, in an industry, is the case of a natural monopoly. A natural monopoly is a firm that has significant economies of scale at all relevant levels of production. The natural monopoly, however, will probably have to come about because of regulation. This regulation can be of many forms, but will generally be imposed such that the natural monopoly will produce a level of output that just generates a normal profit.

A LOOK AHEAD

Monopoly markets are not the only types of imperfectly competitive markets. The next chapter will discuss two other types of imperfectly competitive markets, oligopolies and monopolistically competitive markets. What differs about these firms, as has differed between monopolies and perfectly competitive firms, is how they receive revenues. More precisely, it differs how their revenues are affected by competition. All the firms face similar cost conditions but far different revenue conditions.

MULTIPLE-CHOICE QUESTIONS

1. A natural monopoly will generally be regulated to produce an output level such that
   a. P = MC
   b. MC = ATC
   c. P = MR
   d. P = ATC
   e. MC = MR

2. The demand curve faced by a monopolist is
   a. unitary elastic.
   b. the same as the market demand curve.
   c. horizontal at the market price.

    d. the same as the marginal cost curve.

    e. nonexistent.

3. If a monopoly is producing at a point where MC > MR, the firm should

    a. increase output.

    b. charge a higher price.

    c. reduce output.

    d. shut down in the short-run.

    e. ask for natural monopoly status.

4. A monopsonist will hire more workers up until the point where

    a. MFC = W

    b. MRP = W

    c. MRP = MFC

    d. MFC = 0

    e. MRP = 0

5. The profit maximizing rule, for any type of firm, is to produce where

    a. MC = MR

    b. MC = ATC

    c. P = MR

    d. AFC = 0

    e. AVC = MC

6. A monopolist's short-run supply curve is

    a. the horizontal summation of all of the supply curves in the industry.

    b. the same as the market demand curve.

    c. unitary elastic throughout.

    d. nonexistent.

    e. the marginal cost curve above the shut-down point.

7. A monopoly firm, in order to maintain its market power, must have

    a. excess profits.

    b. excess losses.

    c. normal profits.

    d. relatively elastic demand.

    e. strong entry barriers.

8. Which of the following is not a barrier to entry in a monopoly market?

    a. Increasing marginal costs.

    b. Patent protection.

    c. Economies of scale.

    d. Control of important raw materials.

    e. A government franchise.

9. In a monopoly market, marginal revenue is less than price because

    a. the firm is a price taker.

    b. because price acts as a barrier to entry.

    c. the monopolist can sell more only if it reduces the price on all units sold.

    d. the monopolist wishes to earn large economic profits.

    e. monopolists do not behave rationally.

10. The differences between a monopolist and a competitive firm include the fact that
   a. the monopolist is a revenue maximizer while the competitive producer is a profit maximizer.
   b. the competitive firm is more concerned about the public's interest than the monopolist.
   c. marginal revenue equals price only for the monopolist.
   d. monopoly works in theory but not in practice, and perfect competition works in practice but not theory.
   e. for the monopolist, MR < P, while for a perfectly competitive firm, MR = P.

ANALYTIC EXERCISES

1. Graphically show the total cost and total revenue curves for a monopolist, in the short-run, which is only making a normal profit. Show the average and marginal cost and revenue curves for this same monopolist.
2. If a monopolist cares nothing about profits, but only about revenues, what level of output would the monopolist produce to maximize revenue?
3. True or false: A nonprice discriminating monopolist will never produce along the inelastic portion of the demand curve.
4. Carefully explain why a monopolist does not have a short-run supply curve and why a perfectly competitive firm does have a short-run supply curve.

ESSAY QUESTIONS

1. Comment on the following statement: "Monopolies are bad and perfectly competitive firms are good."
2. In the recent past a major long-distance telephone company was broken up to diminish its monopoly or market power. Economic theory tells us that moves toward more competitive conditions will move society closer to a point of allocative efficiency. Has the telephone industry become more efficient?
3. Other than utility companies, are there any other firms that provide a good example of a natural monopoly?
4. To maintain a monopoly position, in an industry, a firm must have strong barriers to entry. To maintain a monopsonistic position in an input market a firm must also have certain special characteristics, what might those characteristics be?

ANSWERS

Multiple-Choice

1) d,   2) b,   3) c,   4) c,
5) a,   6) d,   7) e,   8) a,
9) c,   10) e.

Analytic Exercises

2) produce where MR = 0
3) true

14

Imperfect Competition: Monopolistic Competition and Oligopoly

LEARNING OBJECTIVES

After you have studied this chapter in the textbook, attended class lectures over this material, and completed this study guide chapter you should be able to answer the following questions.

1. What is a monopolistically competitive firm?
2. Do product differentiation and advertising increase or decrease social welfare?
3. How does a monopolistically competitive firm determine the profit maximizing level of output to produce in both the short-run and in the long-run?
4. Does a monopolistically competitive market lead to allocative efficiency?
5. What is an oligopoly?
6. How does an oligopolistic firm react to the actions of its rivals?
7. Does an oligopolistic market lead to allocative efficiency?

CHAPTER REVIEW

Earlier chapters have discussed the two extreme forms of market structure, perfect competition and monopolies. This chapter continues the discussion of market structure by discussing what falls between these two extremes; firms that have some market power but at the same time face competition. The first type of industry to be discussed is monopolistic competition. A monopolistically competitive market is one in which a large number of firms, with free entry, produce a similar but slightly differentiated product. The second type of market structure presented is that of an oligopoly. An oligopoly is an industry with a small number of large firms each with some degree of market power. The degree of market power each firm has, however, is not complete in that each firm is generally aware of the activities of its rivals in the industry.

What distinguishes monopolistic competition from monopoly and oligopoly (the other two types of firms with market power) is that firms cannot influence market price by virtue of their size. Firms gain control over price in monopolistic competition by differentiating their products. By producing a unique product or establishing a particular brand reputation, no other firm can produce the exact same good.

To be chosen over the competition, products must have positive identities in the minds of consumers, this differentiation is often accomplished through advertising. The advocates of free and open competition, with its differentiated products and advertising, believe that this is what gives the market system its vitality and power to satisfy the enormous range of tastes and preferences in a modern economy. Product differentiation also helps insure high quality and efficient production, and advertising provides consumers with valuable information on product availability, quality and prices that is needed for efficient choice in the marketplace.

There is also a negative side to advertising in that it promotes waste and inefficiency. Advertising raises the cost of products and frequently contains very little information. Advertising can lead to unproductive warfare between firms and may serve as a barrier to entry, thus reducing competition.

The profit maximizing level of output can be found for a monopolistically competitive firm by finding the point where marginal revenue is equal to marginal cost. A monopolistically competitive firm has a downward-sloping demand curve, like a monopolist, but much more elastic. In the short-run the monopolistically competitive firm can earn economic profits, normal profits or excess losses depending on where average costs are in relation to the price of the good. In the long-run, since entry is free, a monopolistically competitive firm will be driven to a point of normal profits. Any excess profits would call forth entry by other firms. Competition would insure that the price of the good is just equal to the average cost of production.

An oligopoly is a market dominated by a few firms that, by virtue of their individual sizes, are large enough to influence the market price. Oligopolies come in a great variety of different structures. What makes an oligopoly so difficult to analyze is the complex interdependence that usually exists among firms in these industries. The behavior of any one firm depends on the reactions of all others. Because individual firms make so many decisions, industrial strategies can be very complicated and difficult to generalize.

A number of different models of oligopoly behavior have been developed. One such model is the cartel model. A group of firms that get together and make price and output decisions is called a cartel. For a cartel to work, a number of conditions must be present: 1) demand for the cartel's product must be inelastic, and 2) the members of the cartel must play by the rules. A similar model is that of price-leadership. In this model one firm dominates an industry and all the smaller firms decide to follow the leader's pricing policy. If the dominant firm knows that the smaller firms will follow its lead, it will derive its own demand curve by simply subtracting from total market demand the amount of demand that the smaller firms will satisfy. A third model of oligopolistic behavior assumes that firms believe that rivals will follow suit if they cut prices but not if they raise them. Firms assume that the elasticity of demand in response to an increase in price is different from the elasticity of demand in response to a price cut. The oldest model of oligopoly behavior was developed by Augustin Cournot almost one hundred and fifty years ago. The newest models of oligopoly behavior are based on what is called game theory and contestable market theory.

With respect to performance, oligopolies are likely to be inefficient. Oligopolies are likely to produce where price is above marginal cost. When price is above marginal cost there is underproduction from society's point of view. Strategic behavior can lead to outcomes that are not in society's best interest. Oligopolies can force themselves into deadlocks that waste scarce resources. To the extent that oligopolies differentiate their products and advertise, there is the promise of new and exciting products. At the same time there remains a danger of waste.

GLOSSARY

MONOPOLISTIC COMPETITION: The most common form of industry (market) structure in the United States. Characterized by a large number of firms, no one of which can influence market price by virtue of size alone. Some degree of market power is achieved by firms producing differentiated products. New firms can enter and established firms can exit such an industry with ease.

PRODUCT DIFFERENTIATION: One strategy that firms use to achieve market power. Accomplished by producing truly different products and by creating differentiated product images by means of advertising.

OLIGOPOLY: A form of industry (market) structure characterized by a few firms that are each large enough to influence market price by virtue of size. Products may be homogeneous or differentiated. The behavior of any one firm in an oligopoly very much depends on the behavior of others.

CARTEL: A group of firms that get together and make joint price and output decisions.

TACIT COLLUSION: The act of joining with other producers in an effort to limit competition and increase joint profits. Tacit collusion occurs when such agreements are implicit.

PRICE LEADERSHIP: The result when one firm that dominates an oligopoly sets prices and all the smaller firms in the industry follow its pricing policy.

KINKED DEMAND CURVE MODEL: A model in which the demand curve facing each individual firm has a "kink" in it. The kink follows from the assumption that competitive firms will follow suit if a single firm cuts price but will not follow suit if a single firm raises price.

STUDY TIPS

1. The distinguishing characteristic between monopolistic competition and oligopoly is not so much the size or number of firms in the industry but how a firm reacts to its competition. Monopolistic competitors are merely price takers who are not generally concerned with the actions of their rivals. Their only concern with market power is in the differentiation of their products. Oligopolies, on the other hand, are quite aware of the actions of their rivals and assume that other firms are aware of their price and output decisions.

2. It should be remembered that the theories of monopolistic competition and oligopoly are what describes the real world. Perfect competition and monopoly are the polar extremes to market structure. The reason why the theory of monopolistic competition and oligopoly is less concise than the competitive and monopoly theories is because it has to explain so much. Most industries have characteristics that are unique to those industries and, as such, a general theory explaining all of this behavior is more difficult to come by.

A LOOK AHEAD

Imperfect competition exists in the real world. In some instances it has been judged bad on either efficiency or equity grounds. In these instances the federal government has taken action to attempt to eliminate imperfect competition or repair the damage caused by imperfect competition. In the next chapter a brief history and explanation of the various federal attempts to deal with imperfect competition is presented.

MULTIPLE-CHOICE QUESTIONS

1. A cartel is most likely to be found in a market characterized as
   a. perfectly competitive.
   b. monopolistic.
   c. monopolistically competitive.
   d. oligopolistic.
   e. contestable.

2. All of the following are characteristics of monopolistic competition except
   a. each firm has a small degree of market power.
   b. there are no barriers to entry.
   c. firms charge exactly the same price.
   d. there are a large number of sellers.
   e. products are differentiated.

3. Monopolistic competition differs from the model of pure competition because
   a. the demand curve faced by perfectly competitive firms is perfectly elastic but perfectly inelastic for monopolistically competitive firms.
   b. there are barriers to entry in a monopolistically competitive market but no barriers to entry in a perfectly competitive market.
   c. perfectly competitive firms produce identical products, while monopolistically competitive firms produce differentiated products.
   d. monopolistically competitive firms earn economic profits in the long-run and perfectly competitive firms earn only a normal profit in the long-run.
   e. none of the above.

4. In a monopolistically competitive market, the marginal revenue from selling another unit of output will be
   a. greater than price.
   b. equal to price.
   c. less than price.
   d. zero.
   e. indeterminate.

5. A kinked demand curve would
   a. discourage nonprice competition.
   b. exist only for a price leader.
   c. discourage frequent price changes.
   d. encourage frequent price changes.
   e. exist because of advertising.

6. The practice of price leadership
   a. makes tacit collusion difficult to detect.
   b. comes about because of diseconomies of scale.
   c. is a device that is used only in perfect competition.
   d. is most common in monopolistic competition.
   e. does not occur in oligopolistic markets.

7. All of the following are examples of nonprice competition except
   a. advertising.
   b. service provided to the customer after the sale.
   c. development of new and improved products.
   d. producing where marginal revenue equals marginal cost.
   e. the development of brand loyalty.

8. When comparing the demand curve faced by a monopolist and the demand curve faced by a monopolistically competitive firm
   a. they will both have the same elasticity of demand.
   b. the demand for the monopolistically competitive firm will be more elastic than the demand for the monopolist.
   c. the demand curve faced by the monopolist will be more elastic than the demand curve faced by the monopolistically competitive firm.
   d. the monopoly demand curve will be perfectly inelastic and the monopolistically competitive demand curve will be perfectly elastic.
   e. it is impossible to compare the respective elasticities.

ANALYTIC EXERCISES

1. In the theory of the kinked demand curve, a firm perceives that other firms will not follow its price increases but will follow its price decreases. Graphically show an oligopoly's demand curve if the firm perceived that its competitors would follow its price increases but not its price decreases.

2. In the discussion of market structure four different types of markets have been discussed: perfect competition, monopoly, monopolistic competition, and oligopoly. For the four firms listed below, explain which type of market structure best describes the activity of this firm.
   a) Billy Bob's Corner Gas Station
   b) The J.C. Penney Company
   c) a diary farmer.
   d) The National Broadcasting Company (NBC)

3. Graphically show a monopolistically competitive firm in long-run equilibrium. Is this firm being allocatively efficient?

ESSAY QUESTIONS

1. If you were made ruler of the country and had to pick just one type of market structure for your country (perfect competition, monopoly, oligopoly or monopolistic competition) what type would you choose and why?

2. Some advertising can be good because it provides information about products, promotes diversity in products and improves quality of products. Some advertising is bad because it wastes resources and promotes consumption of an unnecessary product. With these two things in mind, is political advertising good or bad?

3. Several models of oligopolistic behavior have been mentioned in the text (cartel, price-leadership, kinked demand, game theory and contestable market theory are a few). Which of these is the best general model of the way the real world works?

ANSWERS

Multiple-Choice

1) d,   2) c,   3) e,   4) c,
5) c,   6) a,   7) d,   8) b.

Analytic Exercises

1) the kink would be in the opposite direction
2) a. monopolistic competition
   b. oligopoly (or monopolistic competition)
   c. perfect competition
   d. oligopoly

Imperfect Markets and Public Policy

15

LEARNING OBJECTIVES

After you have studied this chapter in the textbook, attended class lectures over this material, and completed this study guide chapter you should be able to answer the following questions.

1. What was the significance, to antitrust legislation, of the Sherman Act of 1890?
2. What was the significance, to antitrust legislation, of the Clayton Act and the Federal Trade Commission Act of 1914?
3. What government agencies are responsible for antitrust enforcement in this country?
4. What are the arguments for and against antitrust enforcement in this country?
5. How should natural monopolies be regulated and what problems arise in regulating firms of this nature?

CHAPTER REVIEW

When unregulated markets fail to produce efficiently, governments can and do act to improve the allocation of resources. This chapter discusses in some detail the history and theory of government involvement in imperfectly competitive markets. Historically, governments have assumed two basic and seemingly contradictory roles with respect to imperfectly competitive industries: 1) they promote competition and restrict market power primarily through antitrust laws and other Congressional acts and 2) they restrict competition by regulating industries.

The first two significant pieces of legislation dealing with antitrust were the creation of the Interstate Commerce Commission and the Sherman Act. Congress created the Interstate Commerce Commission in 1887 to regulate the railroads and in 1890 passed the Sherman Act that declared monopoly and trade restraints illegal. The biggest problem with the Sherman Act was in its interpretation. The language of the statute declared monopolistic structure, as well as certain kinds of conduct to be illegal, but it was unclear what specific acts were to be considered restraints of trade. It was left to the Supreme Court to decide. The Court's opinion made it clear that the law did not outlaw every action that seemed to restrain trade, but only those that were unreasonable. In clarifying this rule of reason, the court stated that structure alone was not a criterion for unreasonableness. It was possible that an imperfectly competitive firm did not violate the Sherman Act as long as it won its market share using reasonable tactics.

Designed both to strengthen the Sherman Act and to clarify the rule of reason, the Clayton Act of 1914 outlawed a number of very specific practices. First, it made tying contracts illegal. Such a contract binds a customer to buy one product in order to obtain another. Second, it limited mergers that would substantially lessen competition or tend to create monopoly. Third, it banned price discrimination, that is, charging different customers different prices for reasons other than changes in cost or the matching of competition prices.

The Federal Trade Commission (FTC) was given broad powers to investigate the organization, business conduct, practices and management of companies that engage in interstate commerce. In addition, the Commission prohibited unfair methods of competition in commerce, though the determination of what constituted unfair behavior was left rather vague. Finally the FTC was also given the power to issue cease and desist orders where it found behavior in violation of the law.

The Celler-Kefauver Act extended the government's authority to ban mergers. Earlier legislation could only block horizontal mergers in which firms producing the same product joined together. The Celler-Kefauver Act extended the government's power to block vertical mergers, in which firms at various stages in a production process combined, as well as comglomerate mergers in which firms producing unrelated products combined.

The federal government measures competition or market structure with what is called the Herfindahl-Hirshman Index (HHI). To calculate the HHI for an industry, one takes the market share of each firm expressed as a percentage, squares the figures and adds. If the HHI is less than 1000 the industry is considered unconcentrated, and any proposed merger will go unchallenged by the government. If the index is between 1000 and 1800, the government will challenge any merger that would increase the index by 100 points. Herfindahl-Hirshman Indexes above 1800 mean that the industry is considered concentrated, and the federal government will challenge any merger that pushes the index up more than 50 points.

It is fairly easy to build an economic case for having and enforcing prohibitions against unfair and deceptive practices, price fixing, collusion, price discrimination and tying contracts. In recent years, however, antitrust laws have come under increasing criticism. While few complain about the laws that make this kind of conduct illegal, concern is gathering about remedies imposed on concentrated industries that seem to be performing well. These concerns argue that: regulations have become a penalty for success, there is a need for concentrated industries as a protection from foreign competition, concentration is necessary for research and development, barriers to entry are no longer as strong, and many people simply distrust putting power in the hands of government.

When an industry demonstrates very large economies of scale it may be efficient to have only one large firm in that industry. Such a firm is called a natural monopoly as discussed in chapter 13. If a single-firm industry is protected on the grounds that it is a natural monopoly, it must be regulated to prevent exploitation of its monopoly power. The proper role of government in the world of business is hard to define. In the face of monopolies and the consequent social loss they bring about if unrestrained, the government must play a role in the market economy.

GLOSSARY

SHERMAN ACT: Passed by Congress in 1890, the Act declares every contract or conspiracy to restrain trade among states or nations illegal and declares any attempt at monopoly, successful or not, a misdemeanor. Interpretation of what specific behaviors were illegal fell to the courts.

CLAYTON ACT: Passed by Congress in 1914, it clarified the "rule of reason" and outlawed specific monopoly behaviors such as tying contracts, unlimited mergers, and price discrimination.

FEDERAL TRADE COMMISSION (FTC): A federal regulatory group created by Congress in 1914 to investigate the structure and behavior of firms engaging in interstate commerce to determine what was unlawful "unfair" behavior, and to issue "cease-and-desist" orders to those found breaking the law.

HERFINDAHL-HIRSHMAN INDEX (HHI): A mathematical calculation using existing firm market share figures that is currently used by the Antitrust Division of the Justice Department to determine whether a proposed merger is in the public interest.

AVERCH-JOHNSON EFFECT: The observed tendency for regulated monopolies to build more capital than they need. This usually occurs when allowed rates of return are set by a regulatory agency at some percent of fixed capital stocks.

STUDY TIPS

1. In markets where significant economies of scale or limited market demand exist, it may be technically efficient to allow one or only a few firms to produce.
2. Don't assume that government regulation can always efficiently overcome the problems associated with imperfect competition. The resources used by regulators and by business complying with regulations have opportunity costs. Regulations give firms an incentive to lobby for more favorable regulations, using resources that might better be used producing output.
3. The mere size of a firm does not determine if that firm has violated any antitrust laws. Being a large or financially successful firm is not necessarily bad. What should be considered with respect to antitrust legislation is how a firm reacts to its competitors.

A LOOK AHEAD

This chapter has discussed one role the government plays in the economic system, dealing with antitrust and regulation. There are other roles for the government to play in a market economy. It is the subject of the next three chapters to discuss the other functions of the government. Chapter 16 discusses how externalities and public goods can prevent the economy from obtaining a competitive equilibrium or a point of allocative efficiency. As will be seen, the existence of these two conditions can provide another role for government. Chapter 17 discusses the distribution of income. For equity reasons the government may, at times, consider the distribution of income in this country inequitable, and may intervene to change the distribution. Finally, the federal government has a large say in the working of the economy through taxation. Chapter 18 deals with taxation in greater detail.

MULTIPLE-CHOICE QUESTIONS

1. A merger between two firms producing similar products is
   a. a horizontal merger.
   b. a vertical merger.
   c. a conglomerate merger.
   d. a bivariate merger.
   e. impossible to classify without more information.

2. The purpose of antitrust legislation is to
   a. set prices so that all firms earn a fair rate of return or normal profit.
   b. ensure that all industries are perfectly competitive.
   c. prevent firms from unreasonably exerting market power.
   d. establish a bond of trust between business firms and consumers.
   e. guarantee an adequate tax base.

3. Which of the following is most likely to increase an industry's Herfindahl-Hirshman Index?
   a. A horizontal merger.
   b. A vertical merger.
   c. A conglomerate merger.
   d. Regulation.
   e. All four activities will increase the value of the index.

4. Which of the following is not illegal under antitrust statutes?
   a. Collusion among competitors to fix prices.
   b. Tying agreements.
   c. An abusive exercise of market power.
   d. Horizontal mergers that significantly reduce competition.
   e. All four are illegal.

5. The first Congressional Act to make monopoly and restraint of trade illegal was the
   a. Wheeler-Lea Act.
   b. Celler-Kefauver Act.
   c. Clayton Act.
   d. Sherman Act.
   e. Averch-Johnson Act.

ESSAY QUESTIONS

1. Government regulation generally maintains that each community have only one electrical power company. If this regulation did not exist, do you believe there would be competitive power companies in several communities? Would any problems exist if there was more than one power company servicing a community?
2. Price discrimination still exists in several forms. Can you provide an example of when price discrimination has happened to you (recall this implies that you have been charged a different price for a good or service that costs the same to provide for everyone)?
3. If antitrust regulation did not exist would all industries eventually become monopolized?

ANSWERS

Multiple-Choice

1) a,   2) c,   3) a,
4) e,   5) d.

90

Government in the Economy

16

LEARNING OBJECTIVES

After you have studied this chapter in the textbook, attended class lectures over this material, and completed this study guide chapter you should be able to answer the following questions.

1. What is an externality and why do they exist?
2. How can taxes and subsidies be used to correct externalities?
3. What problems exist with using taxes and subsidies to attempt to correct externalities?
4. In order for bargaining and negotiation to work, as a solution to externalities, what conditions have to be met?
5. What problems exist with direct regulation of externalities?
6. What characteristics define a public or social good?
7. How is the market demand curve for a public good different from the market demand curve for a private good?
8. Does an optimal provision of public goods exist?
9. What is social choice theory?
10. Can majority rule voting be used to answer social choice theory questions?

CHAPTER REVIEW

This chapter continues the discussion of market failure in which an allocatively efficient competitive equilibrium cannot be reached. An externality exists when the actions or decisions of one person or group impose a cost or bestow a benefit on second or third parties. Inefficient decisions result when economic units fail to consider these social costs and benefits. In some instances goods are overproduced because individual firms do not look at the marginal social cost of producing a good, they only look at the marginal private cost of producing that good. The marginal social cost of production includes both private costs as well as the costs to society from producing the stated good. In these circumstances one generally says a negative externality exists.

In other instances some external benefit comes from the production of a good. These goods will generally be underproduced because consumers and firms only look at the marginal private benefit from producing a good, not the marginal social benefit. The marginal social benefits include all private benefits plus the benefit accruing to society from the production of a good. These situations are usually referred to as situations of positive externalities.

Four basic approaches have been taken to the problem of externalities: 1) government imposed taxes and subsidies, 2) private bargaining and negotiation, 3) legal rules and procedures such as injunctive relief and liability rules, and 4) direct government regulation. While each approach is best suited for a different set of circumstances, all four provide decision makers with an incentive to weigh the external costs and benefits of all transactions. The first two of these proposals are discussed in more detail below.

Economists have traditionally advocated the use of taxes and subsidies as a direct way of forcing firms to consider external costs or benefits. When a firm creates an external social cost, a tax should be imposed on the firm equal to the damages of each successive unit of output produced. The tax will make the firm internalize the cost of their activity by being set exactly equal to the marginal damage costs generated. The biggest problem with this approach is that damages must be estimated in money terms. The monetary value of damages to health and longevity may be difficult to calculate. It is important to note that taxing externality-producing activities may not eliminate the damages. Taxes on these activities are not designed to eliminate externalities; they are simply meant to force decision makers to consider the full costs of their decisions. Taxes do provide an incentive to use the most efficient technology for dealing with the damage. If the tax reflects true damages, and if it is reduced when damages are reduced, firms may choose to avoid or reduce the tax by using a different technology that creates less damage.

In some situations private bargains and negotiations can lead to an efficient solution, to externalities, without any government involvement. This conclusion is attributed to Ronald Coase or called Coase's Theorem. For Coase's Theorem to hold true, certain conditions must be met: 1) the basic rights at issue must be well defined, 2) there must be no impediments to bargaining, and 3) only a few people can be involved. Coase also pointed out that bargaining will get the participating parties to the right solution regardless of where rights were initially assigned.

Another source of market failure lies in the existence of public goods, often called social or collective goods. These kinds of goods represent a market failure because they have characteristics that make it difficult for the private sector to produce them profitably. Public goods are defined by two characteristics: they are nonrival in consumption and their benefits are nonexcludable. A good is called nonrival in consumption when one individual's consumption does not interfere with another individual's consumption. Private goods are rival in consumption. Public goods also have the property that once the good is produced, people cannot be excluded from enjoying its benefit. For a private profit-making firm to produce a good and make a profit, it must be able to withhold that good from those who do not pay.

Market demand for a private good is simply the sum of the quantities that each household decides to buy. To arrive at the market demand for public goods, one adds up the amounts that individual households are willing to pay for each potential level of output. For private goods, market demand is the horizontal sum of individual demand curves, the sum of different quantities. For public goods, market demand is the vertical sum of individual demand curves, the sum of willingnesses to pay. One problem remains, to produce the optimal amount of each public good the government must know something about everyone's preferences. Because exclusion is impossible, nothing forces households to reveal their preferences.

This introduces the third problem of market failure discussed in this chapter. Defining what society wants is referred to as social or public choice. Social choice theory involves adding up, or aggregating individual preferences and allocating benefits to suit as many of these aggregate preferences as possible. The most common social decision-making mechanism is majority rule. It has been shown, however, that it is impossible to derive a voting scheme that respects individual preferences and gives consistent nonarbitrary results. Defenders of government involvement in the economy acknowledge its failure but believe that we get closer to an efficient allocation of resources with government than we would without it.

GLOSSARY

EXTERNALITY: A cost or benefit resulting from some activity or transaction that is imposed or bestowed upon parties external to the activity or transaction. Sometimes called spillovers or third-party effects. Often externalities are in the form of public goods, falling collectively on many people.

MARGINAL SOCIAL COST: The total cost to society of producing an additional unit of a good or service. MSC is equal to the sum of marginal resource costs and marginal damage costs.

COASE'S THEOREM: The proposition that if bargains were reached costlessly, externalities would not result in an inefficient allocation of resources. Through bargaining and negotiations, private parties can and will arrive at the efficient solution when externalities are present without government involvement.

PUBLIC GOODS: Goods or services that bestow collective benefits on members of society; they are, in a sense, collectively consumed. Generally, since benefits are collective, one cannot be excluded from enjoying them once they are produced. The classic example is national defense.

NONRIVAL IN CONSUMPTION: A characteristic of public goods; one person's enjoyment of the benefits of a public good does not detract from another's enjoyment of them.

NONEXCLUDABLE BENEFITS: Another characteristic of most public goods: their benefits fall on all members of a group or a society and no one can be excluded from enjoying those benefits once the good is produced.

FREE-RIDER PROBLEM: A problem intrinsic to public goods: because people can enjoy the benefits of public goods whether or not they pay for them, everyone is disinclined to pay for them. Consumption is not contingent upon payment.

SOCIAL CHOICE: The problem of deciding what societies want. The process of somehow aggregating or adding up individual preferences to make a choice for the whole.

STUDY TIPS

1. Though the majority of this chapter's discussion of externalities focuses on negative externalities (costs), positive externalities do exist. The important thing to remember is that an externality exists whenever marginal social costs diverge from marginal private costs and when marginal social benefits are different from private marginal benefits.

2. Just because a good is titled a public good does not imply that the good is produced by the public or government sector. Public goods are those goods which are nonrival in consumption and for which the exclusion principle does not hold. Many of the goods provided by the government are not public goods, they are either rival in consumption or the exclusion principle holds.

3. Coase's Theorem is merely an application of the equal marginal principle. Once property rights to a certain good have been defined and the true marginal benefit and marginal cost of that good or activity have been defined, an equilibrium or point of efficiency can be determined.

A LOOK AHEAD

In the next chapter a move is made away from a discussion of pure efficiency and a presentation is made concerning equity and justice. In the next chapter it is argued that the government may wish to change the distribution of income that results from the operation of the unregulated market, on the grounds that it is not fair.

MULTIPLE-CHOICE QUESTIONS

1. When a good's marginal private benefit is less than its marginal social benefit
   a. too many units of the product will be produced.
   b. it will be difficult for producers to generate a fair rate of return on their investment.
   c. there are external benefits associated with the production of this good.
   d. the good could be causing pollution.
   e. the price of the product is too high.

2. When the marginal social cost of a good is greater than the marginal private cost of that good
   a. too many units of the product will be produced.
   b. too few units of the product will be produced.
   c. the price of the good will be too high.
   d. a positive externality is said to exist.
   e. the government should supply the good.

3. One of the characteristics of a public good is that
   a. it is provided solely by the government.
   b. no one really wants the good.
   c. the free-rider effect exceeds and is in the opposite direction to the drop-in-the-bucket effect.
   d. it is rival in consumption.
   e. once it has been produced consumers cannot be excluded from consuming it.

4. When deriving the market demand curve for a private good versus the market demand curve for a public good
   a. the demand for the private good is found by a vertical summation of individual demand curves and the public good demand curve is found through a horizontal summation of individual demand curves.
   b. the demand for the private good is found by a horizontal summation of individual demand curves and the public good demand curve is found through a vertical summation of individual demand curves.
   c. they are both found in the same way.
   d. the demand curve for a private good will be found through a horizontal summation of individual demand curves and the demand curve for a public good will always be perfectly inelastic at the nonexcludable quantity.
   e. public goods do not have demand curves.

5. Arrow's impossibility theorem has shown that
   a. it is impossible to have a public good.
   b. it is impossible to measure the marginal social cost of pollution.
   c. taxes and subsidies cannot solve externality problems.
   d. it is impossible to devise a voting scheme that respects individual preferences and gives consistent nonarbitrary results.
   e. Coase's Theorem is incorrect.

6. At the movie theatre, the person talking during the entire movie two rows ahead of you is a good example of
   a. a public good.
   b. social choice in action.
   c. an imperfectly competitive market.
   d. an externality.
   e. Coase's Theorem.

ESSAY QUESTIONS

1. Many of the readers of this study-guide are enrolled in a state sponsored university. Are state universities public goods since they are provided by the public sector?

2. Some have argued that not enough people go to college after high school. Their argument is based on the fact that the social benefits of a college education are often forgotten. As this chapter explains, when the marginal social benefits of an activity are greater than the private benefits of that activity, the activity is generally under produced or consumed. What are the social benefits of a college education? How should the problem of too few people in college be remedied?

3. Is the optimal amount of pollution no pollution or absolutely clear air? How would Coase's Theorem help answer this question? Who should own the property rights to air?

4. In what ways or in what instances might highways fail to be pure public goods? More specifically is there any situation in which highway travel is rival in consumption or the exclusion principle holds?

ANSWERS

Multiple-Choice

1) c,   2) a,   3) e,   4) b,
5) d,   6) d.

Income Distribution and Poverty

17

LEARNING OBJECTIVES

After you have studied this chapter in the textbook, attended class lectures over this material, and completed this study guide chapter you should be able to answer the following questions.

1. What is equity and why might economists study it?
2. What determines the distribution of income in this country?
3. What are the three general sources of income in this country?
4. How unequal is the distribution of income in this country?
5. How can a Lorenz curve and a Gini coefficient be used to graphically represent the distribution of income?
6. What is poverty and what groups of people fall below the poverty line?
7. What are the basic arguments against the redistribution of income?
8. What are the basic arguments in favor of a redistribution of income?
9. If redistribution is to take place, how is a fair or just distribution to be determined?
10. What are the major policies or programs for redistributing income in this country?

CHAPTER REVIEW

This chapter moves the discussion away from the efficient allocation of resources and focuses on distribution. Consumer choice theory, as presented in Chapter Six, implies that we should talk not about the distribution of material objects but about the distribution of well-being. As one will recall, economists call well-being utility. A consumer chooses on the basis of his or her own utility function. Therefore, society should make distributional choices based on a social welfare function. Unfortunately no such social welfare function, embodying society's ethics, exists. For that reason most discussions of distribution deal with the distribution of income or with the distribution of wealth as an indirect measure of well-being.

The rewards of a market system are linked to productivity, and some people or households in every society are not as productive as other households. For this reason household incomes will differ or the distribution of income will be unequal, some will have more and some will have less. Households derive their incomes from three basic sources: 1) from wages or salaries received in exchange for labor, 2) from property such as land and capital, and 3) from the government. The amount of income received from each of these sources can vary greatly from household to household.

Wage and salary income can vary across households for several reasons. First, some individuals are born with particular skills or through training acquire skills that are absolutely limited in supply and therefore can draw an increased income. Other people take on jobs that are risky or undesirable and command a higher income. Second, some households have more than one wage earner in the labor force and as such have higher household incomes. Third, involuntary unemployment implies that some individuals who would like to work do not have jobs and therefore have lower household incomes.

The amount of income a household earns from property depends upon how much property is owned and what kind of property or assets are owned. These assets or pieces of property are acquired through savings and through inheritance. Savings includes stocks and bonds, as well as the appreciated value of assets such as a residential home.

The final way in which a household generates income is through government transfer payments. Transfer payments are payments made by government to people who do not supply goods or services in exchange. Not all transfer payment income goes to the poor. The single largest transfer program, at the federal level, is social security which goes to all income groups.

The Lorenz curve is a commonly used graphic device for describing the distribution of income. Along the horizontal axis is measured the percentage of families. Along the vertical axis is measured the cumulative percentage of income. If income were distributed equally the Lorenz curve would show a 45-degree line between zero and 100 percent. The more unequal the distribution of income, for an economy, the farther the Lorenz curve will be from the 45-degree line. The Gini coefficient is a measure of the degree of inequality in a distribution. It is calculated by taking the ratio of the area below the 45-degree line and above the Lorenz curve, to the entire area below the 45-degree line. If income is equally distributed the two lines coincide and the Gini coefficient is zero. As income becomes more unequally distributed the Lorenz curve moves to the right and the area below the 45-degree line becomes larger. This increases the value of the Gini coefficient. The maximum value of the Gini coefficient is one, which is complete inequality of income.

A discussion of income distribution cannot take place without a discussion of poverty. In simplest terms, poverty means people with very low incomes. This, however, is an absolute definition of poverty, in that, a very low level of income has to be defined in terms of some dollar amount. A more appropriate measure of poverty might be a relative measure that compares poverty to what is necessary or relative to what others have. Since the early 1960s the government has observed an officially established poverty line. This line is based on the observation that poor families spend about one-third of their incomes on food. The official poverty line has been established at a dollar amount that is simply three times the cost of the Department of Agriculture's minimum food budget.

The most basic argument against government redistribution of income and wealth is based on the notion that everyone is entitled to the fruits of their efforts. Other arguments are based on freedom of contract and property rights. More common arguments are based on the effects of redistribution on the incentive to work, save and invest. The arguments in favor of redistribution are based on the premise that society has a moral obligation to provide the basic necessities of life to everyone. This argument has been more formally developed by writers such as Marx and Rawls.

In this country redistribution and the attempt to correct poverty is accomplished through taxation and a number of government transfer programs. The largest of these programs are social security, public assistance, unemployment compensation, Medicare and Medicaid, food stamps, and various public housing programs.

GLOSSARY

EQUITY: "Fairness." One criterion for judging the final distribution of what society produces.

ECONOMIC INCOME: The amount of money a household can spend during a given time period without increasing or decreasing its net assets. Wages, salaries, dividends, interest income, cash and noncash transfer payments, rents, and so forth are sources of economic income.

LORENZ CURVE: A widely used graph of the distribution of income, with cumulative "percent of families" plotted along the horizontal axis and cumulative "percent of income" plotted along the vertical axis.

GINI COEFFICIENT: a commonly used measure of inequality of income derived from a Lorenz curve. It can range from zero to a maximum of one.

POVERTY: The officially established income level that distinguishes the poor from the non-poor. It is set at three times the cost of the Department of Agriculture's minimum food budget.

UTILITARIAN JUSTICE: The idea that a dollar in the hand of a rich person buys "less" than a dollar in the hand of a poor person. If the marginal utility of income declines with income, transferring income from the rich to the poor will increase total utility.

STUDY TIPS

1. Much of the material in this chapter is descriptive in nature and must be remembered as opposed to being derived from a theoretical model. An informed student of the economy will have a general idea of the sources of income in the economy and the major redistribution programs affecting these sources of income.

2. When discussing poverty the economic distinction between absolute and relative poverty is very important. Absolute poverty has to do with some fixed dollar standard which is set to define what low income levels imply. Relative poverty on the other hand is a more important economic concept because it deals with one's income in relation to what others have or the purchasing power of an individual's income and wealth.

3. The question of what is justice or how fairness should be defined is still an unanswered question in economics. Both economists and philosophers continue to discuss the appropriateness of utilitarian justice, versus Rawlsian justice, versus Marxian justice.

A LOOK AHEAD

Though equity concerns have been mentioned in several chapters throughout the text, this is the only chapter which has dealt with the topic specifically. In general, microeconomics limits itself to a discussion of efficiency concerns because of its attempt to be a positive science. Since well-being or utility is impossible to measure it is difficult for economists to address equity questions without making normative judgments. For this reason economists have spent far less time addressing these issues.

The final three chapters of this text return to the consideration of efficiency questions. Chapter 18 considers the role of government in the taxing of economic activity. Chapter 19 looks at labor markets and the activity of labor unions. Chapter 20 applies the microeconomic model developed in earlier chapters to determining the location of economic activity.

MULTIPLE-CHOICE QUESTIONS

1. The largest income redistribution program in the United States is
   a. Medicaid and Medicare.
   b. unemployment compensation.
   c. public housing.

d. food stamps

e. social security.

2. If the Lorenz coefficient is equal to zero
   a. income is equally distributed.
   b. income is totally unequally distributed.
   c. no one is below the poverty line.
   d. Rawlsian justice has been obtained.
   e. the economy cannot grow.

3. If income is redistributed to make the worst-off individual in society as well-off as possible
   a. Marxian justice exists.
   b. utilitarian justice exists.
   c. Rawlsian justice exists.
   d. Lorenzian justice exists.
   e. the Gini coefficient is one.

4. The largest source of personal income in the United States is derived from
   a. property income.
   b. transfer payments.
   c. social security.
   d. wages and salaries.
   e. stock dividends.

5. Which of the following is not an argument against redistribution of income?
   a. Everyone is entitled to the fruits of their own efforts.
   b. Society has a moral obligation to provide the basic necessities of life to all.
   c. Freedom of contract.
   d. Freedom to own property rights.
   e. Redistribution reduces the incentive to work, save, and invest.

6. If the United States Department of Agriculture determines that the annual minimum food budget, for a family of four, is $3000, then the official poverty line will be set at
   a. $1000.
   b. $3000.
   c. $10,989.
   d. $9000.
   e. $12,000.

ESSAY QUESTIONS

1. Provide a rough sketch of what the Lorenz curve for an economy would look like if the Gini coefficient were equal to one-half. Can different types of income distributions generate a Lorenz curve with the same Gini coefficients?

2. Some have defined the poverty line as the minimum amount of money that is needed for the necessities of life. What is the minimum amount of money that you could live on and feed, shelter and dress yourself? How does this compare to the amount of money that you actually use to support yourself?

3. Why is it so important to discuss relative poverty and not only absolute poverty?

4. Relate the following statement to the discussion in this chapter and to the concept of opportunity cost: "The United States has sent a man to the moon, but they have not eliminated poverty in this country."

5. Karl Marx argued that the income generated from property was injustice; was he correct in his argument?

6. Which is a more important goal for insuring the health and progress of an economy, equity or efficiency?

ANSWERS

Multiple-Choice

1) e,	2) a,	3) c,	4) d,
5) b,	6) d.		

Public Finance
18

LEARNING OBJECTIVES

After you have studied this chapter in the textbook, attended class lectures over this material, and completed this study guide chapter you should be able to answer the following questions.

1. What is the difference between a proportional, progressive and regressive tax?
2. What is the difference between an average tax rate and a marginal tax rate and which rate should be used in economic decision making?
3. What is the difference between the ability-to-pay principle of taxation and the benefits-received principle of taxation?
4. What provides the best tax base; consumption, income or, wealth?
5. What is tax incidence?
6. What group actually bears the burden of the payroll tax?
7. What group actually bears the burden of the corporate profits tax?
8. What group actually bears the burden of taxes, in general, in our country?
9. What is the excess burden of a tax and how is it measured?
10. What would constitute an optimal set of taxes and does an optimal set of taxes exist.

CHAPTER REVIEW

Public finance is one of the major subfields of economics mentioned in chapter 1. Public finance studies many areas of applied microeconomics including taxation. Taxation is the primary way in which the government raises revenues for its operation. Taxation is important to study because it can affect both the allocation of resources and the distribution of income. The important thing to remember about taxes is that they are ultimately paid by people or by households.

In studying taxes there are several new terms which must be learned. For example every tax has two parts: a base and a rate structure. The tax base is the measure or value upon which the tax is imposed. The rate structure determines what percentage or portion of the tax base must be paid to the government in the form of taxes. Taxes are also identified as being proportional, progressive, and regressive. A proportional tax is one in which the tax burden is a constant proportion of income for all households. A progressive tax is one in which the tax burden is a higher proportion of income for higher income households than it is for lower-income households. A regressive tax is one which extracts a lower proportion of income from higher-income households than it does from lower-income households. Finally, tax rates are identified as being average tax rates or marginal tax rates. An average tax rate is found by taking the total amount of tax paid divided by one's total income. The marginal tax rate is the tax rate paid on any additional dollar of earned income.

Equity concerns imply that economists must discuss who should actually pay taxes. One theory of equity, or fairness, states that taxes should be paid on the benefits-received principle. The benefits-received principle holds that taxpayers should contribute to the government according to the benefits they derive from government expenditures. A second principle of equity states that taxes should be based on the ability-to-pay principle. This principle holds that taxpayers should bear tax burdens in line with their ability to pay. The ability-to-pay principle is what is used in tax policy formulation in this country. Given that the ability-to-pay principle is the accepted form of equity criterion, two other principles must be mentioned. The principle of horizontal equity states that those with equal ability to pay should bear equal tax burdens. The principle of vertical equity holds that those with greater ability to pay should pay more.

Three economic aggregates can be used for the tax base: income, consumption, and wealth. Income is anything that enhances one's ability to command resources. Consumption is the total value of things that a household actually consumes during a period. Wealth is the value of all the things that one owns, after one's liabilities are subtracted. There are legitimate arguments for each one of these bases being used. Income provides a measure of one's capacity to command resources today. An income based tax, taxes the ability to consume resources. Consumption provides a measure of the resources actually consumed by an individual. A tax on consumption does not discourage savings. Wealth provides a measure of the power to command resources that arises from income streams that flow from more than one year. Those who have an accumulated ability to pay should be the payers of taxes.

When a tax is imposed on a certain economic unit, that economic unit is not necessarily the unit which bears the burden of the tax. Directly and indirectly, tax burdens are often shifted to others. The ultimate burden of a tax is said to be the incidence of that tax. The imposition of a tax will change economic behavior. Changes in behavior can affect supply and demand in markets and cause prices to change. When prices in input or output markets change, some households are made better off and some are made worse off. These final changes constitute the ultimate burden of the tax. Many empirical studies have been undertaken to measure tax incidence in this country. Using varying assumptions about economic behavior, some generalized results have been found. State and local taxes, which are dominated by sales taxes, tend to be mildly regressive. Federal taxes, which are dominated by the individual income tax, are mildly progressive. The tax system in general is roughly proportional or mildly progressive.

The shifting of taxes and the movement of the incidence of a tax can cause excess burden. When taxes distort economic decisions, they impose burdens on society that in aggregate exceed the revenue collected by the government. The amount by which the burden of a tax exceeds the revenue collected by the government is called the excess burden of the tax. When choosing different types of taxes, the preferred taxes are those which minimize excess burden. The size of the excess burden, imposed by a tax, depends on the degree to which decisions change in response to the tax. The measure of responsiveness that is often used is that of elasticity, either a price elasticity or an income elasticity. Taxes that adhere to the principle of neutrality, that is, that are neutral with respect to economic decisions, are preferred on grounds of efficiency. Broad-based taxes are more difficult to avoid than narrow-based taxes, and low rates distort less than high rates.

GLOSSARY

TAX BASE: The measure or value upon which a tax is levied. Examples include income, sales, and home value.

BENEFITS-RECEIVED PRINCIPLE: A theory of fairness, dating back to Adam Smith and before, which holds that taxpayers should contribute to government (in the form of taxes) in proportion to the benefits that they receive from government spending.

ABILITY-TO-PAY PRINCIPLE: A basis for taxation which stipulates that citizens should bear tax burdens in line with their ability to pay taxes.

TAX INCIDENCE: When we speak of the incidence of a tax, we are speaking of the ultimate distribution of its burden.

TAX SHIFTING: Occurs when tax burdens are transferred from those upon whom taxes are initially levied to others.

EXCESS BURDEN: Often the full burden of a tax to society exceeds the total amount of revenue collected by the tax. The excess burden of a tax is the amount by which its full burden exceeds the total revenue collected. Also called "deadweight losses."

STUDY TIPS

1. Before commenting upon the equity of a tax one has to make explicit what they consider equity to imply for taxation. There are two commonly accepted measures of tax equity: the benefits-received principle and the ability-to-pay principle. The ability-to-pay principle is the most often accepted standard in this country.

2. If the ability to pay-principle is accepted as a measure of equity, then the second criterion to consider is whether the proposed tax is horizontally or vertically equitable.

3. Where a tax is legally imposed is not necessarily and usually not where the incidence of the tax lies. Taxes are most often shifted, or attempts are made to avoid them. The final incidence of a tax generally is determined by the relative elasticities of demand and supply for various inputs and outputs.

MULTIPLE CHOICE QUESTIONS

1. If the tax on $10000 of income is $4000 and the tax rate structure is progressive, what must the tax be on $20000?
   a. $4000.
   b. less than $4000.
   c. $8000.
   d. less than $8000.
   e. more than $8000.

2. If William Robert, III and Muffy-Sue have the same income level and pay the same income tax, then
   a. vertical equity has been achieved.
   b. horizontal equity has been achieved.
   c. the marginal tax rate exceeds the average tax rate.
   d. the benefit-received principle may be applied.
   e. the excess burden of the tax is minimized.

3. Which of the following is not a good candidate for a tax base?
   a. Consumption.
   b. Income.
   c. Leisure.
   d. Wealth.
   e. All are likely candidates.

4. An optimal tax structure is one which
   a. passes both the benefits-received and ability-to-pay principles.
   b. generates the most revenue.
   c. minimizes vertical equity.
   d. minimizes excess burden.
   e. all of the above.

5. The rate of tax paid on any extra amount of income earned is referred to as
   a. the average tax rate.
   b. the marginal tax rate.
   c. the optimal tax rate.
   d. the personal exemption.
   e. the standard deduction.

6. Taxes in general in the United States are
   a. mildly regressive.
   b. extremely progressive.
   c. extremely regressive.
   d. proportional or mildly progressive.
   e. proportionally regressive.

ANALYTIC EXERCISES

1. The Lorenz curve developed in the last chapter was developed net of taxes. Taking a normally shaped Lorenz curve, graphically show the effect of three different types of income taxes; a proportional tax, a progressive tax and a regressive tax.
2. Suppose that three people (call them Winkin, Blinkin and Nod) have income levels of $8000, $12000, and $20000. Further assume that they do not need to pay tax on the first $4000 of their income. Design a proportional tax structure for these three individuals.
3. If a sales tax is imposed on every item sold, with no exceptions, will that tax be proportional?

ESSAY QUESTIONS

1. If a special tax was instituted that used the value of one's automobile as the tax base, would that tax be regressive, proportional or progressive? What assumptions were made in answering this question?
2. Property taxes are based on the market value of one's home. Do property taxes pass either the ability-to-pay principle or the benefits-received principle of tax equity?
3. Are taxes a more effective way to redistribute income or to generate revenue for the government?
4. If taxes are imposed on the sale of alcoholic beverages, list all the possible sources where the incidence of those taxes could be shifted.

5. If one followed a plan of Rawlsian justice (developed in the previous chapter) what type of tax structure would they invoke?

ANSWERS

Multiple-Choice

1) e,	2) b,	3) c,	4) d,
5) b,	6) d.		

19

The Economics of Labor Markets and Labor Unions

LEARNING OBJECTIVES

After you have studied this chapter in the textbook, attended class lectures over this material, and completed this study guide chapter you should be able to answer the following questions.

1. What factors must one consider when making a decision to further one's education?
2. Why might an individual leave a high paying occupation and take a different job at lower pay?
3. How do taxes affect the supply of labor?
4. What are the costs and benefits of extending the search for a new job?
5. What is discrimination, what causes it to arise, and what are the costs of discrimination?
6. How did the labor union movement begin in the United States?
7. What is the appropriate economic model to use in analyzing union behavior?
8. What are the costs and benefits, to both labor and firms, of unionization?

CHAPTER REVIEW

This chapter deals with another subfield of applied microeconomics, labor economics. Labor economics addresses many important questions: how do people and jobs get matched, how are wages determined, under what circumstances will individuals receive training, and when do people lose their jobs? The discussion of labor markets began in chapter 6 with a discussion of labor supply. The discussion continued in chapter 10 when the topic of consideration turned to a firm's demand for labor. A firm's willingness to pay for labor, or its demand for labor, will be based on the value of output produced by labor. That demand was found from the marginal revenue product of labor (MRP). The MRP of any worker is the marginal product of that worker times the price of the output sold. The supply of labor depends on individuals' and households' preferences for work versus nonwork. Nonwork includes, household activities, leisure, and human capital improvement or education. In a competitive labor market equilibrium occurs where the demand for labor is equal to the supply of labor. An individual firm will hire workers up until the marginal revenue product of labor is just equal to the market wage.

Analyzing the labor market is very difficult because the decision to work and the number of hours an individual works is based on preferences or a utility function. Likewise, there are several alternatives to work as well as several alternative types of work. One obvious alternative to working is to continue one's education or to increase one's human capital. In deciding to continue one's education one has to consider whether or not the future benefits of an education exceed the present costs of more schooling. One of the future benefits is the intangible psychological rewards which come from increased education. Public policy affects labor markets through the tax mechanism. Taxing labor income changes both the wage rate and the price of leisure. Whenever the price of a good changes, including the price of leisure, there exists an income and substitution effect to that price change. Empirical studies must sort out if the income and substitution effects, of a change in the price of leisure, are in the same direction or in opposite directions. If the movements are in opposite directions the relative magnitudes of the shifts most also be determined.

Labor market discrimination occurs when one group of workers receives inferior treatments from employers because of some characteristic irrelevant to job performance. Inferior treatment may include being systematically barred from certain occupations, receiving lower wages, or inability to win promotion or obtain training. Occupational discrimination results in a net loss of welfare to the economy. If workers have similar levels of productivity, rules of behavior that force one group into specific occupations are inefficient.

Nearly all eligible workers in a number of major industries belong to labor unions. Workers in several other industries, however, have not been unionized. From their earliest years, union objectives have been higher wages and improved working conditions. One way to analyze union power is to think of a union as a monopolistic seller of labor in a market. The labor union can restrict the supply of labor and charge a wage rate above the competitive equilibrium. This theoretical model can be used to discuss union behavior as long as one keeps in mind that unions look at more than just wage rates. Unions are also concerned about working conditions and the number of people employed. While unions are still a major force in the economy and in American society, they do not enjoy the power or the influence that they once did. As a percentage of those employed, union membership stands at its lowest level since 1938 with the trend being toward less unionization.

GLOSSARY

JOB SEARCH: The process of gathering information about job availability and job characteristics.

DISCRIMINATION: The inferior treatment of an identifiable group, often drawn along racial, ethnic, or gender lines, by employers because of some characteristic irrelevant to job performance.

KNIGHTS OF LABOR: One of the earliest successful labor organizations in the United States, it recruited both skilled and unskilled laborers. Founded in 1869, the power of the Knights of Labor declined after the Chicago Hay Market bombing in 1886.

AMERICAN FEDERATION OF LABOR (AFL): Founded in 1881, the AFL was successfully led by Samuel Gompers from 1886 until 1924. A practical, nonideological union, the AFL existed as a "confederation" of individual craft unions representing skilled workers, each with an independent organization and an exclusive jurisdiction. Now merged with the CIO, the AFL maintains a pre-eminent position among unions today.

NATIONAL LABOR RELATIONS BOARD: A watchdog board established by the Wagner Act in 1935 whose duties include ensuring that all workers are guaranteed the right to join unions and that firm managers participate fairly in collective bargaining if so requested by a majority of their employees.

CONGRESS OF INDUSTRIAL ORGANIZATIONS (CIO): Founded by John L. Lewis, president of the United Mine Workers, after the AFL rejected his plan to organize the steel, rubber, automobile, and chemical industries in 1935, the CIO was the first union to organize semiskilled laborers in the mass production industries. After 20 years of independence, it merged with the AFL in 1955.

STUDY TIPS

1. Many of the ideas presented in this chapter have to be remembered because they deal with the historical development of labor and labor unions in this country. There is no quick and easy way to remember these facts because they are not derived from an economic model but from historical events.
2. The study of labor supply is difficult because supplying labor involves two decisions: whether to work or not and once the decision to work is made, how many hours should be worked. In addition if one decides to work they may increase their market wage by postponing work and acquiring human capital skills through education.

A LOOK AHEAD

Only one microeconomic chapter remains to be studied. The next chapter does not deal with labor markets, which may make the student presume that the topics of this chapter may not be encountered again. This is not the case, the student continuing the study of economics will encounter labor markets and union effects when they study the aggregate or macroeconomy. These markets are important in determining price levels and national output.

MULTIPLE-CHOICE QUESTIONS

1. Which of the following was the earliest successful labor organization in this country?
   a. The American Federation of Labor.
   b. The Congress of Industrial Organization.
   c. The Knights of Labor.
   d. The Taft-Hartley Union.
   e. The National Labor Union.

2. The stock of knowledge, skills, and talents that human beings possess by nature or by education is called
   a. fixed capital.
   b. variable capital.
   c. leisure.
   d. human capital.
   e. a compensating differential.

3. The price of leisure may be measured by
   a. the marginal revenue product.
   b. the marginal physical product of labor.
   c. the average product of labor.
   d. the slope of the supply curve.
   e. the wage rate.

4. If tax rates on wages are lowered, and the income effect of a wage change is in the opposite direction and of a greater magnitude than the substitution effect, what will happen to the supply of labor?
   a. It will go down.
   b. It will increase.

    c. It will depend upon the size of the wage change.

    d. It will remain constant.

    e. It varies from labor market to labor market.

ANALYTIC EXERCISES

1. Historically trace the development of labor unions in this country and predict the state of union activity in the year 2000.
2. Graphically show the affect of unionization on the labor supply curve and the marginal factor cost curve.

ESSAY QUESTIONS

1. In what type of industries would one most likely find a union? What type of industries are most likely not unionized?
2. If you are entering an occupation in which you have never been employed before, would you prefer it to be a unionized occupation or a nonunionized occupation?
3. Wages and salary are not the only benefits to being employed. What benefits other than wages and salaries are important to you when looking for a job? Can a dollar value be placed on these benefits? Namely, how much of a salary reduction would you take to obtain a job which had these benefits?
4. If an employer refuses to hire anyone who does not have a college education is that employer practicing discrimination? From the point of view of the employer why might it be rational not to hire anyone without a college education? From the point of view of society why is it inefficient for the employer to behave in this manner?

ANSWERS

Multiple-Choice

    1) c,   2) d,   3) e,   4) a.

20

The Location of Economic Activity: Cities and Regions

LEARNING OBJECTIVES

After you have studied this chapter in the textbook, attended class lectures over this material, and completed this study guide chapter you should be able to answer the following questions.

1. How has the distribution of people living in urban areas versus rural areas changed since the Industrial Revolution?
2. What economic forces promote urbanization and the growth of cities?
3. What determines the location at which a business firm operates?
4. How do households determine where to locate?
5. Does discrimination exist in the housing market?
6. How is land rent determined?
7. What forms of urban decline have taken place over the last two decades and what has caused this decline?
8. What public policy measures have been undertaken to fight urban decline?

CHAPTER REVIEW

Microeconomic analysis has been used to determine many things: how much to produce, what to produce, how many inputs to hire and various other things. This analysis can be used to determine yet another economic activity, where to locate. Every household must live somewhere, and every business firm must operate somewhere. In making locational decisions individuals and firms act like rational consumers maximizing the utility or profits from every decision they make.

One of the questions that economic analysis can help us answer is, why do we have cities? One of the reasons we have cities is because engaging in exchange is not costless. The cost of engaging in transactions can be minimized when a buyer can engage in many transactions at a single location, such as in a city. A second reason why cities arise is because competition for markets leads directly to the concentration of economic activity. Third, the existence of economies of scale in transportation can bring cities about. Fourth, for certain industries large scale capital-intensive techniques are the most efficient method of production. To have a large number of people employed or working together requires that production take place at a single location or in a city. Fifth, cities grow because businesses service other businesses that locate in one location. Service industries will arise anytime basic industry grows. Sixth, specialized industries need to be located in an area with a lot of people to make a profit, since they sell to such a small percent of the population. Finally, just as specialized products require an urban area so do specialized labor skills. Firms requiring specialized skilled labor will locate within a city, or near it, to obtain those specially skilled laborers.

The choice of a business location for a firm is determined by the level of profits which can be obtained at various locations. Profits will be different at different locations because of differences in both costs and revenues at various locations. Competition and the lack of competition will change output prices, as well as input prices, at alternative locations. Locational cost differentials can arise because of the availability of natural resources at alternative locations and the cost of transporting the goods to market once they have been produced. In addition, public policy can affect the cost and revenue received by firms. Public officials influence the locational choices of firms through various tax and expenditure plans. The most important determinant of firm location may well be land costs.

When discussing the cost of land and land markets one quickly sees that the activity or economic unit that occupies a particular location is the one that is willing to pay the most for it. The rent that a firm or individual is willing to pay for a location is based on how profitable the location is expected to be. Land markets, however, may not always operate efficiently. For this reason zoning laws or planning boards often control the allowable uses of land. The function of these zoning laws or planning boards is to identify all costs and benefits of proposed changes in spatial arrangement so to deal with externalities.

Many cities and urban areas have experienced decline or decay in the last two decades. The lack of both private and public investment in cities has been blamed as the problem. The residential housing market has decayed and industry and business has moved out of the central city. Public policies of tax and expenditure changes have helped to stop this decline, though they have not reversed the process.

GLOSSARY

TRANSACTION COSTS: All the time and money costs, other than production costs and final prices, that are involved in buying and selling: dissemination of product information, advertising, transportation to and from market, and so forth.

EMPLOYMENT MULTIPLIER: A figure used to estimate the total number of jobs in an area created by the introduction of one new job to the area.

GHETTO PREMIUMS: Evidence suggests that during the 1960's and 1970's housing in sections of U. S. cities inhabited predominantly by blacks was more expensive than comparable housing in white areas. The price difference came to be called a ghetto premium.

ZONING: The designation of certain areas for industry, commerce, and housing. Often these categories are broken down into subcategories which specify the kind of business allowed, the number of families allowed within a single residential building, how much land a residence must have around it, and so on.

URBAN DECLINE: The deterioration of the private and social capital stock of a city which results from the lack of investment by both private and public sectors.

STUDY TIPS

1. This chapter would not have to stand as a separate chapter. The material presented here could have been presented in the chapters on consumer theory or firm behavior. The decision of where an individual chooses to live is merely an extension of the utility maximization problem. The consumer chooses a residence that maximizes his or her utility subject to some form of budget constraint. The firm chooses a site location which maximizes its profit level. Profits are affected by the different costs and revenues which vary with location.

2. The material on urbanization since the Industrial Revolution and the material on regional growth and distribution trends must be remembered. This material is historical or descriptive and is not generated from an economic model.

A LOOK AHEAD

This chapter concludes the discussion of microeconomics. That does not mean, however, that microeconomic issues can be forgotten. A continued study of economics, in particular a study of macroeconomics, requires a knowledge of microeconomics. The standard assumption in the study of macroeconomics is that microeconomic markets work. It is assumed that individuals rationally attempt to maximize their utility and firms rationally attempt to maximize their profits. This rational behavior implies that predictions can be made as to how, in the aggregate, individuals will respond to economic stimuli.

MULTIPLE-CHOICE QUESTIONS

1. What is it called when individuals of a certain race pay more to live in a depressed area than members of another race, with comparable means, pay to live in identical housing in a different neighborhood?
   a. Industrial Revolution.
   b. Ghetto Premium.
   c. Zoning.
   d. Urban decline.
   e. Urban renewal.

2. Zoning is often invoked to deal with
   a. urban externalities.
   b. diminishing marginal utility.
   c. transaction costs.
   d. monocentric models.
   e. imperfect competition.

3. Monocentric city models would predict that housing would be least expensive
   a. at the center of the city.
   b. near areas of natural beauty.
   c. immediately next to all other housing.
   d. at the outer edge of the city.
   e. it is impossible for these models to predict.

4. In 1700, approximately what percent of the population lived in agricultural or rural areas?
   a. 12%.
   b. 75%.
   c. 50%.
   d. 15%.
   e. 25%.

5. If a gas station can be built at location A or location B, and profits at location B are higher than profits at location A
   a. rent will be higher at location A than at B.
   b. rent will equalize at the two locations
   c. rent will be high at location B and be zero at location A.
   d. rent must be high at location A.
   e. rent will be higher at location B than at A.

ANALYTIC EXERCISES

1. Consider the metropolitan area in which you grew up or the metropolitan area in which you are now attending school. For this metropolitan area, is business activity distributed along a series of concentric rings around the city center? What occurrences could possibly prevent this type of business distribution in the city?
2. How would the availability of good public transportation affect the results concerning rental values in the monocentric city model?

ESSAY QUESTIONS

1. There are several good economic reasons why urban or city areas are desirable places to live and work. What are the arguments against living and working in a large urban area?
2. Are New York City, Mexico City and Tokyo too large to be economically efficient?
3. Is there a better way to deal with urban externalities than through zoning?
4. What economic factors went into determining were you now live? How will these economic factors change once you have completed school?
5. Why does the state of North Dakota have so few large cities and so relatively few inhabitants?

ANSWERS

Multiple-Choice

1) b,   2) a,   3) d,   4) b,
5) e.

Introduction to Macroeconomics

21

LEARNING OBJECTIVES

After you have studied this chapter in the textbook, attended class lectures over this material, and completed this study guide chapter you should be able to answer the following questions.

1. What is macroeconomics?
2. How is microeconomics related to macroeconomics?
3. What are the major economic problems which concern macroeconomists?
4. What is a business cycle?

CHAPTER REVIEW

Macroeconomics is the study of aggregate economic activity. It is built upon the basic tenets of microeconomics but is mainly concerned with the sum of all microeconomic decisions and transactions, not only by individuals but also by firms. The goal of macroeconomics, however, is one of taking the whole of microeconomic behavior and constructing a working model that can be used to influence the macroeconomy.

Macroeconomics was born out of the Great Depression of the 1930's. The economic conditions which prevailed during that time were not consistent with microeconomic models then in use; for example, conventional microeconomic theory would tell us that in the face of rising unemployment, workers, and especially unemployed workers, would bid down wages to a level at which labor markets would clear. However, unemployment rates were consistently in the teens and occasionally greater than twenty per cent through most of the Great Depression. Macroeconomics developed, largely through the genius of John Maynard Keynes, from a desire to both explain and correct this significant social and economic problem.

Unemployment is just one of the major problems that concerns macroeconomists; others include inflation, the size of the aggregate economy, and economic relationships in the international sector. In attempting to identify and influence each of these areas of concern, macroeconomics recognizes the role of government in the economy. This role was acquired through both the sheer size of government and its ability to direct policy decisions. The policy decisions usually fall into the broad categories of fiscal policy (having to do with the levels of government spending and taxes), monetary policy (influencing the size and composition of the money supply), and incomes policy (assuming direct and indirect control of wages, prices, and profits).

Macroeconomists have developed a series of models to help explain and predict aggregate economic activity. The simplest of these is known as the circular flow model. The significant feature of this model is its ability, in a logical format, to show the relationships among households, firms, government, and financial institutions; doing business in product markets, resource markets, and money markets.

Macroeconomic activity is cyclical over time. Recessions and depressions are examples of time periods when macroeconomic activity is relatively weak, while booms are times when activity is strong. The actual periods of time and magnitude of each extreme varies but the cyclical swing is always observed. One of the goals of macroeconomics would be to influence the timing and magnitude of these extremes.

GLOSSARY

AGGREGATE: The sum or total across individuals in a given category: consumption, investment, and so forth.

FISCAL POLICY: Those changes in taxes and in government purchases that the government can use to expand or contract the macroeconomy.

INFLATION: A general increase in the overall price level.

MACROECONOMICS: The branch of economics that examines the economic behavior of aggregates-- income, employment, wages, taxes, output, and prices--on a national scale.

MONETARY POLICY: Those measures the Fed can use in the money market to influence the quantity of money supplied and hence the interest rate.

STAGFLATION: The existence of low output, or stagnation, and a high rate of inflation at the same time.

STUDY TIPS

1. The successful student will quickly identify the professional background and bias of the instructor. The two sides of economics have a wide range of knowledge and methodology in common; however, there are subtle differences in outlook that may be important to a grade-motivated student.

2. The first difficulty of moving from a study of microeconomics to a study of macroeconomics is to grasp the aggregative way of thinking. When macroeconomists speak of consumption, they are considering the sum of all households. (There is not a time in macroeconomics when a single individual or firm is considered.)

3. Learn the model! As the model is expanded in subsequent chapters, the internal logic remains the same. It is much easier to learn it now, then add to it, rather than learn it in three or four weeks in its final (at this level) form.

4. Do not allow yourself to consider individual exceptions. The definition of inflation is a general rise in prices. Your instructor knows as well as you do that the prices of most electronic equipment from watches to calculators have dropped throughout the last few business cycles, even those times of high inflation. Over this same period of time prices in the health care industry have far outpaced the rate of inflation. As a student of macroeconomics, you are concerned with the overall price picture: prices have generally risen.

A LOOK AHEAD

This chapter is by title an introduction, therefore you must conclude that all of the topics mentioned in the chapter will be revisited later. There are three themes that run through the next twelve or so chapters: the theoretical model, the policy implications of macroeconomics, and a recent history of the U. S. macroeconomy.

The theoretical model started here will be built upon and referred to throughout the rest of the course. Macroeconomic policy has as its goal the control of inflation and unemployment. You will find the historical accounts challenging and helpful, they provide a life to macroeconomics as theory is moved through policy into action, then examined to see what actually happened.

MULTIPLE-CHOICE QUESTIONS

1. Which of the following would be of primary interest to macroeconomists?
   a. relative prices of meat products.
   b. wages in regulated public utility firms.
   c. the general price level.
   d. the impact of Sunday Closing Laws on beer sales.

2. The Great Depression:
   a. was most severe during the decade of the 1930's.
   b. could have been avoided by the group practice of Freudian psychology.
   c. was predicted by the Classical economists.
   d. led to the birth of microeconomics.

3. The idea that the economy can be moved to a desired equilibrium and kept there is known as:
   a. the New Deal.
   b. Reaganomics.
   c. the New Frontier.
   d. fine-tuning.

4. A general _____ in the price level is known as _____.
   a. increase, inflation.
   b. decline, recession.
   c. decline, unemployment.
   d. increase, prosperity.

5. John Maynard Keynes was the author of:
   a. The Wealth of Nations.
   b. The General Theory of Employment, Interest, and Money.
   c. The Grapes of Wrath.
   d. The Law and the Profits.

6. The existence of unemployment:
   a. means that the macroeconomy cannot be in equilibrium.
   b. is not an economic problem but a social problem.
   c. means that not all resources are being used to their fullest.
   d. is a microeconomic concern because the labor market is exactly like the hot dog market.

7. All but which one of the following represent policy tools available to the federal government?
   a. incomes policy.
   b. return policy.
   c. monetary policy.
   d. fiscal policy.

8. In the circular flow model, households:
   a. supply labor and make income payments.
   b. purchase resources.
   c. produce goods and services.
   d. supply labor and receive income payments.

9. Households, government, and businesses interact in:
   a. goods and services and financial markets.
   b. financial and free markets.
   c. labor, goods and services, and financial markets.
   d. goods and services, stock, and labor markets.

ANALYTIC EXERCISES

1. Draw and explain the circular flow model.
2. Consider the impact upon the circular flow model of each of the following microeconomic events:
   a) salad bars increase in popularity by 25%.
   b) the price of wheat doubles.
   c) government stops buying red tape.

ESSAY QUESTIONS

1. It is generally accepted that unemployment increases during one phase of the business cycle, while inflation increases during the other. Why might this be true?
2. Explain the major concerns of the field of macroeconomics.
3. If the macroeconomy is national in scope, why hadn't the field of macroeconomics grown up with the nations over the past six centuries rather than be developed over only the last six decades?

ANSWERS

Multiple-Choice

1) c,	2) a,	3) d,	4) a,	5) b,
6) c,	7) b,	8) d,	9) c.	

Measuring Macroeconomic Activity

LEARNING OBJECTIVES

After you have studied this chapter in the textbook, attended class lectures over this material, and completed this study guide chapter you should be able to answer the following questions.

1. What is the meaning of gross national product, including defining the measure, describing the collection of the measure, and what is and is not included in the measure?
2. What are the other national income accounts?
3. What is the difference between real and nominal GNP?
4. What is the difference between flow concepts and stock concepts?
5. What is the difference between the incomes approach to GNP and the expenditures approach to GNP?
6. How are the various national income accounts calculated?

CHAPTER REVIEW

The focus of chapter 22 is on the generation, interpretation, and significance of the most important measures of the macroeconomy. This study is important because the numbers are the basis for most macroeconomic policy decisions.

The key account is the aggregate measure of the Gross National Product (GNP). GNP is the market value of all final goods and services produced in an economy in one year. In determining what is included in and excluded from GNP, it is well to keep in mind the goal of providing a measure of current domestic economic activity.

There are two basic methods by which GNP is calculated: the expenditures approach and the incomes approach. Either approach leads to the same GNP because of the identity between what is spent and what is earned in the basic circular flow model of macroeconomic activity. The two equations below provide a review of each method:

$$C + I + G + Xn = GNP = W + R + Int + P + (IBT + CCA)$$

Two significant features of the calculation of GNP center around the involvement of other economies and the notion of investment. Purchases of goods and services produced in other economies do not reflect domestic production or employment, and thus should not be included in GNP; conversely, goods produced here and sold there, do contribute to this economy and should be included. Investment includes both the broadly generalized category of business spending as well as current housing expenditures. The logic used in this is that a house is in reality an extremely durable good.

The reason the GNP is such an important statistic is that it indicates the general status of an economy and any changes in the economy. However, the GNP is limited due to the data being reported in current dollar amounts. In order to allow for interyear comparisons, real GNP must be calculated using some constant or base year dollar; the use of constant dollars removes changes in the valuation or purchasing power of the dollar that might either shield or represent real changes in production. The conversion from nominal GNP to real GNP requires a knowledge of the level of production and agreement on a base year dollar; then consists of simply "repricing" the current transactions in the base year currency through the use of an index number. Real GNPs calculated using the same base year may be compared to determine any changes that may have occurred over time in an economy.

The way GNP statistics are defined and collected imposes a limitation on the use of the numbers. There are two other areas that must be addressed: what is current production that is not included? and what is included that the economy would be better off without? The calculation of GNP implicitly excludes all production of illegal activities since these transactions are not reported. The GNP also excludes most of those goods and services that individuals provide for themselves or barter in non-monetary transactions with other individuals.

The GNP is not a perfect indicator of the quality of economic life. An economy that practiced increasing dependence upon purchased child care and food preparation would have an increasing real GNP, ceteris paribus, even though the quality of life may have remained the same. An economy that must spend increasing amounts of money on pollution clean-up and prison construction will have an increasing GNP.

The calculation of per capita GNP, found by dividing the GNP by the population, allows another way of using the statistic as a comparative measure. A constant GNP in an economy that was experiencing population growth would suggest that each individual's "share" was actually shrinking. Per capita real GNP allows a comparison among years that gives an indication of the relative status of individuals in the economy.

GNP is not the only national income account. Careful consideration of disposable income provides an illustration of the flow-of-funds concept. A household's disposable income will either be spent as consumption (note that this is the same personal consumption as seen in the expenditures approach to GNP) or as savings. Savings is a flow into a stock, what one could think of as a pool of savings. This flow of savings for households and all of the sectors is simply the difference between income and expenditures. If all sectors are considered together savings will equal zero; this is because those sectors that have negative savings must borrow out of the stock created by those sectors with positive savings, for example, a portion of individual savings will be in the form of government savings bonds and treasury bills.

GLOSSARY

CURRENT DOLLARS: The nominal value of the dollar. The unadjusted purchasing power of a dollar at the time it is spent.

EXPENDITURES APPROACH TO GNP: The determination of the GNP by summing the dollar expenditures for currently produced goods and services by households, businesses, government, and netting import purchases and export sales.

FLOW VARIABLE: The measurement of the rate or volume of change in some variable. Weekly income, for example, is a flow variable.

GROSS NATIONAL PRODUCT: The market value of all final goods and services produced in an economy in one year. An indicator of economic activity in an economy.

INCOMES APPROACH TO GNP: The determination of GNP by summing the dollar amounts of all income earned in current production of goods and services.

NOMINAL GNP: The measure of the GNP in current dollars.

PER CAPITA GNP: The measure of GNP on a per person basis. Per capita GNP is found by dividing GNP by the population.

REAL GNP: The conversion of nominal GNP to constant dollars. The measure of GNP in constant dollars as opposed to current dollars.

UNDERGROUND ECONOMY: That portion of economic activity which is not accounted for in national income accounting. The underground economy exists primarily because of the existence of illegal activities (gambling, extortion, drugs, prostitution) or for the purposes of tax evasion (cash only or barter arrangements).

STUDY TIPS

1. National income accounting as a topic is one of the few areas where the successful student relies on rote memorization. Beyond reasoning out questions such as the purchase (or any part of the purchase) of a 1956 Packard is included in 1988's GNP, there is no theoretical base in the accounts such as one would find in marginality or consumer preference. Therefore, you should be prepared to learn the composition and decomposition of the various national income accounts. The expenditures approach to GNP can be thought of as the pneumonic "CIGX" pronounced "sig-ex" representing the sum of Consumption, Investment, Government spending, and net exports.

2. The most common mistake made by students in using national income accounts is the distinguishment between real and nominal values. Real GNP is valued in constant, or base year, dollars, while nominal GNP is in current dollars.

3. Similarly, it is important to realize the difference between stocks and flows. Stocks are the sum of flows, the total amount earned during a year is a stock as is the balance in your savings account. The income that you collect at the end of each pay period and the contribution that you make to your savings account from that income are both flows. Savings is a particular problem in macroeconomics because the same term, "savings", is used to refer both to the stock and the flow. For clarity and technical reasons, the flow is saving, while the stock is savings.

4. Remember that in macroeconomics, particularly national income accounting, "investment" is used to denote business spending. The term may refer to business spending regardless of whether the firm borrowed the money, sold equity ownership, or used retained earnings. "Investment" as used here has no relationship and should not be confused with the use of the term in public that refers to purchasing common stock or preserving one's wealth.

A LOOK AHEAD

This chapter is a bit of an anomaly in the study of macroeconomics, almost a necessary evil. The major focus of the chapter, national income accounting, is not closely tied conceptually to the study of economic theory. However, there are some concepts included in the chapter that fall into the economic strain category. A major concept is the nature of stocks and flows as seen first in the preceding chapter in the circular flow model of macroeconomic activity. We will see stocks and flows repeatedly in the identity between savings and investments, leakages and injections, and policy methods in future chapters.

A second concept that is seen in a variety of contexts primarily in macroeconomics, is that of the distinction between measures that are nominal and those that are real. In future chapters you will encounter nominal income, wages, money, and interest rates; as well as real income, wages, money, and interest rates.

MULTIPLE-CHOICE QUESTIONS

1. GNP is:
   a. the measure of the value of all final goods and services produced in an economy in one year.
   b. the sum of all expenditures made by the citizens of a country in one year.
   c. an excellent indicator of the standard of living in an economy.
   d. the sum of all wages and salaries earned in an economy during one year.

2. The significant difference between GNP and the net national product is:
   a. NNP includes both imports and exports.
   b. NNP reflects changes in the capital stock due to its treatment of the capital consumption allowance.
   c. NNP is measured in current dollars because that is the way depreciation is reported.
   d. NNP does not include that portion of personal consumption that is in reality an indirect tax.

3. National Income:
   a. is the same as GNP.
   b. is the amount of money available for personal consumption and savings.
   c. is the sum of all income earned as a result of current production.
   d. is the single best measure of the standard of living of individuals in an economy.

4. Which of the following does not represent investment?
   a. An increase in the quantity of $3.00 ties displayed at K-MART.
   b. The construction of a new house that will be owner occupied.
   c. The purchase of newly issued stock in a genetic engineering corporation.
   d. The construction of a new factory using borrowed funds.

5. If two neighbors decide that one should specialize in lawn mowing and do both lawns, while the other specializes in hedge trimming and does both hedges; are these transactions included in GNP? Why?
   a. No, because these are non-market transactions.
   b. No, due to specialization less effort was expended rather than more.
   c. Yes, because each of the parties was made better off as a result of the transaction.
   d. Yes, because the market accepts and has a price for each of these services.

6. The purchase, in 1988, of a 1958 EDSEL at auction would:
   a. increase the value of the 1988 GNP by the amount of the purchase price.
   b. require the recomputation of the 1958 GNP to reflect the appreciation or depreciation of the value of the car.
   c. would be an investment.
   d. increase the value of the 1988 GNP by the amount of the commission paid to the auctioneer and any expenses associated with the services of the sale.

7. If nominal GNP is greater in 1988 than in 1987 we may conclude:
   a. that the economy has grown.
   b. that the economy has shrunk.
   c. that the economy is stagnant.
   d. nothing.

8. Purchases of intermediate goods _____ included in GNP because:
   a. are not, their value becomes part of the value of a final good.
   b. are not, these are non-market transactions.

c. are, they represent real production in the economy.
   d. are, incomes are earned from the sale of all goods.

9. Which of the following variables represents a stock, rather than a flow?
   a. the quantity of export sales during 1987.
   b. the amount of savings by households during 1988.
   c. 1988 real GNP.
   d. the value of housing held by households at the end of 1987.

ANALYTIC EXERCISES

1. Using the data provided below, calculate gross national product, net national product, national income, personal income, and disposable income.

consumption	$ 1,450
export sales	225
indirect business taxes	135
government spending	675
investment spending	335
personal taxes	365
wages and salaries	1,375
rental income	445
government transfer payments	180
profits	130
dividend payments	70
capital consumption allowance	110
import purchases	290
interest income	200
savings	310
social security contributions	145

2. Using the data provided below, calculate gross national product, net national product, national income, personal income, and disposable income.

wages and salaries	$ 2,345
rental income	820
interest income	465
profits	510
dividends	325
transfer payments	890
capital consumption allowance	480
consumption	3,000
savings	600
personal taxes	610
social security contributions	635
indirect business taxes	335

3. Calculate the nominal GNP for both year 1 and year 2 and the real year 2 GNP, using year 1 as the base year, for the economy represented below.

Year 1   3,000 pizzas @ $10.00 and 45 textbooks @ $20.00
Year 2   3,500 pizzas @ $12.50 and 45 textbooks @ $21.00

ESSAY QUESTIONS

1. Compare and contrast nominal and real concepts.
2. Compare and contrast stocks and flows. Provide examples using flow-of-funds methodology.
3. Outline the differences among the various national income accounts in terms of what is measured and what is shown.

ANSWERS

Multiple-Choice

1) a,   2) b,   3) c,   4) c,   5) a,
6) d,   7) d,   8) a,   9) b.

Analytic Exercises

1) Gross National Product   = $2,395
   Net National Product   =   2,285
   National Income   =   2,150
   Personal Income   =   2,125
   Disposable Income   =   1,760
   (NOTE: you may use either approach)
2) Gross National Product   = $4,955
   Net National Product   =   4,475
   National Income   =   4,140
   Personal Income   =   4,210
   Disposable Income   =   3,600
   (NOTE: you must use incomes approach)
3) Year 1 nominal GNP   = $30,900
   Year 1 real GNP   = 30,900
   Year 2 nominal GNP   = 44,695
   Year 2 real GNP   = 35,900

23

Instability in the Macroeconomy

LEARNING OBJECTIVES

After you have studied this chapter in the textbook, attended class lectures over this material, and completed this study guide chapter you should be able to answer the following questions:

1. How is unemployment measured?
2. What are the major characteristics of a recession?
3. How is inflation measured?
4. Identify the winners and losers during periods of inflation. In what ways are gains and losses due to inflation limited?

CHAPTER REVIEW

The phenomenon known as the business cycle, first introduced in Chapter 21, is seen as an irregular rotation between good economic times and bad economic times. Both extremes present macroeconomists, politicians, and economic citizens with what may be unpleasant problems. The good times, as seen from the standpoint of a growing economy and relatively full employment, carries the potential of rising prices, or inflation. The bad times, seen as a shrinking economy with stable or possibly even falling prices, carries the potential of widespread unemployment.

Recession is the name given to the lower portion of the business cycle. The generally accepted criteria for a recession is any decline in the real GNP that is observed over two consecutive quarters of a year. The decline in real GNP, seen initially as output falls, will be accompanied by a decline in employment, higher unemployment, and a reduction in the amount of plant capacity used. Price changes during most recessions will be either non-existent or downward.

A depression is a severe recession. There is no generally accepted definition of a depression since there is not a depression in every cycle. The Great Depression exhibited several consecutive quarters of unemployment rates in the 20% range as well as falling prices.

Unemployment is idleness in the human resource. The number itself is arrived at through a process of data collection conducted by the Bureau of Labor Statistics. There are three critical definitions to the understanding and interpretation of unemployment. The labor force is the available pool of workers in the economy. In order to meet the definition of being in the labor force, one must be either working or actively seeking work, fall between the ages of 16 and 65, and not be institutionalized. Out of a current population of about 255 million people, the United States has a labor force of about 122 million. The labor force consists of two distinct groups: employed and unemployed. The employed are working, either part or full time, while the unemployed are seeking work. The unemployment rate is the percentage of the labor force that is not working, at current levels each percentage point of the unemployment rate represents about 1.25 million people. The unemployment rate is calculated using the formula shown below:

$$\text{unemployment rate} = \frac{\text{unemployed}}{\text{employed} + \text{unemployed}}$$

There is a portion of the population that is outside of the labor force because they are no longer actively seeking work, but who would go to work if the opportunity afforded itself; this phenomenon is identified as the discouraged worker effect. Discouraged workers have usually exhausted all of the available government benefits so there is no longer a microeconomic incentive to continue registering. Discouraged workers may represent a number as large as 1.5% to 2% of the labor force.

Unemployment falls into three causal categories: structural, cyclical, and frictional. Structural unemployment is that type of unemployment that affects a particular industry or occupational group. The two primary causes of structural unemployment are a lack of demand for the products produced by the workers (derived demand for labor) and the substitution of capital for labor (i.e., automation).

Cyclical unemployment is unemployment that is associated with the general reduction in aggregate demand in the down portions of the business cycle. Cyclical unemployment is seen as relatively uniform unemployment rates across all sectors and industries of the economy.

Frictional unemployment is the measure of the flow of individuals between jobs. Frictional unemployment is not viewed as a negative indicator of the economy. In order for individuals to voluntarily become frictionally unemployed, the economy must be strong enough to afford a reasonable opportunity to move.

The other extreme of the business cycle has relatively full employment but carries the risk of inflation, a general rise in prices. The underlying cause of the inflation is the increase in aggregate demand confronting the economies inability to meet the increased demand. Inflation is measured by use of either a market basket approach, such as the Consumer Price Index, or an aggregate approach, such as the GNP Price Deflator. In either case, the objective is to isolate price changes from all other changes that may be occurring in the macroeconomy.

The Consumer Price Index records the prices of a collection, marketbasket, or bundle, of goods and services monthly. Quantities of the specific items sampled do not change. Price comparisons from year to year reveal differences in price but fail to account for microeconomic decision making which may lead to changes in quantities demanded in response to observed price changes. The CPI is calculated by observing the prices in a specific year as the base year and assigning them the value of 100 (base year prices/base year prices). The index value for subsequent years is found by dividing the price of the current years bundle by the price of the base year bundle then multiplying the answer by 100. For example if the base year bundle cost $38.50 and the observed years bundle cost $43.25 the observed years index would be 111.3 (43.25/38.50 * 100). The rate of inflation between the two years would be found by dividing the observed year's index by the base year's index resulting in an 11.3% inflation rate. The GNP Deflator is a broader measure because it takes account of changes in quantities demanded for all products rather than just a bundle.

Social concern about the effects of inflation generally center around the impact upon individuals that have fixed incomes. Widespread indexing, tying increases in payments to changes in an inflation index, have largely negated this effect. To the extent that individuals and financial intermediaries are good predictors of inflation, thus avoiding unanticipated inflation, the negative effects of inflation are minimized.

GLOSSARY

CONSUMER PRICE INDEX: A marketbasket measure of the change in prices from one period to another. Quantities in the CPI do not change in response to price.

CYCLICAL UNEMPLOYMENT: That unemployment that is attributable to a general downturn or recession in the economy. Cyclical unemployment will be observed across a wide variety of industries.

DEPRESSION: A severe and prolonged recession.

FRICTIONAL UNEMPLOYMENT: That unemployment that is observed as individuals are between jobs and have a reasonable expectation of resuming gainful employment.

GNP DEFLATOR: A broad measure of changes in prices in the economy from one period to another. The GNP deflator reflects adjustments in quantities that are observed in the macroeconomy.

INFLATION: A general rise in prices.

LABOR FORCE: A definitional category that includes all of the noninstitutionalized individuals in an economy that are either working or actively seeking work. The labor force is the denominator used in determining the unemployment rate.

RECESSION: An observed downturn in the macroeconomy in which real GNP declines two quarters in a row.

STRUCTURAL UNEMPLOYMENT: That unemployment that is observed as either demand in a particular industry is down or when technology changes make some job categories obsolete. Structural unemployment will be observed on an individual industry basis rather than across the entire economy.

STUDY TIPS

1. The definitions and measurements of unemployment, labor force, and unemployment rate fall into that small category of concepts in the principles of economics that are best memorized. Common sense will help you in determining such things as the calculable formula for unemployment rate, but generally speaking, there is not a "theory" or "model" available to you as you look at this side of unemployment.

2. The measurement of inflation is also in the category "of its easier to memorize." Theory will help you in determining the winners and losers in inflation if you keep in mind the very significant distinction between anticipated and unanticipated inflation.

3. In performing inflation rate calculations, be especially careful that you maintain the same base year. The concept of assigning base year prices at an index value of 100 is not always inherently obvious to the principles student and it is neither slight of hand nor mystical. All that happens is that the base years prices are observed then divided by the base year prices, which of course always yields an answer of one, then that answer is multiplied by one hundred. The subsequent years' prices are divided by base prices which will almost always yield an answer other than one that is then multiplied by one hundred.

4. Do not fall into the trap of identifying the inflation rate between a year whose index is 112, and the subsequent year whose index is 120, as a year in which the inflation rate was 8%. The inflation rate is found by subtracting the indices (120-112) and then dividing by the earlier year's index (112). The correct inflation rate is about 7.1%.

A LOOK AHEAD

This chapter returns to the major macroeconomic problems of unemployment and recession. Because the primary goal of macroeconomic policy is control of these problems the concepts from this chapter will continue to be seen.

The generation of the numbers that macroeconomists use, and knowledge of how the numbers were generated, prove helpful in determining and evaluating policy in future chapters.

MULTIPLE-CHOICE QUESTIONS

1. The consumer price index:
   a. measures changes in the tastes and preferences of consumers.
   b. generally understates the real inflation rate.
   c. measures price changes while holding quantities of goods and services constant.
   d. is the same as the GNP deflator.

2. The CPI was 298 in 1983 and 311 in 1984. You may then conclude that the rate of inflation in 1984 was about:
   a. 3%
   b. 4.5%
   c. 6.5%
   d. 13%

3. Inflation:
   a. always makes victims of retired people.
   b. is a benefit to creditors.
   c. reduces the purchasing power of the dollar.
   d. always reduces one's real income.

4. The GNP price deflator:
   a. is the broadest based index available.
   b. is a marketbasket measure of prices.
   c. tends to understate inflation.
   d. includes a seasonal adjustment.

5. A recession:
   a. is a period in which the macroeconomy takes time out.
   b. is a return to the good old days.
   c. occurs any time that real GNP declines in two quarters.
   d. has not occurred since the invention of macroeconomics.

6. The labor force participation rate is:
   a. the number of citizens that would be willing and able to work.
   b. the ratio of individuals in the labor force to the total population.
   c. the ratio of individuals employed to the labor force.
   d. the ratio of individuals unemployed to individuals employed.

7. Discouraged workers:
   a. are not unemployed because they are not in the labor force.
   b. are voluntarily unemployed.
   c. are a special category within structural unemployment.
   d. are lazy.

8. The unemployment rate is:
   a. the ratio of employed individuals to the total population.
   b. the ratio of employed individuals to the labor force.
   c. a composite of all non-workers in the economy.
   d. the ratio of unemployed individuals to the labor force.

9. Billy Bob Brown has just voluntarily left his position with the Brown (no relation) Furniture Company and will join the Brown (no relation) Shoe Company in 2 weeks. Billy Bob is:
   a. temporarily out of the labor force.
   b. not loyal.
   c. frictionally unemployed.
   d. structurally unemployed.

ANALYTIC EXERCISES

1. Assume that the rate of inflation between 1987 and 1988 was 5.5%. Your 1987 income was $22,000. What would happen to your real income under each of the following conditions:
   a) you receive no raise in 1988.
   b) you receive a raise to $23,210.
   c) you receive a raise to $26,420.

2. Based upon the following information calculate the labor statistics (to the nearest tenth of a per cent) requested below:

Total population	= 44.5 million
Employed	= 20.5 million
Total labor force	= 23.0 million

   a) labor force participation rate =
   b) unemployment rate =

ESSAY QUESTIONS

1. React to the following statement: If everybody knew what the inflation rate was going to be then inflation would have no effect.
2. Frictional unemployment is sometimes characterized as a positive form of unemployment; how can this be?
3. Compare and contrast the CPI and the GNP price deflator.

ANSWERS

Multiple-Choice

1) c,	2) b,	3) c,	4) a,	5) c,
6) b,	7) a,	8) d,	9) c.	

Analytic Exercises

1. a) real income is reduced
   b) real income is unchanged
   c) real income is increased
2. a) 51.7%
   b) 6.5%

A Simple Model of the Macroeconomy

24

LEARNING OBJECTIVES

After you have studied this chapter in the textbook, attended class lectures over this material, and completed this study guide chapter you should be able to answer the following questions.

1. In the simple model explain why the sum of consumption and investment expenditures is aggregate expenditure.
2. How does one arrive at the conclusion that aggregate output is an identity with aggregate income?
3. What is the consumption function? What is the role of the marginal propensity to consume?
4. What is macroeconomic equilibrium? How does it differ from microeconomic equilibrium?
5. In the simple model, what conditions must be met for macroeconomic equilibrium to exist?
6. Under what conditions might a less than full employment economy be at macroeconomic equilibrium?
7. Explain the multiplier. How is it found? How was it used?

CHAPTER REVIEW

The study of macroeconomics is dependent upon a model of the macroeconomy. Economic models are built upon the premise that they should be simple enough to explain and predict behavior in the macroeconomy yet be complex enough to account for the wide variety of influences in the macroeconomy. The model developed in this chapter is a beginning step in the process of building a comprehensive economic model. This model is limited to two sectors: households and businesses, doing business in only one market, the market for goods and services.

Households have but two behavioral decisions in this model: spending or saving. Household spending is referred to as consumption (the same consumption as was seen in national income accounting); savings is simply income that is not spent. The consumption decision is made on the basis of the set of microeconomic preferences of each household, summed since the concern here is really aggregate consumption. A simplifying assumption concerning consumption is that the portion of income that is spent for consumption is constant across the economy. The portion that is spent is found by identifying the marginal propensity to consume. You are familiar with the marginal concept, propensity simply means tendency; so the MPC is how spending changes in response to the last unit of income. An MPC of .9 implies that the household would spend $90 out of an increase in income of $100.

The second decision, saving, is just a residual of the consumption decision since the household only has these two options. The marginal propensity to save then is simply 1 - MPC. The standard notation for these terms is b = MPC and 1 - b = MPS.

A second assumption concerning consumption is that both individual households and the aggregated households of they macroeconomy would consume some minimal level in the absence of income. This minimal consumption level is identified as autonomous consumption (a). This results in a linear equation form for the consumption function where C = a + b(Y), where Y is the level of national income. In English, this equation states that for any given level of income, consumption is the sum of the level of autonomous consumption and that portion of income that would be spent according to the MPC. In the form of the linear equation, a is the intercept, while b is the slope of the line representing consumption. The MPC, under normal circumstances, has the characteristic of being a proportion that is greater than 0 but less than 1.

The saving decision can also be expressed in this linear form. The saving function (for this simplest model) is -a + (1-b)Y. The -a shows the source of money for autonomous consumption to be the stock of previous year's savings, again reminding us of the similarity between aggregate behavior and individual behavior. The MPS, under normal circumstances, has the characteristic of being a proportion that is greater than 0 but less than 1. The sum of the MPC and the MPS must always be 1, since there is no other choice available to households. For any income, Y, the level of consumption and saving can be determined if autonomous consumption and either the MPS or the MPC is known.

Business spending , the other sector in this simplest model, is given the name investment. Investment includes the full range of spending on any good or service that does not become part of the final product, primarily capital resources. Investment takes one of two forms: either planned or unplanned. Planned investment is that business spending that takes place as a result of the planning process, it is intended. Unplanned investment is a function of changes in business inventories, it is unintended. When businesses produce more goods than they sell, the difference or left-overs accumulate in inventories and are counted as unplanned investment. When, hopefully, these goods are sold out of inventory in subsequent years, they contribute income to the business just as any other investment from a prior year would.

The sum of investment and consumption represent aggregate expenditures or total spending in this simple model. If we assumed that investment expenditures are not effected by national income, so that they were constant over all incomes, then a graph of aggregate expenditures would have a slope equal to the MPC.

Aggregate equilibrium is the condition when there is no force present in the macroeconomy to cause change. The equilibrium condition is one in which national income and aggregate expenditures are equal and neither is changing. Macroeconomic equilibrium occurs when there is no unplanned investment under the conditions of the expenditures for all output is just equal to the sum of all incomes.

A second equilibrium condition is that the amount of money that households divert to savings is just equal to the level of investment; S = I. Equilibrium could then be expressed as Y = C + I and S = I, recognizing that Y = C + S at both equilibrium and disequilibrium.

The unplanned investment of inventory changes is the force that drives the macroeconomy toward equilibrium. If firms over produced, accumulating inventories, the tendency would be for them to curtail production back to a level that consumption expenditures would support and vice versa.

The multiplier explains the mechanism by which the macroeconomy may change equilibria. The identity exists that expenditures become income. Any increase in income then, will be translated into an increase in expenditures according to the MPC. This additional expenditure increases income by a like amount, making even more income to be either spent or saved, again determined by the MPC. Each new level of consumption becomes a new level of income, a portion of which is diverted into the stock of savings according to the MPS. What results from this process is the multiplier effect. Because of the role of the MPC and MPS in determining household behavior and effectively limiting the amount of money added to income from consumption expenditure, the value of the multiplier is 1/1-b or 1/MPS. If the MPC were equal to .9, the MPS would be .1, which means that each new dollar of income would result in an addition to the stock of savings of 10 cents. The multiplier under these conditions would be 10; so that a $10 exogenous increase in investment would ultimately result in a $100 increase in the equilibrium national income.

GLOSSARY

AGGREGATE INCOME: The total income received by all factors of production during a given period.

CONSUMPTION FUNCTION: The relationship between cosumption and income. "Function" refers to a relationship between variables.

EQUILIBRIUM: The condition that prevails when planned aggregate expenditure is equal to aggregate output.

INVESTMENT: Purchase by firms of the new buildings, equipment, and inventories that add to their capital stock.

MARGINAL PROPENSITY TO CONSUME: The fraction of a change in income that is consumed, or spent.

MARGINAL PROPENSITY TO SAVE: The fraction of a change in income that is saved.

SAVINGS: That part of household income that a household does not consume during a given period. Money earned but not spent.

STUDY TIPS

1. Spend enough time with the model that you can prove to yourself that aggregate output does in fact equal aggregate income. They are exactly the same thing looked at from the other side of all transactions. They constitute an identity.

2. The most difficult part of any science is the language. The most difficult word for most economics students is "investment." We use the word in a radically different way from the rest of humanity. Investment is business spending for currently produced plant and equipment which will be used in the production process but which will not become part of the product.

3. In thinking about macroeconomic equilibrium, keep in mind that savings equals planned investment only at equilibrium. It is always true that the sum of consumption and savings is disposable income. For ease of learning in future chapters you may want to generalize the equilibrium condition to one of leakages equals injections.

4. Memorize either the likely values of the multiplier (i.e. 2 (when MPC = .5), 4 (MPC = .75), 5 (MPC = .8), 10 (MPC = .9)) or the formula for deriving the multiplier (1/1-b).

5. Always confirm your conclusions about changes in equilibrium income in response to changes in investment with the simple circular flow model. Common sense tells you that if businesses increase their investment spending, aggregate spending increases, so equilibrium income increases. You should never have to worry about the direction of change, once you have thought the change through. This leaves you free to worry only about the numerical value for which you are solving.

A LOOK AHEAD

The multiplier will be seen in subsequent chapters as government is added to the model. With the government added, you will find the multiplier is the same, only its application has changed. The working of the multiplier remains the same, with only the formula and resultant values changing when a consideration of taxes is added to the model.

The money multiplier encountered in chapters 26 and 27 relies upon the same logic, but starts from a different set of premises.

Equilibrium is a term with which you are familiar from microeconomics. The macroeconomic equilibrium developed in this chapter will be expanded to include other variables as the model grows in subsequent chapters.

MULTIPLE-CHOICE QUESTIONS

1. As income increases:
   a. consumption and savings both increase.
   b. consumption increases and savings decreases.
   c. consumption increases and savings is unchanged.
   d. one cannot say for sure how consumption changes, if at all.

2. The consumption function:
   a. describes the relationship between consumption and saving.
   b. is a + b(Y).
   c. was a hit song from Sesame Street.
   d. is the opposite of the savings function.

3. The marginal propensity to save is:
   a. 1 - MPC.
   b. the sum of all previous periods saving.
   c. the source of all borrowed funds.
   d. MPC - 1.

4. It is always true that:
   a. roses are red.
   b. MPC + MPS = 1 and Y = C + I(intended)
   c. Y = C + S and 1 - MPS = MPC
   d. S = I(intended) and Y = C + I(intended)

5. The difference between actual investment and _____ investment is:
   a. perceived, important.
   b. planned, small when the economy is at equilibrium.
   c. perceived, zero when the economy is growing.
   d. planned, composed of inventory adjustments.

6. If aggregate output is greater that aggregate expenditures then:
   a. the economy is growing.
   b. inventories are increasing.
   c. savings is greater than actual investment.
   d. inventories are decreasing.

7. If consumption when income is $1.5 million is $1.75 million and is $2.5 million when income is $2.5 million then:
   a. dissaving is occurring.
   b. the MPS = .25.
   c. there is no money left over for investment.
   d. equilibrium income is $2.5 million.

8. The multiplier:
   a. is always 4.
   b. shows that any change in investment will lead to a greater change in equilibrium income.
   c. is 1/1 - MPS.
   d. has no effect on consumption.

9. If the MPC = .9, then:
   a. the multiplier must be 10.
   b. a $200 increase in I will lead to an $1800 increase in Y.
   c. the MPS = -.1.
   d. the multiplier must be 9.

10. Macroeconomic equilibrium is attained when:
   a. full employment is reached.
   b. all available resources are being used to their fullest.
   c. Y = C + S
   d. S = I(actual).

ANALYTIC EXERCISES

1. Fill-in the blanks below:

MPC = .8

Y	C	S	I	C+I
0	100	____	20	120
100	180	____	20	____
200	____	____	20	____
400	____	____	20	____
equilibrium = ____	____	____	20	____

2. If the initial equilibrium in an economy is $1,000 when the MPC = .75, a $20 increase in investment would cause the new equilibrium income to be _____.
3. When the MPS = .1, what size and direction of change in investment would be required to increase the equilibrium income by $400?

ESSAY QUESTIONS

1. Compare and contrast microeconomic and macroeconomic equilibrium.
2. Discuss the role of inventory in moving a macroeconomy toward equilibrium.
3. Explain the multiplier effect.

ANSWERS:

Multiple-Choice

1) a,	2) b,	3) a,	4) c,	5) d,
6) b,	7) b,	8) b,	9) a,	10) d.

Analytic Exercises

1) when $Y = 0$, $S = -100$
   when $Y = 100$, $S = -80$, $C + I = 200$
   when $Y = 200$, $C = 260$, $S = -60$, $C + I = 280$
   when $Y = 400$, $C = 420$, $S = -20$, $C + I = 440$
   at equilibrium, $Y = 600$, $C = 580$,
   $S = 20$, $C + I = 600$

2) $1,080.

3) $40.

Government in the Macroeconomy
25

LEARNING OBJECTIVES

After you have studied this chapter in the textbook, attended class lectures over this material, and completed this study guide chapter you should be able to answer the following questions.

1. How does the consumption function change to accommodate the inclusion of government in the model?
2. Explain (and use) the government expenditures multiplier.
3. Explain (and use) the tax multiplier.
4. In the model, why is the government spending multiplier always larger than the tax multiplier? Explain the balanced budget multiplier.
5. Describe the budgetary process of the federal government.
6. What role do state and local governments play in the macroeconomy?

CHAPTER REVIEW

The model of the macroeconomy is being expanded to include the government sector. Microeconomists and macroeconomists view the government in distinct ways. The microeconomic role of government includes the provisions of services, regulation, and the calculus of the political process. The macroeconomic role of government is based upon the concept of aggregate spending developed earlier as the sum of consumption spending, investment spending, and government spending.

Fiscal policy is the use of government to influence the size of the macroeconomy. There are three basic tools available to fiscal policy makers: government spending, taxation, and transfer payments. In terms of government spending the government acts as any other economic agent, but has the ability to act out of a whole host of motivations. An increase (decrease) in government spending, ceteris paribus, will be a direct increase (decrease) in aggregate spending not unlike an increase (decrease) in investment or autonomous consumption.

Tax changes take the form of adjustments in average tax rates and lump-sum tax amounts. Personal income tax rate increases (decreases) have the effect of decreasing (increasing) consumption expenditures due to a decrease (increase) in disposable income. The volume of tax collections, however, is a function of both the tax rate and national income (aggregated individual incomes). A shrinking economy would provide smaller tax revenues to the government if rates remained unchanged, for example; the same result could occur if the economy remained the same size while the rates were decreased.

Transfer payments are subsidies to individuals in the economy that are not tied to current production; welfare, veterans' benefits, and social security payments are just some of the more common transfer payments. Transfer payments become a tool of fiscal policy in the same way that government spending is. Transfer payments become a part of disposable income and as a function of the MPC, personal consumption. An increase (decrease) in transfer payments will result in an increase (decrease) in aggregate demand.

The multiplier developed in Chapter 24 is applicable to changes in government spending because this policy option directly affects aggregate spending. A $1 increase (decrease) in government spending becomes a $1 increase (decrease) in national income (remember the identity between spending and income). That $1 increase (decrease) in income is then subject to the MPC and the MPS. Given an MPC of .9, we would observe an additional $.90 in consumption expenditures which, in turn, become income, leading to $.81 of additional consumption expenditures. This process would continue until $10 had been added to national income; the multiplier for an MPC of .9 is 10 (found by dividing one by the MPS or 1/1-b).

Taxes, on the other hand, are subject to a further constraint. Tax changes are first encountered at the income side of the model, rather than at the demand for goods and services side. A $1 change in taxes is going to lead to a $1 change in income rather than to a $1 change in aggregate spending. The $1 change in taxes is subject to the MPC, so consumption is changed by $.90 (assuming an MPC of .9), therefore the initial change in aggregate spending is $.90 rather than $1. Ultimately, any change in taxes has a smaller impact on the macroeconomy than an equal change in government spending. The tax multiplier is always one less than the corresponding government spending multiplier because of the lag effect of tax changes showing up as changes in aggregate spending. If we thought of the circular flow model, a tax change has a diversion or leakage into savings prior to the change in aggregate spending, whereas a change in government spending changes aggregate spending prior to the initial diversion into savings. The tax multiplier is found by the formula: -b/1-b, and always assumes a value one less than the multiplier. In the example cited above, the ultimate impact on the macroeconomy of a $1 increase in taxes would be a $9 decrease in equilibrium national income.

Tax increases (decreases) work in the opposite direction of government spending increases (decreases). If the goal is to increase the size of the macroeconomy, this goal could be accomplished by either increasing government spending or decreasing taxes. The magnitudes of the changes are determined by the desired change and the appropriate multiplier; 1/1-b for government spending changes and -b/1-b for tax changes.

Because the multipliers have different impacts upon the macroeconomy, assuming different mathematical values, there is a change in the equilibrium level of national income when both government spending and taxes changed by the same amount in the same direction. A balanced budget change will cause the size of the economy to change in the same direction and by the same amount as the change in government spending. If one observed an economy in equilibrium while the MPC is .8; an increase of $250 million in both government spending and taxes would lead to an increase of $250 million in the equilibrium level of national income. In this case the government spending multiplier is 5, so that the increase in government spending would add $1.25 billion to national income; the tax multiplier is 4, so that the increase in taxes would reduce national income by $1 billion, leaving the net effect of a $250 million increase. Thus, the balanced budget multiplier is 1.

Automatic stabilizers include transfer payments and tax changes that occur in conjunction with changes in the business cycle and are consistent with the general pattern of fiscal policy. As the economy is declining along the business cycle, fiscal policy would prescribe measures that increased aggregate spending; as a function of the increased cyclical unemployment, transfer payments are increased, partially restoring lost incomes to households. As the economy is growing along the business cycle and both employment and income are increasing; taxes increase due to the progressive income tax system, and transfer payments decrease as individuals are removed from unemployment and welfare rolls.

GLOSSARY

AUTOMATIC STABILIZERS: Revenues and expenditures items in the federal budget that automatically change with the state of the economy: tax revenues that rise during an expansion, for example, and expenditures for transfers that fall.

BALANCED-BUDGET MULTIPLIER: The multiplier by which the equilibrium level of output (income) changes for every dollar of change in government spending that is balanced by a dollar change in taxes so as not to create any deficit. This multiplier is equal to one: the change in Y resulting from the change in G and the equal change in T is exactly the same size as the initial change itself.

DISPOSABLE INCOME: Income minus taxes: the amount available to spend on current consumption /or to save.

TAX MULTIPLIER: The multiple by which the equilibrium level of output (income) increases (decreases) for every dollar of a decrease (increase) in taxes.

STUDY TIPS

1. The basic logic of the model has not changed, it is simply a case that the model has been expanded to include the effects of government action in spending policies and taxation.
2. If you learned the investment multiplier in chapter 24, then you know the government spending multiplier.
3. The tax multiplier is always one less than the government spending multiplier. Go back to the circular flow model, start with a $1 change in taxes, trace the effect around the model three or four times to convince yourself that this is true.
4. Be very careful in assigning positive and negative values to the multiplied results. The safest method here is to check with your logic. You know that a tax increase will cause aggregate income to decrease.

A LOOK AHEAD

The marginal propensity to consume of the consumption function is expanded upon later through the average propensity to consume in an effort to more directly tie household consumption patterns to the macroeconomy.

Investment will show up again in the context of the impact of firm behavior upon the macroeconomy.

MULTIPLE-CHOICE QUESTIONS

1. Which of the following is NOT a tool of the federal government in trying to direct the macroeconomy?
   a. government spending.
   b. tax rates.
   c. national income.
   d. transfer payments.

2. When tax receipts exceed government expenditures:
   a. the federal budget is balanced.
   b. there is a budget surplus.
   c. there is a budget deficit.
   d. a climatological extreme has been reached.

3. When government is added into the model of macroeconomic activity, the equilibrium condition is expressed as:
   a. Y = C + S + G - Tx + Tr.
   b. Y = C + I + G and S = I.
   c. S + Tx = I(actual) + G.
   d. a balanced federal budget.

4. The government spending multiplier:
   a. applies to all actions taken by the government.
   b. is the opposite of the tax multiplier.
   c. is equal to 1/b.
   d. is equal to 1/1 - b.

5. The tax multiplier:
   a. is the negative of the government spending multiplier.
   b. is one less than the MPC.
   c. is equal to b/1 - b.
   d. is equal to 1 - (1/b).

6. The balanced budget multiplier:
   a. is always equal to 1.
   b. does not exist because under conditions of a balanced budget there is no change.
   c. is equal to (1/1 - b) - 1.
   d. is the inverse of the difference between the MPC and the MPS.

7. Taxes have a _____ impact on the macroeconomy than government spending because:
   a. smaller, of the existence of widespread tax evasion.
   b. larger, of the difference in the multipliers.
   c. smaller, individuals pay taxes prior to making the consumption savings decision.
   d. larger, a lot of government money is spent in other countries.

8. All of the following are automatic stabilizers except:
   a. defense spending.
   b. unemployment compensation.
   c. progressive income tax.
   d. welfare programs.

ANALYTIC EXERCISES

1. Fill-in the blanks:

   MPC = _____   MPS = _____

Y	Tx	DI	C	S	I	G	C+I+G
0	10	-10	50	-60	20	10	80
100	10	____	____	-40	20	10	____
300	10	____	____	____	20	10	____
equilibrium = ____	10	____	____	____	20	10	____

2. The current equilibrium income in the macroeconomy is $1,000 with an MPC of .75, what would be the new equilibrium after an increase in government spending of $60?

3. Recommend a combination of a tax change and government spending change that would cause an economy to grow by $2,000 when the MPC is .8.

4. If both taxes and government spending are increased by $25 when the MPC is .9 by how much and in what direction does the equilibrium national income change, if at all?

ESSAY QUESTIONS

1. Explain the two major tools of fiscal policy.
2. Explain why the tax multiplier is smaller than the government spending multiplier.
3. React to the following statement: "If we just had a balanced budget requirement, government could spend or not spend as much as it wished without having an impact upon the macroeconomy."

ANSWERS

Multiple-Choice

1) c,   2) b,   3) c,   4) d,   5) c,
6) a,   7) c,   8) a.

Analytic Exercises

1)

MPC = .8 MPS = .2

Y	Tx	DI	C	S	I	G	C+I+G
0	10	-10	50	-60	20	10	80
100	10	90	130	-40	20	10	160
300	10	290	290	0	20	10	320
equilibrium = 400	10	390	370	20	20	10	400

2) $1,240.
3) wide variety of correct answers.
4) increases by $25.

Money and the Financial System

26

LEARNING OBJECTIVES

After you have studied this chapter in the textbook, attended class lectures over this material, and completed this study guide chapter you should be able to answer the following questions.

1. What is money?
2. What are the functions of money?
3. How do banks create money?
4. What is the money multiplier and how does it work?
5. Why do individuals hold money?
6. What constitutes excess, required, and total reserves?

CHAPTER REVIEW

The definition of money is anything that meets some basic criteria serving as a medium of exchange, a store of value, and a unit of account; most of the world's currencies conform to these criteria.

United States currency is in the form of coins and Federal Reserve Notes. Coins, to the extent of containing a limited amount of precious metal, have some intrinsic value. Federal Reserve Notes, on the other hand, derive their value strictly from the willingness of other individuals to accept them as payment (and even covet them). Federal Reserve Notes fall into an additional category of money that is called "fiat money." Fiat money is "designated" money that not only has no intrinsic value, but is irredeemable, that is, it may either be exchanged for goods and services or other notes--it has no backing in gold or silver.

"Money" is not limited to just currency and coins but includes such things as checking account balances, since all three criteria are met. A bank credit card would not fit the criteria because the balance is not there, it serves as near-money, fulfilling only the medium of exchange function of money.

Banks are profit-seeking businesses that are the primary institutions for the creation of money. The two enabling features in the money creation process are the willingness of individuals to accept checks and the fractional reserve banking system. With regard to checks, we have already seen that checks constitute money, so that the simple definition of money that we will use (the sum of publicly held cash and checking account balances) forces us to recognize that most (as much as 80%) of what we call money is not even "fiat." Fractional reserve banking is an outgrowth of warehouse receipts, for gold and other precious metals, that became negotiable. Goldsmiths, who provided this warehousing function, soon learned that there would always be some gold on deposit and there was little risk in issuing warehouse receipts for more gold than was in storage. The "extra" warehouse receipts would be issued in the form of loans with confidence that the gold itself would never be demanded. Fractional reserving, then, is the practice of holding back only a portion of each deposit rather than the entire deposit.

Modern banks have reserve requirements equal to 12% of all checking account balances. A $100 deposit would require a set-aside of $12, leaving $88 upon which the bank may attempt to earn a profit. The $88 is identified as excess reserves where the sum of excess reserves and required reserves would equal total reserves. A prudent banker (have you ever known one who wasn't?) could legally loan up to the amount of excess reserves, in this case $88. If the bank made the loan, then we would observe an increase in the money supply (stock of money) of $88. The new $88 was created by the bank in response to the demand for the loan by a customer. There is a net increase of $88 to the basic M1. There is also a "shifting" of $10.56 (12% of the new demand deposit of $88) from excess reserves to required reserves; total reserves remain at $100.

This shifting in reserves continues as more loans are made and potentially up to the point where there are no excess reserves, all reserves being in the form of required reserves. The simple money multiplier predicts the total amount of money that could be created through a series of these transactions as a multiple of the stock of reserves.

The major motivation for individuals' holding of positive cash balances is for transactions purposes. The size of the cash balance increases (decreases) with increased (decreased) income due to the concommitant increase (decrease) in consumption. The lengthening (shortening) of time between income payments will also increase (decrease) the size of the cash balance. A third influencing factor is the interest rate; at relatively high (low) interest rates, individuals become less (more) willing to hold cash or demand deposit balances.

GLOSSARY

BARTER: The direct exchange of goods and services for other goods and services.

COMMODITY MONEY: Items used as money that also have intrinsic value on their own.

EXCESS RESERVES: The difference between a bank's actual reserves and its required reserves.

FIAT MONEY: Items designated as money that have no other intrinsic value.

FINANCIAL INTERMEDIARIES: Banks and other institutions that make available money from those who have money to lend to those who want to borrow money.

FRACTIONAL RESERVE BANKING: a banking system under which banks are not required to hold the whole of all deposits but may use a fraction of each deposit as a source of income.

MEDIUM OF EXCHANGE: A function of money; it is exchanged for goods and services when people want to buy things and goods and services are exchanged for it when people want to sell things.

MONEY AGGREGATES: the various measures of the stock of money that exists in an economy. M1, the most basic measure of money is composed primarily of the sum of publicly held cash and demand deposit balances.

MONEY MULTIPLIER: The multiple by which deposits can increase for every dollar increase in reserves; basically, one divided by the required reserve ratio provided there is no leakage out of the system.

REQUIRED RESERVES: The percentage of its total deposits that a bank must keep as reserves.

STORE OF VALUE: Another function of money: it transports purchasing power from one time and place to another.

TRANSACTIONS MOTIVE: The main reason that we hold money--to buy things.

UNIT OF ACCOUNT: Another function of money: its use as a standard unit provides a consistent way to quote prices.

A LOOK AHEAD

In chapter 26, the concept of the multiplier has been employed in the relationship between money creation and fractional reserve banking. The logic of the money multiplier and the fiscal policy multiplier previously studied is that a marginal input into the economy, whether in the form of increased spending or new reserves, will have a multiplied impact on the macroeconomy. The arithmetic rule is the same because once one has grasped the actual number of the multiplier, then the value of the change is simply multiplied by the multiplier. Additionally, each of the multipliers is found by using the reciprocal of a fractional value; either the marginal propensity to save or the required reserve ratio.

The marginal concept from both the microeconomics portions of the book and more recent chapters are continually employed in the chapter.

The concepts of stocks and flows reappear in this chapter. Monetary aggregates are measuring the stock of money. The transactions demand for money is related to the flow concepts of consumption and income payments.

MULTIPLE-CHOICE QUESTIONS

1. The largest component of the simplest definition of money, or M1 is:
   a. publicly held cash.
   b. Federal Reserve Notes.
   c. demand deposit balances.
   d. bank credit card balances.

2. Checkable deposits are money because they are:
   a. legal tender.
   b. denominated in dollars.
   c. backed by gold.
   d. a medium of exchange.

3. Which of the following best describes the backing of U.S. currency?
   a. the gold stored at Ft. Knox, KY.
   b. the belief that holders of goods and services will accept it in trade.
   c. the willingness of the government to surrender something of value in return for it.
   d. the faith and confidence in the ability of the government to pay its debts.

4. The total quantity of money demanded is:
   a. directly related to National Income and the rate of interest.
   b. directly related to National Income and inversely related to the rate of interest.
   c. inversely related to National Income and directly related to the rate of interest.
   d. inversely related to National Income and the rate of interest.

5. The goldsmiths became bankers when:
   a. they accepted deposits of gold for storage.
   b. they issued receipts for gold that was stored.

    c. gold receipts became negotiable.

    d. they issued paper money in the form of receipts for more gold than was in storage.

6. When cash is deposited in a demand deposit account in a bank there is:

    a. a decrease in the money supply.

    b. an increase in the money supply.

    c. a change in the composition of the money supply.

    d. a decrease in the rate of interest.

7. If the required reserve ratio is 25%, the value of the multiplier is:

    a. 8.

    b. 5.

    c. 4.

    d. indeterminate without knowing the size of the deposit.

8. Excess reserves are all but which one of the following?

    a. the difference between total reserves and required reserves.

    b. the source of bank capital for expansion.

    c. equal to the potentially largest single loan of an independent bank in a banking system.

    d. that portion of a deposit in excess of the required reserve at the time of deposit.

9. The functions of money include all but the following:

    a. a medium of exchange.

    b. the generation of wealth.

    c. a store of value.

    d. a unit of account.

ANALYTIC EXERCISES

1. A commercial bank that is a member of the banking system has current deposits of $100,000 while holding total reserves of $31,000. If the bank is subject to a required reserve ratio of 20%, what is the size of the largest loan that it can make? If the bank extends that size loan, what is the maximum potential increase in the total money supply if all subsequent banks follow the same strategy?

2. The commercial banking system has excess reserves of $700 and makes loans of $2800, maximizing the money creation process; what is the required reserve ratio for the banking system?

3. What is the average transactions account balance for an individual who earns and consumes $24,000 per year if the income is earned monthly? Yearly?

ESSAY QUESTIONS

1. Explain the three criteria used in the definition of money.

2. Illustrate the money creation process assuming an initial deposit of $1,000 and a required reserve ratio of 25%.

3. Why are banks the only institutions in the U. S. economy that can create money?

4. Why do individuals hold money? What determines how much money individuals hold?

ANSWERS

Multiple-Choice

1) c,	2) d,	3) b,	4) b,	5) d,
6) c,	7) c,	8) b,	9) b.	

Analytic Exercises

1) The independent bank may make a maximum loan of $11,000. A loan of $11,000 has the potential of leading to a maximum of $55,000.
2) 25%
3) $1,000; $12,000

The Federal Reserve ————————— 27

LEARNING OBJECTIVES

After you have studied this chapter in the textbook, attended class lectures over this material, and completed this study guide chapter you should be able to answer the following questions.

1. What is the structure of the Federal Reserve System?
2. What are the duties of the Federal Reserve System?
3. Explain the operation of the major tools of monetary policy available to the Federal Reserve System.
4. Explain the functioning of the interest rate market.

CHAPTER REVIEW

The Federal Reserve System is the central bank for the United States economy. The Board of Governors of the Federal Reserve System is a politically independent, presidentially-appointed group of seven members each serving a fourteen year term. The Chairmanship of the Fed is a four year appointment and constitutes one of the most powerful positions in the U. S. government. The Fed has twelve district banks each serving a unique geographic region; through the district banks the Fed provides the central banking function of being the bankers' bank. The Fed also serves as the government's bank, the lender of last resort, regulator of the domestic banking industry, facilitator of international currency transactions, issuer of the currency and monetary policy agent.

The Federal Open Market Committee (F.O.M.C.) is composed of seven members of the Board of Governors, the President of the New York Federal Reserve Bank and four other District Bank Presidents. The F.O.M.C. determines the course of monetary policy. Monetary policy is conducted in order to control the supply of money. The primary method used to control the money supply is through the control of bank reserves. A secondary method is adjustments in reserve requirements, largely made obsolete by the Depository Institutions Deregulation and Monetary Control Act of 1980.

The discount rate is the rate of interest at which banks borrow from the Fed. Changes in the discount rate tend to influence market interest rates even though banks display a general reluctance to borrow from the Fed. Changes in the discount rate are subject to the phenomenon of the announcement effect, sending a clear signal through the financial community of the intentions of the Fed. Relatively high (low) discount rates discourage (encourage) bank borrowing for reserve expansion, thus making less (more) money available for loans, driving market interest rates up (down).

Open market operations directly impact upon banks' reserve positions. Open market operations consist of the buying and selling of government securities from and into the Fed's portfolio (government securities are the major asset of the Fed). A sale of government securities by the Fed would result in a decrease in bank reserve balances as the checks for payment were cleared out of the banking system and into the Fed. A reduction in bank reserves, through the operation of the money multiplier, would reduce the capability of money creation by banks and possibly drive interest rates up to dissuade individuals from demanding loans. A purchase of securities would have the effect of injecting reserves into the system because bank reserves accounts would be increased by the amount of the purchase by the Fed.

The Fed has influence over the money supply through the tools of monetary policy. The actual amount of money that is demanded and supplied is the result of a relatively simple microeconomic-like market in which the interest rate functions as the (rental) price of money. Fed action, in making money available for creation is not a function of the interest rate; but the decision to create money, made between a consumer and a bank, is a function of the interest rate. An equilibrium interest rate would be a rate that equates the amount of money demanded with the amount of money supplied, within the constraint of the Fed's willingness to make money available.

GLOSSARY

DISCOUNT RATE: The interest rate that member banks pay when they borrow from the Fed.

FEDERAL RESERVE SYSTEM: The central banking system in the United States.

INTEREST RATE: The "price" that borrowers pay to lenders for the use of money; it provides a link between the money market and the goods market.

LENDER OF LAST RESORT: One of the functions of the Fed. It may provide funds to a bank in trouble.

OPEN MARKET OPERATIONS: The purchase and sale by the Fed of government securities in the open market; a tool to expand or contract the amount of reserves in the system and hence the money supply.

STUDY TIPS

1. Keep in mind that the reserve account serves two purposes: as a part of monetary policy and as member banks' deposit accounts. All interdistrict checks are cleared through member banks' reserve accounts; you may want to read the back of a check that you have written to determine where it has been in the clearing process and how long it took (this is called the transit record).

2. Memorize the likely money multipliers or the formula for deriving the money multiplier (1/reserve ratio).

3. The logic of the money multiplier is the same as that of the fiscal policy multipliers.

4. The monetary policy of discount rate changes fits very well with common sense as you think about the relationship among interest rates, consumer spending, and investment.

5. Work your way through the process of the monetary policy of open market operations. Keep in mind that the goal is to influence the money supply and the medium is the banks' reserve accounts. A purchase by the Fed puts reserves into the banking system. Reserves always have the potential of becoming created money (loans).

A LOOK AHEAD

The model of interest rate determination and the Fed's role in influencing interest rates will be important in the considerations in Chapter 28 and subsequent chapters as the model is expanded.

The tools of monetary policy continue to be important as the macroeconomists "tool-kit" is growing. As policy options are developed and historical decisions reviewed the tools will take on an expanded meaning.

MULTIPLE-CHOICE QUESTIONS

1. A Federal Reserve Note:
   a. is an asset of the Federal Reserve System.
   b. is fully backed by the gold in Ft. Knox, KY.
   c. may be exchanged for silver.
   d. may be a exchanged for another Federal Reserve Note.

2. A change in the required reserve ratio from 20% to 10% when the required reserve account balance is $400:
   a. increases the money multiplier from 5 to 10.
   b. increases the amount of money in excess reserves by $200.
   c. decreases the potential for money creation.
   d. both a and b.

3. The discount rate:
   a. is the rate of interest at which banks borrow from the Fed.
   b. is the rate of interest at which banks borrow from each other.
   c. is the inventory turnover rate at K-Mart.
   d. is a tool of fiscal policy.

4. Open market operations are conducted:
   a. in order to control the international price of the dollar.
   b. as a tool of fiscal policy.
   c. in an effort to influence bank reserves.
   d. by each of the 12 District Banks.

5. The F.O.M.C. is:
   a. composed of interested members of Congress.
   b. established to set interest rates and regulate banks.
   c. the deposit insurance corporation for central banks.
   d. the monetary policy group of the Fed.

6. A purchase of securities by the F.O.M.C. will ultimately lead to:
   a. dissatisfaction in the banking community.
   b. an increase of reserves in banks.
   c. a decrease in the money supply.
   d. government ownership of the national debt.

7. The announcement effect:
   a. increases the probability of discount rate changes being effective.
   b. allows banks to avoid being audited.
   c. is the same as moral suasion.
   d. is a tool of monetary policy.

8. A bank's reserve account at the Fed:
   a. is fully insured up to $100,000 by an agency of the Federal government.
   b. consists of required reserves and vault cash.
   c. serves as both a reserve and as a clearing account for checks drawn on the bank.
   d. cannot contain both required and excess reserves at the same time.

9. An increase in the money supply would have the best possibility of occurring if:
   a. the required reserve ratio were increased.
   b. the discount rate were lowered.
   c. if taxes were lowered.
   d. if the F.O.M.C. sold securities in the open market.

ANALYTIC EXERCISES

1. Calculate the potential money supply change under each of the following conditions assuming a required reserve ratio of .8.
   a) a $750 purchase of securities by the F.O.M.C.
   b) an increase in the discount rate from 7% to 7.5%.
   c) a $600 sale of securities by the F.O.M.C.

2. Calculate the additional maximum amount of money that could be created by the banking system under the following conditions:

   total deposits = $5,000   reserve ratio = .1
   total reserves = 1,000

ESSAY QUESTIONS

1. Explain the mechanism through which changes in the discount rate might affect the macroeconomy.
2. Explain the mechanism through which open market operations by the Fed might affect the macroeconomy.
3. React to the following statement: "The Fed is to blame if there is not enough money in the economy; but blame profit-seeking bankers if there is too much."

ANSWERS

Multiple-Choice

1) d,   2) d,   3) a,   4) c,   5) d,
6) b,   7) a,   8) c.

Analytic Exercises

1) a. +$3,750.
   b. indeterminate.
   c. -$3,000.
2) another $5,000. ($500 of total reserves is excess; the multiplier is 10)

28

The Determination of Income and the Interest Rate

LEARNING OBJECTIVES

After you have studied this chapter in the textbook, attended class lectures over this material, and completed this study guide chapter you should be able to answer the following questions.

1. How do the goods market and money market interact?
2. What is the role of the interest rate in the goods market? In the money market?
3. What is the role of real output in the money market? In the goods market?
4. Why do expansionary (contractionary) fiscal and monetary policies impact the interest rate differently?
5. What is the role of the price level in the goods market? in the money market?

CHAPTER REVIEW

This chapter is a synthesis of the previous two chapters in which the goods market and money markets are combined to provide a better model of macroeconomic activity. These two markets are inter-related because of the role of money as a determinant of demand in the goods market and the concept of aggregate demand determining the demand for money.

The linkages between the two markets may be reduced to two primary areas: the interest rate and real output. The interest rate is important in the goods market because we find that investment decisions are largely a function of the interest rate. As interest rates increase (decrease), the cost of borrowing increases (decreases), and projects that would (not) have been undertaken are not (are). You will recall that investment spending is a profit-motivated business decision in which consideration is given the interest rate even if the firm chooses not to borrow the funds. The interest rate may also impact consumer spending to the extent that households are willing to assume higher levels of debt, thus indirectly affecting goods markets.

The level of real output, on the other hand, is a function of the level of investment; in real terms, business spending increases (decreases) must precede production increases (decreases). Therefore the goods market depends upon the interest rate, while the interest rate is itself determined in the goods market.

The interest rate is simply a microeconomic equilibrium between the demand for money, as determined by consumers, and the supply of money, as influenced by the Federal Reserve System.

The inter-relationship between these two markets allows us to conclude that there is a unique combination of a level of real output and an interest rate that will simultaneously lead to equilibrium in each market. Reducing the discussion to one that centers around the interest rate, we can think of this unique equilibrium representing a single interest rate at which the demand for (as determined by real output) and supply of money (as controlled by the Fed) are in equilibrium; and that the level of real output at that equilibrium is the unique level at which the goods market clears, also at the original interest rate.

The policy implications of this inter-relationship are strong. We find that expansionary (contractionary) fiscal policy leads to increases (decreases) in interest rates because of the increase (decrease) in aggregate demand. A potentially serious problem with increases in the interest rate associated with expansionary fiscal policy come int the form of crowding out. Crowding out occurs when government, in an effort to follow an expansionary policy course, bids the interest rate up, making some projects unfeasable, thus "crowding out" private borrowers.

Theoretically, monetary policy has just the opposite effect on the interest rate as that of fiscal policy. An expansionary (contractionary) monetary goal is accomplished through a reduction (increase) in the interest rate, simply because the interest rate is one of the variables that falls most easily under the influence of the Fed (remember that it is the Fed that controls the discount rate). Any crowding out that occurs will have the effect of reducing the impact of the multiplier.

The aggregate demand curve itself depends upon the general price level in the economy. Increases (decreases) in prices have the effect of increasing (decreasing) the demand for money. Under the ceteris paribus condition of holding government spending, taxes, and the money supply constant, we find that increases (decreases) in the price level accompany decreases (increases) in real output.

GLOSSARY

CROWDING OUT: The decline in planned investment spending induced by a higher interest rate when that increase in the interest rate is caused by rising output and income (and therefore increased money demand) accompanied by no expansion in the money supply.

FISCAL POLICY: Those changes in taxes and in government purchases that the government can use to expand or contract the macroeconomy.

INTEREST SENSITIVITY: Interest sensitivity occurs when planned investment spending changes a lot in response to small changes in the interest rate.

MONETARY POLICY: Those measures the Fed can use in the money market to influence the quantity of money supplied and hence the interest rate.

STUDY TIPS

1. Since this chapter is primarily a synthesis of the previous two chapters the best study tip would be to quickly review the previous two chapters. The most common error made in confronting the integration of two markets is failure to recognize the interdependence of variables. Keep in mind that if consumer demand for goods and services is to be met, the goods market must respond by producing the goods while the money market must respond by supplying the money.

2. It is well to always bear in mind the distinction between real and nominal values. Once discussion of the price level is encountered then you have a method for determining real values. In this chapter real values are used because it is at that level that the goods and money markets interact.

3. When considering the effects of various changes in policy, use the tools that you have learned in previous chapters. The circular flow model is particularly helpful in trying to decide if a particular policy is contractionary or expansionary. An increase in interest rates, for example, would be contractionary because it would reduce the level of investment as well as the level of consumer spending; both conclusions are almost automatic if you put them in the context of the model.

A LOOK AHEAD

As suggested earlier, this chapter is a synthesis of the previous two chapters. The economic strains then are a continuation and amplification of previously encountered concepts. Of particular importance here are the policy options and implications. Previously the policies were considered in a vacuum, whereas now they are shown to have significant differences in the way they work, i.e., the impact upon the interest rate.

This chapter relies heavily upon a clear understanding of the distinction between real and nominal values.

The addition of the concepts of aggregate demand and aggregate supply show a similarity to the microeconomic concepts of supply and demand, especially in the solution of equilibrium.

MULTIPLE-CHOICE QUESTIONS

1. Which of the following would not affect aggregate demand?
   a. the Fed increases the discount rate
   b. Congress passes a tax decrease
   c. inflation increases
   d. a new gold mine is discovered

2. Which of the following would increase aggregate demand?
   a. individuals expect to enter a period of rising inflation
   b. Fed purchase of securities in the open market
   c. decreased disposable income due to tax policy
   d. a decrease in government spending

3. Generally speaking, increases in the price level;
   a. have no impact on the economy as a whole.
   b. decrease the real money supply, ceteris paribus.
   c. lead to increases in aggregate demand.
   d. are good for the economy.

4. An exogenous variable:
   a. does not normally have a significant impact on the macroeconomy.
   b. is derived from the difference between imports and exports.
   c. is one whose determinants lie outside the model under consideration.
   d. can be accurately predicted.

5. The equilibrium interest rate is determined:
   a. at the point where money demanded is equal to the quantity supplied.
   b. is subject to Fed policy, exclusively.
   c. is determined by consumers since money does not become money until an individual demands it.
   d. by the Fed.

6. The effect of crowding out depends to a large extent on:
   a. the willingness of businesses to be bullied.
   b. interest rate sensitivity.
   c. the power of the Presidency.
   d. the strength of international trade.

ANALYTIC EXERCISES

1. Determine the effect of each of the following policies on interest rates and output.
   a) a tax decrease
   b) an open market sale of bonds by the Fed
   c) a government spending decrease
   d) a decrease in the discount rate

ESSAY QUESTIONS

1. Why does the interest rate respond differently to monetary and fiscal policy? How?
2. Explain the price level and its role in the determination of an equilibrium between aggregate demand and aggregate supply.
3. How are the goods market and the money market interdependent?

ANSWERS

Multiple-Choice

1) d,   2) b,   3) b,   4) c,
5) a,   6) b.

29

Household Behavior in the Macroeconomy

LEARNING OBJECTIVES

After you have studied this chapter in the textbook, attended class lectures over this material, and completed this study guide chapter you should be able to answer the following questions.

1. Explain the life-cycle and permanent income models of household consumption.
2. What determines the supply of labor?
3. Compare and contrast the income and substitution effects as they are applied to labor markets.
4. Distinguish between nominal and real wages.
5. What is money illusion?
6. How do governmental policy on taxes and transfer payments effect labor markets and consumption?
7. Review the recent history of household consumption and labor supply functions.

CHAPTER REVIEW

The concept of the marginal propensity to consume does not adequately explain the breadth of consumer behavior within the macroeconomy. The average propensity to consume (APC) is the ratio of consumption to income. In a microeconomic sense, an individuals' APC decreases as income increases, even though total consumption will continue to increase as income increases. Keynesian theory is based upon the dependence of consumption upon current income, thus the APC is very important.

The assumption that current income is the sole determinant of consumption is relaxed in the life-cycle consumption model. In this model, current consumption is seen as a reflection of anticipated lifetime earnings. In this model, consumption patterns by pre-professional students or young professionals are more consistent with anticipated future incomes than with current incomes. Likewise, consumption patterns of the elderly may be more similar to those of their high income years, rather than the APC of their retirement income (remember that social security payments and business transfers are not current income). This model is frequently referred to as the permanent income hypothesis; that is, the individual household makes a calculation of permanent income and adjusts spending patterns accordingly.

Households, as participants in the resource market, are responsible for making the supply of labor decision. One way of constructing the supply of labor function is to view labor and leisure as interchangeable uses of time. The cost of leisure is the opportunity cost of foregoing additional hours of work. At relatively high wage rates, the opportunity cost of leisure increases. The substitution effect, as seen in chapter 6, shows us that one response to increased wages would be an increase in hours of work over hours of leisure due to the increased opportunity cost of leisure.

The income effect, again from chapter 6, suggests that workers can work fewer hours and still have the same income. The result of the income effect is that the supply of labor would be reduced. As you can see, in the absence of other influences, the income and substitution effects have opposite results. In practice, the substitution effect is dominant, for most individuals; thus increased (decreased) wages lead to increases (decreases) in the labor supply.

The real wage rate is the amount of purchasing power available in the wage. The best proxy for the real wage rate is to wages with respect to a price index, such as the CPI or the GNP pric deflator. Nominal wages that increase at the same rate as the index represent no change in real wages. Money illusion, a phenomenon to which most of us are susceptible, is mistaking an increase in the nominal wage for an increase in the real wage. Widespread money illusion could lead to increasing levels of consumption during a period of inflation. Normally, money illusion is a temporary condition. Because the effects of money illusion are limited, the model assumes that both the supply of labor and consumption patterns are based upon real wages and real prices. An increase (decrease) in the real wage will increase (decrease) both the supply of labor and consumption.

Consumption is not solely a function of earned, permanent, past, or anticipated future income. The existence of a stock of wealth has a positive influence upon consumption as well as a negative influence upon the supply of labor. Another influencing factor would be the earning of nonlabor income, what the IRS now calls passive income. This income source would also increase consumption and decrease an individuals willingness to work.

Transfer payments are a source of nonlabor income as well as a function of the political process. Through changes in transfer payments the government has an affect, in addition to the government spending component, on both consumption and the supply of labor. Increases in transfer payments, ceteris paribus, will increase consumption while possibly decreasing the supply of labor. Government tax policies also impact consumption through the adjustments made in disposable income. A tax increase (decrease) would decrease (increase) disposable income, thus decreasing (increasing) consumption.

The interest rate influences consumption to the extent that the direct cost of borrowing to purchase is viewed by the consumer as a portion of the consumption price. Furthermore, the opportunity cost of reducing one's stock of savings to consume will reduce consumption levels at high interest rates; individuals will choose to leave money in the form of interest earning instruments, rather than withdraw to consume. As interest rates fall (rise), consumers will increase (decrease) consumption.

Households are not limited to consumption and savings; but also make capital investment when purchasing housing. You will recall from national income accounting that the housing purchase is not included as consumer spending. The housing purchase is a function of both the interest rate and income. Increases (decreases) in interest rates tend to reduce (increase) housing purchases (note that there is an employment implication here that is important to the macroeconomy). Increases (decreases) in income tend to increase (decrease) the demand for new and additional housing.

GLOSSARY

AVERAGE PROPENSITY TO CONSUME: The proportion of income that households spend on consumption.

LIFE-CYCLE MODEL: The theory that households make lifetime consumption decisions based on their expectations of lifetime income.

MONEY ILLUSION: The term used to describe any change in the amount of labor supplied or in the amount of consumption based only on a change in nominal wages (rather than real wages). It may appear in the very short term due to lack of information but it (is) generally incompatible with microeconomic theory of consumer behavior.

PERMANENT INCOME: Expected long-ryun future income.

SUBSTITUTION EFFECT: What happens when a wage increase leads to a substitution of labor for leisure because leisure now has a higher opportunity cost (or a wage decrease leads to a substitution of leisure for labor since leisure has a lower opportunity cost).

STUDY TIPS

1. It is extremely important in this chapter to remind yourself that you are studying macroeconomics. It is very easy to fall into the trap, when thinking about consumption and consumption patterns, of thinking about an individual household rather than the aggregate. The reason for studying consumption theory in macroeconomics is in order to understand and have a frame of reference for the summation to aggregate consumption.

2. Keep in mind the distinction between real and nominal wages.

3. In studying the income and substitution effects, remember that there are some individuals in the macroeconomy that are susceptible to each of the effects. A macroeconomist must recognize that each of the effects exist, then try to determine which is dominant across the economy when making policy decisions.

A LOOK AHEAD

The household behavior chapter warrants a look back in addition to the usual look ahead. On top of renewing our interest in consumption, we are calling up topics from as far back as chapter 6 in this study.

Consideration of these topics gives us a feel for both the microeconomic foundations and the wide variety of decisions that are reduced into the aggregated numbers of macroeconomics. The role of the households is particularly important in making policy decisions in the areas of transfer payments and taxes.

MULTIPLE-CHOICE QUESTIONS

1. The average propensity to consume is:
   a. the sum of all individual marginal propensities to consume.
   b. larger than the MPC.
   c. is the opposite of the average propensity to save.
   d. consumption divided by aggregate income.

2. The theory that consumption is not tied to any one period's _____ but is a function of expected income over a long period of time is:
   a. income, the life-cycle model of consumption.
   b. needs, the life-cycle model of consumption.
   c. consumption function, the permanent income model.
   d. planned expenditures, wealth model.

3. Permanent income:
   a. is that income that one can count on year in and year out.
   b. includes income from the stock of wealth.
   c. decreases the APC.
   d. precludes the possibility of permanent savings.

4. The substitution effect:
   a. is seen in some restaurants that display signs "no substitutions please."
   b. causes some individuals to choose increased leisure over increased work when real wages decrease.
   c. causes some individuals to substitute work for leisure as real wages increase.
   d. allows macroeconomists to determine the opportunity cost of unemployment.

5. The income effect:
   a. explains why tax rates increase as nominal wages increase.
   b. causes some individuals to choose increased leisure over increased work when real wages decrease.
   c. causes some individuals to substitute work for leisure as real wages decrease.
   d. leads to class differences in a free market society.

6. Failure to recognize the difference between real and nominal wage increases is responsible for:
   a. money illusion.
   b. consumer ignorance.
   c. the consumption function.
   d. the wealth effect.

7. Generally speaking, _____ interest rates lead to higher levels of _____.
   a. higher, consumer spending.
   b. lower, consumer spending.
   c. stable, permanent income.
   d. higher, consumer debt.

8. Fiscal policy decisions:
   a. are not directly related to consumer spending.
   b. are made by producers rather than consumers.
   c. on government spending have no relationship to consumer spending.
   d. on taxation affect the disposable income available for consumption.

9. Housing:
   a. is a luxury good for some individuals.
   b. is a consumption good.
   c. is considered an investment.
   d. consists of both food and shelter.

ANALYTIC EXERCISES

1. If the rate of inflation is 12% and you receive a wage increase from $1,000 to $1,200 per month, what has happened to your real wage?
2. What is the APC in an economy where the national income is $4.5 billion and the level of savings is $1 billion?

ESSAY QUESTIONS

1. Compare and contrast the simple Keynesian consumption function and the life-cycle model of consumption.

2. In July of 1988, 13 U. S. Postal Service workers in New York were indicted on charges of diverting the mail after being observed dumping first class mail rather than sorting it. The explanation offered was that they wanted to shorten their working day. Evaluate the workers' motive in terms of the income and substitution effects under each of the wage assumptions below:

   a) that postal workers are paid by the hour.

   b) that postal workers are paid a monthly salary based on seniority.

ANSWERS

Multiple-Choice

1) d,   2) a,   3) b,   4) b,   5) c,

6) a,   7) b,   8) d,   9) c.

Analytic Exercises

1) real wages increased by about 8%.

2) APC is about .778.

30

Firm Behavior in the Macroeconomy: Investment and Labor Demand

LEARNING OBJECTIVES

After you have studied this chapter in the textbook, attended class lectures over this material, and completed this study guide chapter you should be able to answer the following questions.

1. What are the effects of expectations on investment decisions made by firms?
2. What are the effects of interest rate changes on the investment decisions made by firms?
3. What is the role of government in influencing investment decisions made by firms?
4. What is the relationship between the cost of capital and the cost of labor in capital spending decisions?

CHAPTER REVIEW

Investment, as we have seen in previous chapters and as the word is used by economists, denotes that business spending in which business is the final consumer. Not all business spending is investment; labor, overhead, raw materials, and packaging all become part of the product. The bulk of investment is the addition to the capital stock of the firm and the macroeconomy in the form of purchases of plant and equipment. Specifically, macroeconomists would be most concerned with net investment, identifying those additions to plant and equipment that represent expansion rather than replacement. In an accounting sense, the allocation for depreciation is deducted from actual investment spending. The aggregated result of this accounting procedure is the same as the change in the economy's capital stock.

In earlier models that have been constructed, investment has been first considered as an exogenous variable and then shown as being a function of the interest rate. The interest rate is still a major consideration in any firm's investment decision, because the anticipated profit created by the new plant and equipment must be greater than the cost of borrowing (irrespective of the use of either internal or external funds) the funds to construct the new plant and purchase the new equipment. However, if we look closely at that statement we observe that anticipated profit introduces uncertainty into the decision making process. The combination of the long-life nature of capital and the need to be able to predict the future broaden the scope of the investment decision beyond a simple comparison of rate of return with the current market interest rate.

The Marginal Efficiency of Investment schedule is couched in terms of the quantity of investment that would occur at each and every interest rate. The MEI is similar to all demand curves in that it is unique to a certain set of conditions, tastes and preferences in the case of most consumer goods. The condition that is most relevant is the expectation on the part of the investment decision maker about the future. An optimistic outlook would cause the MEI to shift to the right since more projects would become profitable at each interest rate due to the perceived increase in profitability.

Another of the factors influencing the MEI is current tax treatment of investment. Government, as a minor tool of fiscal policy, recognizes the link between new plant and equipment and the level of employment to be positive. Tax policies can be used in an effort to increase the level of investment; it is true that using the MEI as the schedule this leads to the conclusion that government must also have a goal of increasing the profitability of firms. The tax treatment of depreciation is one example of this behavior. For tax purposes firms are required to spread investment costs over a number of years. The smaller the number of years that a firm is allowed to depreciate capital, the lower the tax burden of the firm. Accelerated depreciation allows firms to depreciate a larger portion of the capital investment during the early years of the life of the machine, effectively wearing out the machine for tax purposes and thus encouraging the firm to expand more rapidly than under straight-line depreciation. Increased depreciation capability causes the MEI to shift to the right as a result of the increased willingness of firms to invest.

A second, similar, tax-based policy to increase investment is the investment tax credit. The investment tax credit allows a portion of any new capital investment to be used as a tax credit. A tax credit is a direct reduction in the tax bill of a firm; for example, a firm that had a tax liability of $50,000 and a tax credit of $15,000 would pay the government only $35,000, effectively using the tax credit as a coupon. Depreciation, on the other hand, is a tax deduction, reducing the taxable income of the firm.

The cost of labor is important in investment decision-making because of the relative substitutability of capital and labor. A high relative wage rate will tend to increase the investment schedule. Conversely, relatively high costs of capital will increase the demand for labor.

Labor markets play a particularly important role in the conduct of the firm during times of falling sales, output, and inventory build-ups. If labor is in short supply or has high training costs, a firm may choose to continue producing at possibly lower levels of output rather than shutdown. Recovery from these slack times clearly reduces the amount of capital expenditures that will be made in the macroeconomy.

GLOSSARY

DEPRECIATION: The process of allocating the cost of a long-term asset over the life of the asset.

INVESTMENT: Purchase by firms of the new buildings, equipment, and inventories that add to their capital stock.

INVESTMENT TAX CREDIT: Another provision of tax law that allows firms to deduct a certain percentage of the cost of a new investment from its tax liability in the year the investment is made.

MARGINAL EFFICIENCY OF INVESTMENT: A curve that shows the total amount of investment that would be undertaken in an economy in a given period of time at every possible interest rate.

PRODUCTION FUNCTION: The relationship betweenoutputs and inputs--that is, how much output can be produced given a variety of combinations of capital and labor and other inputs.

A LOOK AHEAD

This chapter is the first of two on the role of the firm in the macroeconomy. As such, almost every topic covered will be seen again. Of particular importance for future consideration is the production function. As subsequent chapters examine employment levels and wage rates, a major determinant is the relative cost and substitutability of labor and capital.

The idea of the role of expectations is increasingly important in macroeconomics. Expectations will be emphasized in the discussion of the rational expectations school of thought in chapter 35.

MULTIPLE-CHOICE QUESTIONS

1. The stock of capital is:
   a. the aggregate money supply.
   b. the Dow-Jones Index.
   c. plant and equipment.
   d. the flow of investment funds.

2. The marginal efficiency of investment schedule:
   a. allows manufacturing firms to compare the efficiency of different types of equipment.
   b. is a demand for investment curve where the interest rate is the price.
   c. increases as interest rates increase.
   d. shows the trade-offs between capital and labor at various wage and interest rates.

3. At _____ interest rates, investment _____ due to _____.
   a. higher, decreases, government regulation.
   b. lower, increases, crowding out effect.
   c. higher, increases, profitability of fewer projects.
   d. lower, increases, profitability of more projects.

4. Tax laws may influence investment by changes in _____ and/or _____.
   a. IRAs, capital gains laws.
   b. windfall profits taxes, depreciation.
   c. depreciation, investment tax credits.
   d. investment tax credits, capital gains laws.

5. In general, the faster firms may _____ capital goods, the _____ the level of investment.
   a. depreciate, higher.
   b. repair, lower.
   c. repair, higher.
   d. depreciate, lower.

6. Once a firm has committed itself to a particular form of capital equipment, then we may assume:
   a. they are using fixed-proportions technology.
   b. wages will not change in the future.
   c. all future production adjustment will be made by either adding or subtracting units of labor.
   d. they are using variable-proportions technology.

7. In general, the _____ the cost of labor relative to the cost of _____, the greater the number of _____ used.
   a. lower, raw materials, machines.
   b. higher, capital, workers.
   c. higher, capital, machines.
   d. lower, raw materials, workers.

8. Adjustment costs:
- **a.** refer to down time in the factory as capital equipment is being maintained.
- **b.** more than ever before.
- **c.** influence the rapidity with which production management will react to changes in demand for products.
- **d.** are normally included in labor contracts to maintain real wages.

ANALYTIC EXERCISES

1. Draw a marginal efficiency of investment schedule, then adjust it for each of the events below:
- **a)** there is widespread agreement among economists that the next four years will be more prosperous than any four years in history.
- **b)** the government eliminates the investment tax credit.
- **c)** the IRS agrees to allow firms to depreciate all capital equipment on a two year schedule.
- **d)** the minimum wage is doubled.

ESSAY QUESTIONS

1. What is the relationship between the flow of investment and the stock of capital?
2. What is the role of expectations in determining the investment schedule?
3. React to the following statement: "Keynes had it right to start with, investment is, in the end, simply a function of the interest rate."

ANSWERS

Multiple-Choice

1) c,	2) b,	3) d,	4) c,	5) a,
6) a,	7) b,	8) c.		

Analytic Exercises

1) **a.** outward shift in the MEI.
b. inward shift in the MEI.
c. outward shift in the MEI.
d. indeterminate.

31

Firm Behavior in the Macroeconomy: Output, Prices, and Wages

LEARNING OBJECTIVES

After you have completed this chapter in the textbook, attended class lectures over this material, and completed this study guide chapter you should be able to answer the following questions.

1. How do firms make input/output decisions?
2. What is the microeconomic role of inventory balances in firm decision making?
3. How are wages determined?
4. What are the macroeconomic factors that firms must be aware of in decision making?
5. What are the effects of individual firm behavior on the macroeconomy?

CHAPTER REVIEW

For simplicity and clarity, this chapter considers the models of the firm in two forms: perfectly or imperfectly competitive. The type of market in which an individual firm competes determines to a large extent its behavior pattern with regard to wages, prices, and output. The perfectly competitive firm has no control over price and accepts the price as a given in decision making. Given the rules of profit maximization with which you are already familiar, every decision that involves price is altered because of this lack of control. Marginal revenue is uniquely equal to price so that in making the output decision, an individual firm will seek that output level where the marginal cost is just equal to price. An externally determined price will also impact the labor market as firms hire workers according to their marginal revenue product, which in this case is a function of constant marginal revenue.

The firm that is operating in an imperfectly competitive environment will have some control over price, depending upon a wide variety of microeconomic factors. The central characteristic of firms in imperfect competition is that each one faces a downward-sloping demand curve. There are two implications present in the downward-sloping demand curve: marginal revenue is declining and divergent from the demand curve no longer equal to the price of the product) and concommitantly, the price must be lowered, for all purchasers, in order to sell an additional unit of output.

The output decision for an imperfectly competitive firm is still at a level of output where marginal revenue is just equal to marginal cost. Again, the difficulty faced by these firms is brought about by their control over price and the dependence of marginal revenue upon the price. Profit maximizing firms will still seek that price and output combination at which marginal revenue equals marginal cost.

The wage constraint for imperfect competitors is one of a consistently rising marginal cost curve, in the absence of what we could call a normal supply curve. A second wage problem that these firms encounter is one of the market-place itself; larger firms tend to be more susceptible to union activity or wage behavior that resembles it; specifically, large firms tend to prefer to classify labor into rather large and general groups with similar wage patterns. Size of firms and institutional constraints make it difficult to practice good marginal decisions in the hiring, firing, and paying of laborers; thus, losing mobility in the labor market.

In previous chapters we have referred to the importance of expectations in both macroeconomic and microeconomic decisions. An expectation of the general level of prices is critical in the determination of individual firm behavior in the areas of price, output, and wages. Additionally, imperfectly competitive firms, particularly in small geographic or large oligopolistic markets, must form an expectation concerning the price of their competitors' product(s). If the expectation across the macroeconomy is for generally rising prices it becomes relatively easier for a firm to raise prices. An expectation of generally rising prices would also decrease a firm's tenacity in holding wages and associated costs.

The existence or absence of inventories has a direct impact upon the level of output. A large inventory may cause a firm to reduce current output even though current sales would seemingly justify expansion. Firms tend to operate with a goal of maintaining a stable level of inventory, which may mean that they could increase output at a time when sales are slowing down. Determining factors of the level of inventory and reliance upon inventory include the cost of maintaining inventory and the flexibility of the output process; as we have seen in previous chapters, firms with a highly specialized and expensively trained labor force may be less flexible than firms using common labor. As we consider the inventory question from a macroeconomic point of view, the conclusion is still that a general slowdown in economic activity will lead to an inventory build up and firms will typically respond by reducing output.

GLOSSARY

IMPERFECTLY COMPETITIVE MARKETS, OR INDUSTRIES: Industries in which individual firms do have some degree of control over the prices that their products sell for. Imperfectly competitive firms decide on a price/quantity combination.

MARGINAL COST: An increase in total cost that results from producing one additional unit of output; a per unit cost measure.

MARGINAL REVENUE: The additional revenue that a firm would earn by raising its level of output by one unit.

PERFECTLY COMPETITIVE MARKETS, OR INDUSTRIES: Industries made up of many small firms producing homogeneous products. Competitive firms take prices as given and decide how much to produce.

STUDY TIPS

1. Review the microeconomic theory of firm behavior paying particular attention to the determination of wages.
2. Be very careful in this chapter, as you were in chapters 29 and 30 to maintain a macroeconomic outlook. In the discussion of the role of inventories pay special attention to both the microeconomic fact of inventory accumulation and its impact upon output by the firm as well as the impact of overall inventory accumulation on the macroeconomy.

3. Keep clear two distinctions: the microeconomic market that is being considered, either perfect or imperfect competition and the condition of the macroeconomy, either at full employment or not.

A LOOK AHEAD

In future chapters we will return to consider the overall impact, causes, and responses of unemployment. The model for determination of wages will be referred to again. The consideration of domestic prices will also continue to be held for the next several chapters.

MULTIPLE-CHOICE QUESTIONS

1. For a firm operating in a perfectly competitive market all but which of the following are decisions the firm must make
   a. what to produce.
   b. price at which to sell.
   c. quantity to produce.
   d. where to locate the plant.

2. The level of demand for the firm's product tends to restrain the ability of a firm operating in an imperfectly competitive market to
   a. set price.
   b. control quality of the product.
   c. set output.
   d. engage in institutional advertising.

3. Diminishing returns means that competitive firms
   a. earn less total revenue each year that they are in business.
   b. are price takers.
   c. as output increases, plant size must also increase.
   d. as output increases, ceteris paribus, marginal costs eventually rise.

4. Marginal revenue for imperfectly competitive firms is always less than price for a given level of output greater than one because
   a. of price discrimination.
   b. in order to sell an additional unit price must be lowered for all units.
   c. they are only equal in perfect competition in the very long run.
   d. profits are maximized when marginal cost is equal to marginal revenue and everyone knows that you cannot make a profit if price is equal to cost.

5. Expectations by firms in imperfectly competitive markets that prices will increase tend to be self-fulfilling prophecies because
   a. the firm will perceive both itself and its competitors to be on a demand curve that has shifted outward to the right.
   b. both the firm and its competitors will shift the demand curve inward to the left.
   c. all firms in the industry that share this expectation will collude to set price.
   d. price is determined by the resource prices and all firms in any one industry purchase in the same resource market.

6. The optimal level of inventory is found by balancing
   a. a crystal ball.
   b. the cost of production against the cost of firing and rehiring employees.
   c. the risk of running out of a product against the good will gained by always having product in stock.
   d. the cost of lost sales and increased storage from lowering inventories against the gain in revenue and decreased storage cost of raising inventories.

7. The demand for labor is
   a. always inelastic.
   b. derived demand.
   c. a function of both the nominal and the real wage rate.
   d. is the same as marginal revenue.

8. When expectations get built into the wage system we see
   a. high nominal wages.
   b. lowered supplies of labor at each and every wage.
   c. wage-setting.
   d. collective bargaining.

9. The difference between output and sales is
   a. inventory investment.
   b. always greater than one.
   c. net profit.
   d. not relevant in macroeconomics.

10. Firm profits, ceteris paribus, are high when
   a. sales are high and prices are stable.
   b. nominal wages are high and productivity is high.
   c. sales are high and real wages are low.
   d. the economy is experiencing a boom but never during a recession.

ESSAY QUESTIONS

1. Under conditions of perfect competition, describe the method by which a profit maximizing firm will determine the level of output.
2. What is the role of inventories in the output decision of a firm?
3. What is the effect of expectations on wages?
4. Describe the effects that price, nominal wage, real wage, and sales have on the profits of a firm.

ANSWERS

Multiple-Choice

1) b,	2) a,	3) d,	4) b,	5) a,
6) d,	7) b,	8) c,	9) a,	10) c.

32

A Complete Model of the Macroeconomy

LEARNING OBJECTIVES

After you have studied this chapter in the textbook, attended class lectures over this material, and completed this study guide chapter you should be able to answer the following questions:

1. What are the macroeconomic forces determining the shape of the aggregate demand curve?
2. What are the economic forces that determine the shape of the aggregate supply curve?
3. Explain equilibrium in the complete model of the macroeconomy.
4. Using the complete model, what are the effects of a change in fiscal policy?

CHAPTER REVIEW

The complete model developed in this chapter is simply an addition of the consideration of price to the income/interest rate model previously used. In the complete model we again see that macroeconomic markets are the summation of microeconomic activity and that macroeconomic markets are highly interrelated. You will recall that the income/interest rate model relied upon the cross-market impacts such things as the effect of interest rates, a money market variable, had on consumer spending and consumer spending, a goods market variable, had on the supply of money. As the model is expanded, price is shown as a factor in each of the markets.

Price, as it is used in this chapter and in all of aggregate demand/aggregate supply modeling, refers to the general price level as it has been defined previously. The price level assumes the characteristic of a price on the graphical depiction of aggregate demand/aggregate supply, and is shown as the vertical axis; just as it would appear in a microeconomic format. However, the responses that are observed in aggregate demand and aggregate supply to changes in price do not always follow simple microeconomic reasoning.

The aggregate demand curve has a downward slope that suggests that at higher price levels total demand in the economy decreases; however, the higher price level has caused an increase in the interest rates due to the inflationary expectation component of interest rates. The increase in general prices does not, in and of itself, cause individuals to reduce spending; consumption decisions are made on the basis of individual product prices, not the aggregate price level.

The aggregate supply curve becomes steeper as the sum of individual firms' output increases. This steepness is a function of the limitation of resources rather than an increase in the general price level. The finiteness of resources and the law of diminishing returns lead to increases in resource prices (costs) which are reflected on the vertical axis.

Equilibrium in the complete model exists at the intersection of the aggregate demand and aggregate supply curves. Equilibrium implies a unique combination of a national output and a general price level at which all of the markets under consideration are clearing. This macroequilibrium includes a money market that has equilibrium interest rate, demand for money, and supply of money; as well as a goods market in which national income is in equilibrium. Equilibrium may occur at either full or less-than-full employment.

Changes in the price level are both a result of other macroeconomic forces, such as changes in costs of production and a cause of other macroeconomic changes, such as the interest rate. The simplest way to observe the changes of price is to consider the impact upon aggregate demand; because there is a direct relationship between changes in aggregate demand and the price level. If aggregate demand shifts outward (to the right), ceteris paribus, the general price level will increase. If aggregate demand shifts inward (to the left), ceteris paribus, the general price level will decrease.

In evaluating the effects of various fiscal policies, it is important to first observe the relative level of employment or resource utilization in the macroeconomy. If the economy is at or near the full employment level for all resources, then the aggregate supply curve will be steep; thus any increase in aggregate demand will be absorbed in increased prices rather than in increased output. However an economy which had a significant level of unemployed resources, thus having an aggregate supply curve that was relatively flat, would find that increases in aggregate demand would lead to increases in output.

The effect of monetary policy is less predictable because the Federal Reserve Board may choose to exercise policy as a positive force; for example, what we have previously looked upon as contractionary and expansionary policy options or may choose to react to either support or counteract the actions taken by fiscal policy agents. If the Fed generally supported the macroeconomic goals of the administration, then an expansionary fiscal policy that lead to an increase in the demand for money would be accommodated by a Fed that would make money available; the result being a reduction in the upward pressure on interest rates. A Fed that opposed expansion could tighten the money supply, driving up interest rates and prices in the process.

GLOSSARY

AGGREGATE DEMAND CURVE: A curve showing the relationship between the level of output in the economy and the price level.

AGGREGATE OUTPUT: The total quantity of real goods and services produced (or supplied) by all factors of production during a given period.

AGGREGATE OUTPUT (INCOME): The combined term used to remind you of the exact equality between aggregate output and aggregate income.

INFLATION: A general increase in the price level.

STUDY TIPS

1. Learn to think in terms of the macroeconomic usage of "price." Price refers, unless otherwise specified either specifically or in context, to the general price level. Although, the concept is not economically correct, it is easy to think of this "price" as if it were the average price of all goods and services in the economy.

2. As in previous (and future) chapters before you consider the effects of a policy, make sure that you know the general economic conditions: either full employment or not.

3. The most difficult part of this chapter is accomplishing the task of thinking about all of the macroeconomic markets that now fit into this one model. Keep in mind that none of the macroeconomic variable exist in isolation; consumer expenditures impact aggregate demand, money markets, and the general price level at the same time they are a function of the general price level. The safest avenue for a serious student of macroeconomics is to carefully learn the determinants of each of the major variables.

A LOOK AHEAD

This model will be used in subsequent chapters in looking at the different ways in which major macroeconomic problems are dealt with in the real world. Topics from this chapter help explain the similarities and differences among the various schools of economic thought which will be examined later.

The study of the international economic relationships of the macroeconomy undertaken in chapters 37 and 38 demand a thorough understanding of the closed model presented here.

MULTIPLE-CHOICE QUESTIONS

1. The shape of the aggregate supply curve gets
   a. steeper when the economy is in a recession.
   b. flatter when the economy is at full capacity.
   c. smoother over time.
   d. steeper as the economy nears full capacity.

2. In the aggregate supply and demand model, macroeconomic equilibrium occurs when
   a. supply equals demand in all markets.
   b. when money markets and labor markets clear.
   c. only at full employment.
   d. aggregate supply equals aggregate demand.

3. When aggregate demand shifts in the aggregate supply and demand model
   a. there will be some unemployment.
   b. there are changes in both the goods and money markets.
   c. aggregate supply will immediately adjust.
   d. there is a respondent change in the quantity supplied in each market.

4. In the aggregate supply and demand model, cost shifts are
   a. only possible in the goods market since the interest rate is a price rather than a cost.
   b. both contractionary and inflationary, ceteris paribus.
   c. temporary in nature, ceteris paribus.
   d. due primarily to union wage-setting activity.

5. One policy that would combat inflation by shifting aggregate demand to the _____ is
   a. left, increasing taxes.
   b. right, increasing government spending.
   c. left, decreasing interest rates.
   d. right, decreasing government spending.

6. One advantage, although it is rarely used as such, of using government spending as a tool of policy is that
   a. the debate in congress about fiscal policy is conducted in public.
   b. government spending benefits all of the citizenry.
   c. its effect is direct and the initial impact is clear.
   d. changes in government spending are not inflationary.

7. Because taxes _____ due to an expansion of government spending, we conclude that the deficit
   a. increase, increases less than the government spending change.
   b. increase, decreases.
   c. are not changed, increase but at its old rate.
   d. decrease, increases more than the government spending change.

8. The magnitude of the effect of an expansionary fiscal policy is
   a. greater when the Federal Reserve Board is following an accommodative strategy.
   b. the same under all assumptions.
   c. a function of the economic theory accepted by the political party in power.
   d. always less than expected.

9. Interest rates
   a. rise during expansions.
   b. fall during monetary expansions.
   c. are unchanged during monetary expansions.
   d. follow a cycle of their own.

ANALYTIC EXERCISES

1. Assuming that the Fed is accommodative and that congress is following a contractionary fiscal policy, identify the change that you would predict in each of the following variables:
   a. national income
   b. interest rates.
   c. general prices.
   d. employment.

2. Assuming that the Fed is not accomodative and that congress is following an expansionary fiscal policy, identify the change that you would predict in each of the following variables:
   a. gross national product
   b. nominal money supply.
   c. general prices.
   d. unemployment.
   e. the demand for labor.

ESSAY QUESTIONS

1. What are the forces that drive the aggregate supply and demand model toward equilibrium?
2. Why does the interest rate change in different directions when fiscal policy rather than monetary policy is employed?
3. How does the impact of expansionary policy change as an economy reaches full employment? Why?

ANSWERS

Multiple-Choice

1) d,   2) d,   3) b,   4) b,   5) a,
6) c,   7) a,   8) a,   9) b.

Analytic Exercises

1) a. decrease
   b. decrease
   c. no change
   d. decrease
   e. decrease
2) a. increase
   b. no change
   c. increase
   d. decrease
   e. increase

Unemployment and Inflation

33

LEARNING OBJECTIVES

After you have studied this chapter in the textbook, attended class lectures over this material, and completed this study guide chapter you should be able to answer the following questions.

1. What are the factors that make it difficult for macroeconomic theory to explain the causes of unemployment?
2. Why are wages less responsive to external pressure to change than other prices?
3. What is the role of expectations in determining the inflation rate?
4. What is the monetarist explanation of inflation?
5. Explain the Phillips curve? Is it still applicable?
6. What is stagflation? Why does it occur?

CHAPTER REVIEW

Unemployment and inflation have been characterized in previous chapters as the polar extremes of the business cycle. Inflation, or generally rising prices, is a symptom of a boom. Unemployment is a symptom of a trough, recession, in the business cycle. Previously the discussion has been centered around the types of each of these phenomenona; in this chapter we try to place them in the context of their root causes, macroeconomic significance, and relation to each other.

Unemployment is simply another way of looking at resource utilization in labor markets. Previous chapters have discussed the measurement of various types of unemployment. The particular type of unemployment with which we are most concerned here is cyclical unemployment; that unemployment that is a function of aggregate macroeconomic activity. Cyclical unemployment decreases (increases) as the macroeconomy grows (shrinks). We have also seen previously, both in macroeconomics and microeconomics, that wages theoretically are determined on the basis of the marginal revenue product; however, the existence of some unemployment under conditions of prosperity suggests that the level of employment may not be completely responsive to macroeconomic conditions.

The classical school of economic thought held to a theory that said that workers would willingly accept wage changes both upward and downward. During times of prosperity, as there was upward price pressure, workers would accept wage increases, and during times of recession, when cyclical unemployment set in, workers would willingly accept, and even bid down, wage cuts in order to keep working. However, we find in a complex economy that workers are less willing to accept lower wages, sometimes apparently preferring unemployment. The institutional force of the minimum wage also works as an absolute barrier to falling wages. The presence of labor unions and the power of large firms in the absence of unions, each operate in their respective markets to create a stickiness to wage changes. The role of expectations cannot be ignored in causing wage rigidity; both workers and employers must make an expectation calculation in the formulation of future wages.

Inflation, as we have previously defined it, is a general rise in prices. The measurement of inflation is done in terms of prices. In microeconomics, we learned that firms have three choices when confronted with increased demand for their products: raise prices, increase output, or both raise prices and increase output. You will note that two of these possible responses involve increasing prices; if all firms followed one of these strategies, then inflation would be observed in the macroeconomy. In looking at the increase in demand brought about by an increase in aggregate macroeconomic activity; the primary question becomes, as it was in the previous chapter, at what level is unemployment? If the economy is at or near full employment, then increased demand will have a greater impact upon price than upon output; an economy with a relatively large level of unemployment will observe a larger relative change in output than in price.

Inflation is particularly susceptible to events that may occur outside of the domestic economy. The general measures of inflation, the Consumer Price Index and the GNP Price Deflator, both measures prices without regard to country of manufacture; therefore, an increase in price in another country that is reflected in a domestic price of an imported good, could lead to the observance of inflation here. A second impact that import prices may have on inflation is in the importation of raw materials and other non-final goods. An increase in the price of imported intermediate goods that lead to an increase in domestic costs of production and then domestic prices would contribute to inflation.

The role of expectations is again critical. The expectation of inflation tends to become a self-fulfilling prophecy. Lenders who expect inflation will build that expectation into the interest rate and retailers who expect inflation will increase prices now in an attempt to gain enough to soften the burden of inventory restocking.

Stagflation is a particularly vexing macroeconomic problem. Stagflation is a compound name combining stagnant and inflation, meaning a period of inflation when there is little or no growth and continued unemployment. The existence of stagflation implies that a long held tenet, the trade-off of unemployment and inflation may not be absolute. The Phillips Curve charts the relationship between unemployment and inflation. For most mature economies through most of their histories, a clear trade-off has existed. However, the U.S. economy experienced stagflation during the 1970's. Some explanations for this phenomenon include an increase in the full-employment level or vice-versa, an increase in the permanent unemployment rate; concommitant increases in aggregate demand and decreases in aggregate supply, usually as a result of supply shocks; or an increase in the ability of individuals to anticipate increases in aggregate demand and accepting the entire increase in the form of increased prices rather than increasing output.

GLOSSARY

CYCLICAL UNEMPLOYMENT: The increase in unemployment that occurs during recessions and depressions.

INTERMEDIATE GOODS: Those products that are produced by one firm for use in further processing by another firm.

PHILLIPS CURVE: A graph with either the rate of wage inflation or the rate of price inflation on the vertical axis and some measure of demand pressure, such as the unemployment rate, on the horizontal axis. The curve implies a trade-off between inflation and unemployment, a trade-off which broke down in the 1970s and 1980s.

RECESSION: Formally, a period in which real GNP declines for at least two consecutive quarters. Marked by falling output and rising unemployment.

STAGFLATION: The persistence of high unemployment (stagnation) at the same time that the price level is rising rapidly.

STICKY WAGES: The downward rigidity of wages as an explanation of unemployment.

STUDY TIPS

1. Do not accept the assumption that this chapter is just a replay or synthesis of previous chapters and parts of chapters where unemployment and inflation were topics. Each new study of these vital macroeconomic problems is taken in new light and stands independently.

2. It is very easy to fall into the trap in macroeconomics of viewing unemployment and inflation as opposite phenomenon. Learn in this chapter that they are generally thought of as symptoms of opposite sides of the business cycle but in and of themselves they are separate problems with different causes and policy solutions.

3. Stagflation is a good example of being prepared to follow the advice in 2 (above). Stagflation is a particular case in which an economy does not inflate its way out of unemployment, and as such, is not really a third example of a bad thing that can happen in the macroeconomy.

A LOOK AHEAD

This chapter has focused and summarized the major problems confronting macroeconomists. However, the problems of unemployment and inflation continue to be an integral part of this study. In the chapters on the role of the international sector in the macroeconomy we see the implications of price of foreign goods in influencing the domestic inflation. Imports and exports also have widespread employment effects. A major justification for import quotas is to protect domestic levels of employment.

MULTIPLE-CHOICE QUESTIONS

1. Under the classical assumption, it is always true that there will be full employment, no involuntary unemployment, because
   a. workers will always bid wages downward.
   b. wages are sticky.
   c. bargaining power is in the hands of owners.
   d. there was no unemployment insurance system then.

2. The existence of sticky wages suggests that
   a. workers have most of the bargaining power.
   b. there will be some unemployment as workers and firms are unwilling to accept wage cuts.
   c. wages are constant over the business cycle.
   d. workers are no better off than they were in the past.

3. The nominal wage is
   a. the lowest wage at which it is legal to either hire a worker or work.
   b. an expression showing the purchasing power of income.
   c. the wage actually paid to the worker.
   d. is the wage earned by the average worker in the economy.

4. The expectation errors explanation of unemployment suggests that
   a. workers regularly change jobs (frictional unemployment) with the reasonable expectation of getting a better one.
   b. there are times firms may set wages too high.
   c. workers quit work to avoid the humiliation of being fired.
   d. workers make employment decisions based upon nominal rather than real wages.

5. As individual firms produce closer to full capacity they are _____ likely to contribute to inflation as
   a. more, demand for products increases.
   b. more, output decreases.
   c. less, costs of capital increase.
   d. not, there is no need for them to raise prices.

6. Import prices may contribute to inflation because
   a. the competition from imports drives domestic prices up.
   b. of consumer ignorance.
   c. increased demand for imports puts American workers out of work, causing unemployment.
   d. they are included in the Consumer Price Index.

7. Stagflation
   a. exists only in theory.
   b. is a period of time of generally rising prices with little or no change in employment.
   c. only occurs at full employment.
   d. is a seasonal phenomenon that occurs prior to Christmas.

8. The Phillips curve shows one possible relationship between
   a. the Old and New Testaments.
   b. prices and interest rates.
   c. inflation and unemployment.
   d. prices and wages.

9. A major weakness of the Phillips curve is that
   a. there are many more factors than unemployment that affect inflation.
   b. it has never been observed in the real world.
   c. it only explains the economy in the 1980's.
   d. prices and interest rates are measured in different units.

ANALYTIC EXERCISE

1. Analyze the conditions that might have to exist in the U.S. economy for the Phillips curve relationship to be restored, or be as it was prior to the 1970's.

ESSAY QUESTIONS

1. Why is there unemployment in the economy?
2. What is the difference between nominal and real wages? Is it important?
3. What is the role of imports in determining the level of inflation?
4. Is there always an identifiable relationship between inflation and unemployment? Why or why not?

ANSWERS

Multiple-Choice

1) a,	2) b,	3) c,	4) b,	5) a,
6) d,	7) b,	8) c,	9) a.	

Analytic Exercise

1) answers will vary.

34

Analysis of Other Macroeconomic Issues

LEARNING OBJECTIVE

After you have studied this chapter in the textbook, attended class lectures over this material, and completed this study guide chapter you should be able to answer the following questions.

1. What is the relationship of the stock market to the macroeconomy?
2. How does the multiplier change through the different phases of the business cycle?
3. What is the federal deficit? How might it be controlled?
4. Compare and contrast the lags in monetary and fiscal policy.

CHAPTER REVIEW

The common stock market exists primarily as a source of capital for corporate America. The transaction of purchasing a new issue of common stock represents the purchase of a part ownership in the corporation, if there are distributed profits those profits are in the form of per share dividends. Stock exchanges give order and location to the buying and selling of common stocks among individuals and institutions. Sudden changes in the value of common stocks may effect individuals' willingness to provide capital through these markets.

The issues traded on the exchanges have already generated the capital flow toward the firm and are just forms of ownership. The total volume of dollar transactions represent a sizeable amount of the stock of wealth of this economy. In general, as the price level of common stocks increases (decreases), wealth is generated (destroyed). Another important impact of the stock market upon the macroeconomy is the relationship between the stock of wealth and the level of consumption. In general, the loss (gain) of wealth decreases (increases) the level of consumption.

A third possible impact of the stock market is on the general level of expectations in the macroeconomy. A decline (rise) in the price level of common stocks could have the effect of producing negative (positive) expectations. There is little evidence to suggest that the most recent stock market crash (October, 1987) has had a lasting effect upon expectations.

Theoretical macroeconomics in its simplest form provides a value for the multiplier that is arithmetically easy to determine. However, the actual multiplier that is observed in the contemporary U.S. economy is much smaller than the ten that would be determined if the savings rate were actually ten percent. The reaction and role of the interest rate works to limit the size of the multiplier, as does the reaction of prices and the effect of prices upon consumer spending patterns. The multiplier will also be smaller if there is slack in the economy; output can be expanded without the use of new capital and employment. The actual multiplier, as it is observed may be as low as 1.5.

In analyzing the relationships among macroeconomic variables, one must be mindful of the complexity of the macroeconomy itself. Although the specific tradeoff value in terms of the relationship between output and unemployment cannot be found, there is a great deal of evidence to support the generalization that increases in output are accompanied by increases in employment. However, on a percentage basis, increases in output are larger than the increases in employment. The relative level of macroeconomic activity at any one time has a lot to do with the strength of this relationship. If the economy is at relatively full-employment, then an increase in output will be more closely matched by an increase in employment than at a time when there was considerable slack in the macroeconomy.

The national debt, or the accumulated deficits over time, provides a drag on the level of macroeconomic activity. The issue of the deficit has long been both a political and economic concern. A political solution to the problem comes to the economy in the form of the Gramm-Rudman-Hollings Bill. This law sets a legal maximum for any additions, not the absolute size, to the deficit, with the goal being deficit reduction. In evaluating deficit reduction programs, the impact of a cut in government must be estimated both for any reduction that would occur in aggregate demand and the effect on GNP after the full effect of the appropriate multiplier has been felt. The Federal Reserve Board, and its view of the effect of the deficit will influence its willingness to either support the deficit reduction program or compensate for it.

It is difficult to determine in the analysis of macroeconomic policy how long it takes for the effect of a policy to be completed. There are three lags that are extant in both monetary and fiscal policy. The first of these is the recognition lag: the length of time that it takes for decision-makers to recognize that a macroeconomic problem exists. The second lag is the implementation lag: the length of time during which decision-makers formulate a policy to combat the perceived problem. The third lag is the response lag: the length of time it takes a policy to work, or show that it will not work.

In general, the recognition lag for monetary policy is much shorter than that for fiscal policy. The reason is that monetary policy is forged by only a few individuals, each having training, expertise, and experience in monetary policy; unlike Congress, which has 435 House members and 100 Senators, representing a wide variety of backgrounds and constituencies. The implementation lag is also shorter for monetary policy than for fiscal policy. The Federal Reserve Board is not subject to the political pressures that prey upon Congress and has a few simple tools of monetary policy that can be applied quickly and in relatively small increments. Response lags for each policy are difficult to determine because ultimately each policy has the goal of changing a variable as large as the GNP. Most economists agree that the full effects of monetary policy taken as a package may have a slightly longer response lag than do fiscal policies.

GLOSSARY

CAPITAL: Anything that is produced by the economic system which is used subsequently as an input in the production of future goods and services.

CAPITAL MARKETS: The input, or resource, markets in which households supply their savings, for interest or for claims to future profits, to firms who demand funds in order to invest in capital.

IMPLEMENTATION LAG: The time that it takes to put the desired policy into effect once economists and policy makers recognize that the economy is in a slump or a boom.

MULTIPLIER: The multiple by which the equilibrium level of output increases or decreases when some variable, such as planned investment, changes.

RECOGNITION LAG: The time it takes for policy makers to recognize the existence of a boom or slump.

RESPONSE LAG: The time that it takes for the economy to adjust to the new conditions after a new policy is implemented; the lags that occur because of the operation of the economy itself.

STUDY TIPS

1. In this chapter it is very easy to fall back into the blur of using the world's language rather than economic language. Remember that here we are discussing the economic role of the stock market both as a generator of capital and a bellweather of general economic activity. The economists use of the word "investment" is still reserved for expenditures on capital and does not refer to the personal "investment" in the stock market.

2. The discussions of the multiplier included here are designed to show you the way theory becomes applied. The concept of the multiplier first introduced in chapter 23 is still valid because it shows the flow of changes in variables into and out of the economy.

3. Always know what the macroeconomic conditions are at the time of consideration of a particular problem. Again in this chapter, we encounter the ongoing problem that responsiveness depends upon the current level of employment and general economic activity. The relationship between increases in output and employment are different depending upon the state of the economy.

4. Do not be confused by the treatment of the deficit in the Gramm-Rudman-Hollings Bill. The limitation is on the incremental additions to the deficit rather than the absolute size of the national debt.

5. The significant differences in terms of the policy lags between fiscal and monetary policy are in recognition and implementation. The response lags are most closely similar because in both cases the goal becomes more general ultimately leading to an altered GNP, for example.

A LOOK AHEAD

There are two significant economic concepts from Chapter 34 that are important to consideration of the topics remaining. The first of these is the idea that the multiplier effect and specifically the arithmetically derived multiplier is subject to change given the economic environment in which a policy is invoked. The multiplier effect is present but the size of the multiplier at any one time is difficult to predict.

The second important note that will be used in the future is the lags involved in policy decisions. Awareness of the lags may alter the choice of policy instruments.

MULTIPLE-CHOICE QUESTIONS

1. Common stock holdings are
   a. a part of the stock of wealth of households.
   b. regulated by the Federal Reserve.
   c. guaranteed by the Securities and Exchange Commission.
   d. not related to the macroeconomy because they are basically microeconomic decisions and transactions.

2. The value of common stock holdings is important in the study of macroeconomics because
   a. there is a relationship between stocks and international trade.
   b. the stock of wealth is a determinant of consumption spending.
   c. the federal deficit is financed in the stock market.
   d. the stock market represents the level of interest in the macroeconomy.

3. A stock market crash tends to
   a. cause firms to be more conservative in expansion plans.
   b. be followed by a boom in the market.
   c. be accompanied by widespread bank failures.
   d. follow a period of steady declines in the value of the market.

4. The existence of excess _____ and _____ will lessen the effect of the multiplier.
   a. money, inventory
   b. wages, capital
   c. labor, capital
   d. capacity, exports

5. Most economists estimate the actual multiplier to be no larger than
   a. 1.
   b. 2.
   c. 5.
   d. 7.

6. Because of the ability of firms to _____ the average number of hours worked per worker, employment _____ increase as rapidly as does output.
   a. increase, does
   b. decrease, does not
   c. increase, does not
   d. decrease, does

7. The Gramm-Rudman-Hollings Act is designed to
   a. control the size of the federal deficit.
   b. control inflation.
   c. increase tax receipts for the federal government.
   d. provide jobs in the inner city.

8. The implementation lag in policy is the length of time between _____ and _____.
   a. recognition of the problem, the ultimate resolution of the problem
   b. agreement on what the problem is, putting a policy into action that is designed to solve the problem
   c. a boom, recession
   d. the presentation of the federal budget, approval of the budget

9. Because the change occurs directly in aggregate demand, the _____ lag for fiscal policy is _____ than that for monetary policy.
   a. implementation, longer
   b. implementation, shorter
   c. response, longer
   d. response, shorter

ESSAY QUESTIONS

1. What is the role of the stock market in the macroeconomy?
2. What is the relationship between output and employment under the conditions of full employment? Less than full employment?

3. What is the primary intent of the Gramm-Rudman-Hollings Act?
4. Compare and contrast monetary and fiscal policy in terms of the recognition lag? Implementation lag? Response lag?

ANSWERS

Multiple-Choice

1) a,	2) b,	3) a,	4) c,	5) b,
6) c,	7) a,	8) b,	9) d.	

35

Debates in Macroeconomics and Supply-Side Economics

LEARNING OBJECTIVES

After you have studied this chapter in the textbook, attended class lectures over this material, and completed this study guide chapters you should be able to answer the following questions.

1. What does the tautology, MV = PY mean?
2. In the monetarist school of thought, what is the role of money in the macroeconomy?
3. What are the basic tenets of supply-side economics?

CHAPTER REVIEW

This chapter is concerned with the areas in macroeconomics about which there is ongoing debate and around which economists have rallied into separate schools of thought.

Monetarism is a school of thought that believes that money is a central determinant of the level of economic activity; the leading force in the macroeconomy. The central theoretical tenet of monetarism is found in the tautology sometimes referred to as the equation of exchange: MV = PY. In this tautology, M is the nominal money supply, most easily thought of as the sum of publicly-held cash and demand deposits or M1. The velocity of money, represented by the letter V, is the number of times that each dollar in M is spent in one year, or the number of times that each dollar goes through (around) the circular flow model. Velocity is a measurement of the frequency at which money is spent rather than the rapidity with which it is spent. The product of M and V then is the total amount of money spent in a year.

The gross national product could be loosely expressed as the real output of the economy, Y, times the general price level, P. PY then is the number of final goods and services produced and sold in an economy at the average price of a good or service. The tautology is simply that the dollar value (PY) of goods and services sold is exactly the same as the total amount of money spent (MV).

The initial debate over monetarism revolves around the constancy of the velocity of money. If velocity is constant, then algebraically, any change in the money supply, a function of Federal Reserve Board policy, would lead to an equal change in the product of output and price. The second question is how would a change in M be distributed across P and Y. If we assume that Y is constant, then any change in M will result in an equal percentage change in P; thus, by deduction, the Federal Reserve Board is capable of accomodating inflation. A Federal Reserve Board that was inflation averse could simply not allow the money supply to expand, thus holding down increases in the general price level; remember that the initial assumption is that velocity is constant. In reality, V is not constant, but it is very slow to change.

The reaction of P and Y to changes in the money supply are to some extent a function of the level of economic activity in the economy. An economy that is experiencing some unemployment is more likely to accept increases in the money supply, which would show up in the market place as increases in aggregate demand, in the form of increases in output. Whereas an economy operating closer to full employment will most likely translate an increase in the money supply into increased prices, and of course, at full employment we know that the economy will always shift to higher prices since output cannot expand.

An emerging school of thought, rational expectations, is built upon what is called the rational expectations hypothesis. The hypothesis states, as we have seen throughout the book, that expectations play a large role in decision making. The rational expectationists assign rationality to the formulation of individual expectations. Expectations are a product of past experience observed and reduced to average levels. So that economic plans are based upon what has happened in the past under similar conditions. Deviations from the expectations are surprises, which are factored into future decisions. An example of this phenomenon can be seen in the Lucas supply function, where output is a function of the difference between anticipated prices and actual prices. This phenomenon can also be seen in the money illusion discussions of earlier chapters.

The macroeconomic implications of rational expectations are such that if the participants in the economy are good predictors, then there will be a high level of stability. It is also possible that included in the rational expectations of individuals is a calculus of what the government might do in monetary and fiscal policy when the macroeconomy is less than stable. To the extent that individuals can predict policy decisions; they can also work to either profit from or circumvent policy. Under strict adherence to rational expectations the ability to perform policy operations and even the need for policy is questioned. Overall, there is no reason to doubt that individuals are rational, the issue may be the extent to which individuals are informed and have access to information.

Supply-side economics is based upon a redefinition of the way in which the macroeconomy and specifically, changes in the macroeconomy are viewed. Supply-siders believe that output and the willingness to change output determine the size of the macroeconomy. They first make the assumption that incentives must be provided to produce, contrary to the demand-side theory which suggests that incentives must be provided to increase aggregate demand. Incentives to produce would come in the form of tax cuts, increase in savings, and reductions in government regulation.

The tax cuts are based upon the Laffer Curve which theorizes that individuals will produce more, have a greater incentive to work, if they are allowed to keep a larger portion of their income. The tax cuts are not designed to directly stimulate demand as we found in Keynesian theory. In fact, it is believed that the increased income would be either saved or invested in order to provide for an increase in the capital stock of the economy, thus further enhancing the supply side of the macroeconomic equation.

The supply-siders see government regulation as adding additional costs to the production process. These costs provide no benefits to the producers and represent a disincentive to increase production.

GLOSSARY

LAFFER CURVE: The graph, named after Arthur Laffer, with the tax rate on the vertical axis and tax revenue on the horizontal axis, assumes that there is some tax rate beyond which the supply response is large enough to lead to a fall in tax revenue for further increases in the tax rate.

LUCAS SUPPLY FUNCTION: The supply function, originated by Robert Lucas, that embodies the idea that output (Y) depends on the difference between the actual price level and the expected price level, or the price surprise.

RATIONAL-EXPECTATIONS HYPOTHESIS: The hypothesis that people know the "true model" of the economy and that they use this model to form their expectations of the future.

VELOCITY OF MONEY: The number of times a dollar bill changes hands, on average, during the course of a year; the ratio of nominal GNP to the stock of money.

STUDY TIPS

1. The various schools of thought in economics, or for that matter, any discipline, typically differ only in their interpretation of the significance and cause of historically observed phenomenon. Because of this difference the study of schools of thought requires a high level of concentration to keep the interpretations separate. The monetarist explanation of inflation is a perfect example of the need to learn the particulars of one interpretation.

2. Supply-side theory is particularly difficult to master in the simplified form presented at the undergraduate level. The main problem that must be guarded against is the temptation on the part of the student to slip from the supply-side interpretation back to the more familiar demand-side theory of the Keynesian chapters preceeding. This problem is especially acute in the discussion of taxes; tax cuts work on the supply-side for supply-siders.

A LOOK AHEAD

The focus of this chapter has been on the frontier theoretical work within the economics profession. As we move into future chapters on growth and then international economics, we will find that these theories have not yet been fully integrated into these issues.

This chapter is very important in the continuum of the study of macroeconomics because the new approaches, interpretations, and explanations demand a high level of understanding of the present theories upon which most of the work in macroeconomics is based.

MULTIPLE-CHOICE QUESTIONS

1. The velocity of money is
   a. always one.
   b. the number of times a dollar bill changes hands during one year.
   c. equal to GNP divided by the number of goods and services traded in one year.
   d. constant in the real world.

2. If we make the assumption that _____ is constant or at least fairly stable over time, then the equation $MV = PY$ can be used to explain _____.
   a. money supply, inflation
   b. velocity, prices
   c. money supply, real GNP
   d. velocity, nominal GNP

3. The theoretical viewpoint that believes velocity is constant and that there is a direct relationship between the size of the money stock and the level of inflation and/or growth in the economy is
   a. the quantity theory of money.
   b. the classical school of thought.
   c. Okun's Law.
   d. aggregate supply and demand theory.

4. Under which of the following assumptions could we say that inflation is purely a monetary phenomenon?
   a. velocity is constant
   b. output is constant
   c. both output and velocity are constant
   d. the change in prices is greater than the change in output

5. The rational expectations theory assumes
   a. that full employment always exists because rational actors would always realize that they should accept wage changes.
   b. no unanticipated inflation.
   c. that all decision makers have a theoretical model of how the economy works.
   d. nothing.

6. Generally, people are said to have rational expectations if they
   a. are right in predicting the future.
   b. use all available information.
   c. consult other rational people.
   d. have inquiring minds.

7. Supply-siders identify the most significant problem in the macroeconomy as
   a. inflation.
   b. the abandonment of Say's Law.
   c. a general lack of control of aggregate output.
   d. high rates of taxation and regulation that destroy the incentives to produce.

8. According to supply-side theory the most important and probable result of a cut in personal taxes would be
   a. increased consumption spending.
   b. increased personal savings.
   c. increased number of hours worked.
   d. a revenue neutral fiscal policy.

9. The Laffer curve
   a. shows the relationship between tax rates and inflation.
   b. is currently in effect.
   c. shows the relationship between government revenue and tax rates.
   d. shows the relationship between productivity and aggregate demand.

ESSAY QUESTIONS

1. Critically evaluate the quantity theory of money.
2. Outline the basic tenets of monetarism.
3. What are the forces that fostered the acceptance of rational expectations?
4. Critically evaluate rational expectations as an explaining model of macroeconomic behavior.
5. Outline the basic tenets of supply-side theory.
6. Compare and contrast Keynesian and supply-side theories.

ANSWERS

Multiple-Choice

1) b,   2) d,   3) a,   4) c,   5) c,
6) b,   7) d,   8) c,   9) c.

Economic Growth 36

LEARNING OBJECTIVES

After you have studied this chapter in the textbook, attended class lectures over this material, and completed this study guide chapter, you should be able to answer the following questions.

1. Compare and contrast economic growth in primitive economies with growth in developed economies.
2. Outline the causes of growth.
3. Identify the major growth and non-growth periods in the U.S. economy. Has this economy completed growing?
4. What is the role of public policy in fostering growth? in hindering growth?

CHAPTER REVIEW

The best definition of growth is a period of sustained increase in real per capita gross national product. Real output per capita insures that any changes in real GNP will be measured against any changes that may have taken place in the population and would thus be tied to an increase in population. This is an important distinction because an economy with a growing population could have an increasing real GNP, but if GNP were growing at a lower rate than the population, we cannot conclude that there has been real growth.

The key ingredient in determining the capability for growth is the resource endowment of the economy and the individuals in the economy. There are two basic ways in which growth can take place: either the economy discovers new resources and sources of resources or the economy uses its endowments of resources more efficiently. Primitive societies typically achieve economic growth as capital is acquired and investments in human capital are made. Developed economies tend to rely more on adjustments in the way the existing resource base is used, through new technology and innovation, than in discovery of additional resources.

Specifically, there are six factors identified that cause economic growth. An increase in the supply of labor, through immigration, maturity of the population, increased health standards, and natural population growth leads to growth to the extent that the capital-labor substitution ratio can absorb more labor. Likewise an increase in physical capital will lead to growth. Physical capital increases may represent the ability of a society to move to more efficient capital, consider the quantum leaps that are seen in the agricultural output of relatively primitive economies as tractors and harvesters are introduced as substitutes for laborers.

Increases in the investment in human capital lead to growth. A better educated labor force will be more productive and more amenable to and capable of the acceptance of increased capitalization. Health standards, reflected in increased levels of infant mortality, increased length of life expectancy, and overall physical fitness of the labor force are all parts of the investment in human capital necessary for economic growth. The adaptation of technological changes allow the more effective use of both human and capital resources, thus promoting growth.

Recent years have seen the introduction of a number of new managerial techniques that have spurred growth. There have been advances in both the way to properly train, manage, and motivate workers, as well as scientific management methods that have reduced the burden of inventories and the logistics of the production process. Finally, as economies grow, both individual firms and the aggregate economy have available economies of scale; either in the form of absolute size or agglomeration of many industries engaged in the same or similar pursuits.

Public policies to stimulate growth are completely separate from those designed to influence the business cycle. By its very nature, growth is a long-term process; the goal being to cause a fundamental change in the economy. The growth process must work over the course of the business cycle with a goal to increase the absolute value of the bottom of the recession as well as the top of the boom. The major political difficulty with growth policies is divorcing them from a short-term evaluation. A policy to cause the economy to grow 15-20% may take a decade or more, and operate through times of inflation, high unemployment, and even stagflation, as we have seen in the recent economic history of the U.S.

Growth is not a universally accepted goal. Among the major arguments against growth is that growth does not necessarily imply an improvement in the quality of life. Growth may be accompanied by pollution and alienation and dehumanization of the worker. Big business may abuse the goal of growth by inducing demand for products or planning product obsolescence. A growth goal may speed up the depletion of the worlds resources. Finally, growth may simply serve as an income redistribution vehicle, widening the gap between the economic haves and have-nots.

GLOSSARY

ECONOMIC GROWTH: An increase in the total output of an economy. Often the term is used to refer to increases in output per capita.

HUMAN CAPITAL: A form of intangible capital that includes the skills and other knowledge that workers have or acquire through education and training and which yields valuable services to a firm over time.

STUDY TIPS

1. Economic growth is a topic that is built upon the cultural literacy that you have developed over the past several years. Before you began the study of this chapter you could have, with a small investment in deep thinking, made a good list of the forces that cause an economy to grow. Therefore, do not let the rather lofty discussion we present or the theoretical framework within which growth is discussed discourage you.

2. As you solidify and refine the determinants of growth watch for the pitfalls inherent in growth as a goal. The difficulty here is not being able to match the determinants with a problem. The problems presented as being associated with growth truly represent a different set of concerns altogether.

A LOOK AHEAD

The issue of growth is again addressed in chapter 39. In that chapter we will look specifically at growth for developing countries. The determinants of growth are basically the same, you will find that the differences are a function of the level of development that is extant in the developing economy.

MULTIPLE-CHOICE QUESTIONS

1. In terms of the aggregate production function, gross national product depends upon
   a. the stock of labor of an economy.
   b. savings rates in prior periods.
   c. both the capital stock and the labor stock.
   d. the rate of acceptance of immigrants.

2. In general, output increase when there are additions to the
   a. labor force.
   b. per capita income.
   c. stock of money.
   d. import purchases.

3. The law of diminishing returns suggests that increases in the _____, ceteris paribus, may not lead to increased _____.
   a. stock of capital, employment
   b. number of workers, output per capita
   c. number of workers, efficiency of capital
   d. stock of capital, money supply

4. Because _____ generally enhances the productivity of labor, an increase in _____ can increase _____.
   a. incentives, output, income
   b. competition, population, output
   c. training, capital, income
   d. capital, capital, output

5. Increased human capital result from all but which one of the following?
   a. education
   b. health
   c. age
   d. job training

6. The ability of technological change to affect productivity depends upon both
   a. the discovery and acceptance of new technology.
   b. the stock of capital and acceptance of new technology.
   c. the number of new patents and quality of the labor force.
   d. the willingness of the population to accept change and the overall level of macroeconomic activity.

7. A public policy designed to increase productivity could include
   a. a package of tax increases.
   b. increased Social Security funding.
   c. personal and corporate tax cuts.
   d. stricter immigration laws.

8. The amount of capital accumulation in an economy is ultimately constrained by
    a. the savings rate.
    b. interest rates.
    c. tax rates.
    d. disposable income.

9. Among the major anti-growth arguments are all but which one of the following?
    a. increased choices available to the economy
    b. reduced quality of life
    c. growth is not spread evenly across all income levels
    d. increased creation of artificial needs

10 Real growth is seen as an increase in _____ that is _____ than the increase in _____.
    a. income, greater, prices
    b. output, less, pollution
    c. output, greater, population
    d. income, greater, output

ANALYTIC EXERCISES

1. Prepare a set of public policies designed to increase the level of economic growth.
2. At what point in its development should an economy consider dropping economic growth as a goal?

ESSAY QUESTIONS

1. Describe the general process of economic growth. How is it measured?
2. What are the major determinants of growth?
3. Outline the public policies available to encourage economic growth.
4. Critically evaluate the common arguments in favor of economic growth; opposed to economic growth.

ANSWERS

Multiple-Choice

1) c,	2) a,	3) b,	4) d,	5) c,
6) a,	7) c,	8) a,	9) a,	10) c.

Analytic Exercises

Answers will vary.

37

International Trade and the Theory of Comparative Advantage

LEARNING OBJECTIVES

After you have studied this chapter in the textbook, attended class lectures over this material, and completed this study guide chapter, you should be able to answer the following questions.

1. What are the significant macroeconomic impacts of importing goods and services into an economy?
2. What are the significant macroeconomic impacts of exporting goods and services from an economy?
3. How is macroequilibrium determined in an open economy?
4. What is the theory of comparative advantage?

CHAPTER REVIEW

This chapter introduces the rest of the world into the study of the macroeconomy, thus making our consideration complete. In previous chapters as we have considered the variables that make up aggregate demand, consumption, investment, and government spending, we have simply assumed that these expenditures were made on goods and services produced in this economy. However, as we move into the real world with our model, we observe that sometimes when households make consumption expenditures they buy goods and even services that are the products of other economies. The purchase of a BMW creates jobs in West Germany, where the cars are made, to a much greater extent than jobs created at the dealership from which the purchase was made. Both payment for the car and the profits from the sale are removed from this economy to another. Businesses, as they make capital expenditures, may also buy imports, as does government. In all cases, as we have seen in earlier chapters, these import purchases represent leakages out of this economy.

Likewise, the sale of exports out of our economy into other economies represents the creation of jobs and profits here, even though the goods and services are consumed in other countries. This exporting and the subsequent return of profits and payments into this economy are injections into the simple circular flow model. In order to reconcile these two sides of import-export transactions, we use the concept of net exports, subtracting out those cases where we purchase goods and services produced in other economies from those cases where we sell goods and services in other economies.

Introducing a new set of variables into the model changes the conditions under which we would observe equilibrium and makes equilibrium more difficult to attain and sustain. An economy that participates in international trade is identified as an open economy, although we will see that openness is a relative term in international trade.

Trade surpluses occur when the value of exports exceeds the value of imports. Under conditions of surpluses there is usually very little political or economic pressure to make adjustments in trade policies. Trade deficits, in which the value of imports exceeds the value of exports, are more politically arousing. The standard response to prolonged trade deficits is protectionism. Protectionism takes the form of tariffs and other import restrictions such as embargoes and quotas, designed to allow domestic producers greater access to domestic markets and drive foreign producers out of domestic markets.

The principal argument to counter protectionism is couched in the theory of comparative advantage. Simplified, the theory of comparative advantage states that a producer, usually viewed as a producing country in these debates, has among the various products which it produces a wide array of opportunity costs of production. The comparative advantage in the production of any one good resides with the lowest opportunity cost producer in each product. The theory of comparative advantage was first proclaimed by David Ricardo.

Absolute advantage exists when a producer is superior at the production of all goods in question among trading partners. The existence of an absolute advantage does not negate the possibility of there being a comparative advantage producer for each commodity. The determination of comparative advantage is the value of what is given up, opportunity cost, rather than the absolute amount of what is produced.

The theory of comparative advantage explains why the second baseman, shortstop, and third baseman in baseball are almost always righthanded throwers. The most important and frequent throw made by an infielder is to first base; left-handed throwers take comparatively longer (have a higher opportunity cost) to turn and throw than do right-handed throwers, who simply throw across the body toward first.

In international trade situations, where trade is free, trade takes place according to the theory of comparative advantage. The trading price is a function of the strength of the trading partners but we always recognize that the price is bound by the option of either partner producing the product and paying the relatively higher opportunity cost.

A second feature of modern international transactions is the need to obtain the preferred currency of the country in which goods are produced. This currency problem leads to international trade being conducted in what turns out to be a two-tiered market. The price that a U.S. resident is going to pay for a BMW is not just a function of the price of BMWs in West Germany and the market conditions for BMWs in the U.S., but is also a function of the relative values of the two currencies involved. The maker of BMWs will want payment in Deutschmarks, not dollars. Unlike the purchase of a Chrysler, whose price is quoted to you in dollars and you have dollars. The purchase price of the BMW will be quoted in dollars but at some point a conversion has to be made into the other currency.

Currency markets are simple microeconomic supply and demand markets where trade of currency takes place and relative values change daily. If the price of a countries currency goes up against the dollar it means that it takes more dollars to buy the currency of the other country and thus should take more dollars to buy the products of that country. The other side of this currency equation says that at the same time the products of the U.S. can now be purchased by foreigners for fewer units of their currency. A rising Deutschmark makes BMWs more expensive here and Chryslers less expensive there.

GLOSSARY

COMPARATIVE ADVANTAGE: The advantage in the production of a product enjoyed by one country over another when that product can be produced at lower cost than in the country in terms other than goods.

NET EXPORTS: The difference between exports (sales to foreigners of U. S.-produced goods and services) and imports (purchases of goods and services from abroad.) The figure can be positive or negative.

PROTECTION: The shielding of some sector of the economy from foreign competition through the use of tariffs or quotas.

TRADE DEFICIT: The situation when a country imports more than it exports.

TRADE SURPLUS: The situation when a country exports more than it imports.

STUDY TIPS

1. Be very careful in thinking about imports and exports that you learn the difference. Imports are products produced in other economies but consumed here. Exports are products produced here but consumed in other countries. Imports and exports are not opposite sides of the same equation but have separate determinants.
2. Learn the difference between the balance of trade, which is only goods and services, and the balance of payments, which includes all international transactions.
3. Simplify the theory of comparative advantage down to a question of opportunity costs. The person, firm, or country with the lowest opportunity cost of a product will hold a comparative advantage in that product. Then, expand the conclusions to the implications for international trade.
4. In making comparative advantage determinations it is easiest to disregard any knowledge that you have of absolute advantage. Only use the concept of absolute advantage if that is the concern of a particular question.

A LOOK AHEAD

Understanding of the principle of comparative advantage and the implications of interrupting or fostering free trade is absolutely essential to an understanding of the open economy presented in Chapter 38. Exchange rate markets are dependent upon the demand for goods produced in other countries as well as a desire to hold other currencies; exchange rate discussion assumes that comparative advantage is clearly understood.

In both chapters on growth (one past, one future), it is interesting and helpful to note that resource utilization is reduced to a question of comparative advantage. Investments in education to upgrade the human resource are attempts to reduce opportunity costs.

The balance of payments is a focus in Chapter 38.

MULTIPLE-CHOICE QUESTIONS

1. An open economy is one which
    a. has no secrets.
    b. has exports to and imports from the rest of the world.
    c. has no import quotas or tariffs.
    d. keeps public records.

2. Net exports are
   a. exports minus imports.
   b. always a positive number.
   c. imports minus exports.
   d. not included in GNP.

3. A big decrease in exports, ceteris paribus, would result in
   a. an increase in output.
   b. an increase in inventories.
   c. a decrease in imports.
   d. a decrease in taxes.

4. A trade surplus means that a country is
   a. a net debtor to the rest of the world.
   b. importing more than it is exporting.
   c. exporting more than it is importing.
   d. erecting trade barriers against the rest of the world.

5. A country that holds a comparative advantage in the production of one good
   a. must also have an absolute advantage in the production of that good.
   b. will never import that good.
   c. will be able to control the world price of that good.
   d. is the lowest opportunity cost producer of that good.

6. The major arguments in favor of free trade rely upon
   a. the relative strength of trading partners.
   b. the law of diminishing returns.
   c. comparative advantage.
   d. mutual interdependence.

7. In order to buy a foreign produced good
   a. comparative advantage calculations must be performed.
   b. you have to test drive it.
   c. one must show that a domestic good is unavailable.
   d. foreign currency must be obtained.

8. In a two-good, two-currency world, an increase in the exchange rate of currency A for currency B means that
   a. A's goods appear to be relatively less expensive to the citizens of B.
   b. B's goods appear to be relatively less expensive to the citizens of A.
   c. A has lost any comparative advantage that she might have had.
   d. any additional rise will result in a stoppage of trade between A and B.

9. A tariff is
   a. a tax on imports.
   b. a quota on imports.
   c. a tax on exports.
   d. a prohibition on international trade.

10. All but which one of the following are arguments in favor of protection?
    a. it saves jobs
    b. foreign competition is unfair because foreign labor works for lower wages
    c. it allows infant industries time to grow
    d. it increase the choices available to consumers

ANALYTIC EXERCISES

1. Suppose that the United States can produce three personal computers or 3,000 cases of wine with one unit of resource, while Italy can produce 1 personal computer or 5,000 cases of wine with one unit of resource.
    a. Identify the absolute and/or comparative advantages.
    b. Speculate as to how trade will take place and what the terms of trade will be.

2. Assume the following production data per unit of agricultural labor:

	bananas	nuts
Argentina	10	3
Brazil	5	4

    a. Identify the absolute and/or comparative advantages.
    b. Speculate as to how trade will take place and what the terms of trade will be.

ESSAY QUESTIONS

1. What is the role of imports and exports in the open economy?
2. Explain the law of comparative advantage.
3. Outline and critically evaluate the major arguments in favor of free trade. opposed.

ANSWERS

Multiple-Choice

1) b,	2) a,	3) b,	4) c,	5) d,
6) c,	7) d,	8) b,	9) a,	10) d.

Analytic Exercises

1) a. The United States has a comparative advantage in the production of computers, while Spain has a comparative advantage in the production of wine.
   b. Answers will vary.
2) a. Argentina has a comparative advantage in the production of bananas, while Brazil has a comparative advantage in the production of nuts.
   b. The price at which Brazil will purchase bananas is between 3/10 and 8/10 the price of nuts.

38

Open Economy Macroeconomics

LEARNING OBJECTIVES

After you have studied this chapter in the textbook, attended class lectures over this material, and completed this study guide chapter you should be able to answer the following questions.

1. What is included in the current account?
2. What is included in the capital account?
3. What is the role of exchange rates in the open economy?
4. What are the economic factors that determine exchange rates?

CHAPTER REVIEW

In Chapter 37 we opened up the macroeconomy to international trade and introduced the concept of the two-tiered market: one for goods and one for currency. In this chapter the discussion is expanded to a study of the role of foreign trade in the macroeconomy.

In microeconomic terms each import-export transaction is one in which one currency, a dollar, for example, is traded for another currency, a Japanese yen. When we consider the macroeconomic implications of these transactions it is just as easy and correct to simply consider all other currencies as a class identified as foreign exchange. The demand for foreign currencies then is simply a function of our demand for the goods and services whose prices are quoted in those currencies. The supply of foreign currency arises out of their purchasing goods and services from us that are priced in dollars. The account of international transactions is known as the balance of payments.

The balance of payments is kept in the standard accounting format of debits and credits. Any transaction that brings in foreign exchange is a credit, while any transaction that allows domestic currency to leave is a debit. The balance of payments is divided into two broad accounts: the current account and the capital account.

The current account measures the import-export flows of goods, services, and transfer payments. Exports of merchandise earn foreign exchange for this economy in addition to creating jobs domestically as was seen in Chapter 37. Imports of merchandise involve the loss (transfer offshore) of foreign exchange. This portion of the current account is most commonly referred to as the balance of trade. The export and import of services and the payment and receipt of transfer payments have the same respective effects in terms of foreign exchange. If the current account does not balance, then the economy is either a net debtor (if outflows of foreign exchange exceed inflows) or creditor (if inflows exceed outflows).

The current account being out of balance gives rise to the capital account. The capital account is divided into private sector capital flows and government sector capital flows. As domestic banks and other lenders provide capital to other countries and businesses, make investments in other economies, foreign exchange is lost. U.S. firms that borrow from foreign banks and institutions and foreign firms that invest here, cause the gain of foreign exchange. Likewise, the U.S. government, when it sells a portion of the national debt, in the form of Treasury bills, for example, to foreign citizens and institutions, attracts foreign exchange. Official U.S. government loans to other countries and agencies represent the outflow of foreign exchange.

The observation of the accounts still leaves the question of the actual determination of the value of the currencies that are traded unanswered. Since the early 1970's most of the economies of the world have left the determination of the value of their currency up to the free market. However, frequently governments and central banks intervene to help determine the value of the currency, usually intervention takes place in an effort to control the balance of trade rather than the balance of payments, per se. In all cases the determination of the value of particular currencies continues to follow the microeconomic rules of supply and demand without regard to the motivations of the participants in the exchange market.

In Chapter 37 we introduced the concept of net exports, in which an accounting is made for domestic production that is sold offshore and foreign production that is consumed here. The motivations for imports and exports are different. Imports tend to increase as national income increases. A part of this can be explained that since import purchases are a part of the household consumption expenditure and since consumption itself is a function of income, then it stands to reason that imports would increase. There is also evidence to support increased import consumption with increased income since there are a wider variety of consumption options available to a society with higher income. Exports, similarly, are a function of the importing (foreign) countries income; therefore, exports will assume a role determined outside the model, or exogenously.

The multiplier for an open economy must include recognition that any increase in national income, that might come from an expansionary policy, for example, would be partially distributed toward the purchase of imports. This effectively reduces the value of the multiplier by the portion of marginal income that would be diverted to import purchases. Because of the exogenous determination of export sales, there is no consideration of either exports or net exports in the open economy multiplier. This phenomenon leads to the conclusion that the multiplier for an open economy is smaller than that for a closed economy.

We have seen previously that governments may allow exchange rates to be flexible or may attempt to maintain a fixed exchange rate. If exchange rates are allowed to move freely, then currency prices will adjust in the same way that product prices do. Under flexible exchange rates, production for international trade is subject to the law of comparative advantage. If exchange rates are fixed then price adjustments that otherwise would have been distributed between the product price and the change in the exchange rate, must now be accounted for entirely in relative product prices among trading nations. Fixed exchange rates shift a portion of the adjustment process into domestic economies; whereas flexible exchange rates allow for adjustments among economies.

GLOSSARY

CAPITAL INFLOW: The situation when foreigners buy U.S. IOU's such as Treasury bills and give up some of their currency in exchange for dollars.

CAPITAL OUTFLOW: The situation when Americans buy IOU's of other countries and give up dollars in exchange for other currencies.

EXCHANGE RATE: The ratio at which two currencies are traded, one for the other.

FOREIGN EXCHANGE: All currencies other than the domestic currency of a given country.

STUDY TIPS

1. Foreign exchange transactions and the consideration of the impact of international trade on the foreign exchange holdings of an economy is most easily thought of as the inflow and outflow of dollars. Any transaction that results in the outflow of goods and services is a gain in foreign exchange while any transaction that results in the inflow of goods and services is a loss of foreign exchange.
2. In considering the macroeconomic impacts of international trade be mindful of the conditions of the economy. Not only should you be aware of the current state of the economy but you must also be prepared to ask and answer two other questions: is the economy open or closed? and are exchange rates free? The answers to these two questions determine the level of influence that international trade has on the domestic economy.

A LOOK AHEAD

The concept of the open economy is important in consideration of economic growth in developing countries as well as a distinguishing characteristic among different economic systems.

MULTIPLE-CHOICE QUESTIONS

1. Foreign exchange is
    a. a general term for international trade.
    b. the name given to the lump sum of all currencies other than the domestic currency.
    c. the result of foreign trade in goods and services.
    d. any transaction which takes place at a border.

2. The current account includes all but which one of the following?
    a. merchandise
    b. capital investment
    c. tourism
    d. shipping

3. The balance on current account shows
    a. the relationship between sales of export goods and services and purchases of import goods and services.
    b. up as a negative number.
    c. that the U.S. is always a net creditor nation.
    d. the direction and amount of gold flows between the nation and its trading partners.

4. If a nation is neither an international borrower nor lender, then
    a. it must not be an open economy.
    b. it has a balanced budget.
    c. its current account balance is zero.
    d. then it is using an international currency.

5. Imports are considered as an _____ variable in the model of an open economy because imports _____.

   a. exogenous, increase as other countries purchase our exports
   b. exogenous, are a function of comparative advantage which has more to do with an economy level of native endowments
   c. endogenous, are a function of domestic income
   d. endogenous, and exports are both included in the GNP

6. Exports are considered as an _____ variable in the model of an open economy because exports _____.

   a. endogenous, increase as other countries sell us imports
   b. endogenous, are a function of the relative value of currencies between trading partners
   c. exogenous, are determined by the wages and productivity of our workers
   d. exogenous, are a function of other nations' national incomes

7. The multiplier in an open economy is generally _____ than in a closed economy because _____.

   a. larger, there is a wider market available.
   b. smaller, some increase in income is spent on imports.
   c. larger, our exports become more attractive to the rest of the world.
   d. smaller, there is less need for fiscal policy.

8. The supply of dollars for foreign exchange _____ the same as _____.
   a. is, the demand for dollars for foreign exchange
   b. is not, the supply of dollars in the U.S.
   c. is, the supply of dollars in the U.S.
   d. is not, the product of the price of imports and the quantity of imports

9. Freely floating exchange rates
   a. reach equilibrium in the same way as any other microeconomic market.
   b. ignore the principle of comparative advantage.
   c. contribute to the international problem of nations being either debtors or creditors.
   d. are responsible for the law of two prices.

ANALYTIC EXERCISES

1. Complete the table below, the Qd is quantity demanded in Germany.

exchange rate	$ price	DM price	Qd	total $ expenditure
4DM = $1	5	_____	500	_____
3DM = $1	5	_____	1000	_____
2DM = $1	5	_____	1200	_____

2. Compute the balance of payments position for the economy shown below:

purchase of foreign securities from foreigners	50
imports of goods and services	80
exports of goods and services	100
sale of domestic securities to foreigners	40

ESSAY QUESTIONS

1. Explain the effect of opening an economy upon the multiplier.
2. Explain the major components of the current account, the capital account.
3. Under what conditions might an economy operate with a surplus in the current account but have a deficit in the capital account?
4. How are exchange rates determined?
5. "Since imports are just the exports coming into an economy rather than going out, they must have the same set of determinants." REACT.

ANSWERS

Multiple-Choice

1) b,	2) b,	3) a,	4) c,	5) c,
6) d,	7) b,	8) b,	9) a.	

Analytic Exercise

1)

DM price	total $ expenditure
20	2500
15	5000
10	6000

2) trade surplus of 10

39

Economic Growth in Developing Nations

LEARNING OBJECTIVES

After you have completed this chapter in the textbook, attended class lectures over this material, and completed this study guide chapter you should be able to answer the following questions.

1. Compare and contrast economic conditions in developed and developing countries.
2. What are the factors that determine economic growth in the Third World?
3. Outline three possible strategy options to enhance Third World economic growth.
4. What is the role of population growth in Third World development? of agriculture?

CHAPTER REVIEW

The nations of the world can be divided into two levels of development status: developed (industrialized) and developing. A developing nation is one in which there is a relatively low level of material well-being: the average amounts of food, clothing, shelter and other commodities the average person consumes. The best, albeit crude, measure of this level in developing countries is the per capita GNP. Developing countries usually have lower general health and education levels than do developing countries. In terms of the distribution of wealth, a high concentration of the population living in poverty and a very small portion of the population that is relatively wealthy is a complicating characteristic of developing nations.

A second classification system that is typically applied to the world's nations is based on both political and economic differences. In this scheme the mixed-capitalist, non-Communist countries are the "First World"; the communist bloc nations, regardless of level of economic development, are the "Second World"; all other nations are the "Third World". Separating out the communist economies does not eliminate the presence of economic planning from our consideration, as we shall see later.

Although there is not a well-developed theory of economic development, we can identify some general characteristics of developing nations, similar to what we did in Chapter 36. The common economic denominators among developing nations include insufficient capital formation, a shortage of human resources, a lack of social overhead capital, and economic dependency on developed nations.

The saving-investing identity model that has been developed in macroeconomics provides the explanatory link to the problem of insufficient capital. Capital formation depends upon the availability of a pool of savings. Developing countries typically have such a low level of per capita income that there is simply no saving in the economy; an economy that suffers in this way may be locked out of development according to the "vicious-circle-of-poverty" hypothesis. A second explanation may be that there are no domestic incentives for any wealthy individuals in the economy to invest; instability, lack of capital markets, and the desire for immediate gains may cause individuals to remove wealth from developing to developed economies.

As you will recall from earlier study, the production function consists of combinations of both labor and capital. Developing countries typically have an abundance of labor but a shortage of human capital. The stock of human capital is a function of education, skill acquisition, and health standard. The goal of investment in education and vocational training is to increase productivity. Another feature of the human capital shortage is in the form of a general lack of entrepreneurship in developing countries in developing countries: either due to a lack of individuals with entrepreneurial ability or the absence of sufficient rewards to the risk-taker.

Developing countries characteristically have a shortage of social overhead capital. Social overhead capital is the network of public goods: transportation, communication, and regulation systems that provide an environment productive businesses can profitably operate. The complicating factor in the provision of social welfare overhead capital is the status and strength of the government.

Dependence theory suggests that developed nations deal with developing nations in a way that makes the developing nations dependent. To the extent that developing countries are seen merely as markets for export sales, outside help for development will be retarded. There is no widespread agreement on the level of dependence by developing countries.

In addition to the obvious strategy of simply identifying the characteristics of developed economies outlined above and striving to attain development through upgrading; there are at least three major questions that any economy must answer as it seeks development.

The first development question is should the focus of the economy be industrial or agricultural? Because developed countries are industrialized, industrialization is usually the chosen answer. However, there are some pitfalls in an industrial goal; if industrialization is sought at the expense of agricultural production, the economy risks becoming a net importer of food. Secondly, an industrial strategy may be highly capital intensive and thus provide neither jobs nor the impetus for increased investment in human capital.

A second question is on which side of the export-import equation to attempt changes. The choice is either to promote the production of exports or reduce imports through import substitution. The export option requires an identification of consumer demand in other countries coupled with sufficient capital to provide a manufacturing base. The major risk in this strategy is the uncertainty of meeting trade barriers erected by developed nations.

The other option, import substitution, involves identifying those goods which the developing nation imports and creating policies to produce those goods domestically. The specific strategy may involve protective barriers or import quotas, driving the price of imports up to a price where the good can be produced profitably domestically; or direct subsidization of the domestic industry. The major risk of import substitution is one of economies of scale in manufacturing; the market may simply not be large enough to support an efficiently-sized domestic industry.

A third option is one of degree of reliance upon market forces: is there to be planning or is the marketplace to determine the direction of development? Recalling our classification system of First, Second, and Third Worlds, it would be easy to say that those Third World economies that desire development determine whether they want to be First or Second World, then simply follow the appropriate system. However, this question is not really that simple. Even an economy based upon the principles of economic freedom may opt for planning to guide early development in an effort to concentrate resources in those areas that show the greatest promise. Individual decision-makers may rely upon short-term motives and/or not have enough information to make microeconomic decisions in the long-run interest of development.

Population and population control introduce another problem into a developing economy. In many developing countries, children provide an economic function similar to resources: they are both laborers and the retirement system for their parents. Children also represent a drain on the economies resources in terms of demands on the food supply. Since growth is measured in per capital GNP, in order for growth to be seen, GNP must increase at a higher rate than does population.

GLOSSARY

IMPORT SUBSTITUTION: An industrial trade strategy that favors developing local industries that can manufacture goods that replace imports.

SOCIAL OVERHEAD CAPITAL: Basic infrastructure projects such as roads, power generation, and irrigation systems.

VICIOUS-CIRCLE-OF-POVERTY: The hypothesis that suggests that poverty is self-perpetuating since poor nations are unable to save and invest enough to accumulate the capital stock which would help them grow.

STUDY TIPS

1. The focus of this chapter is on the ways in which developing countries become developed and the problems that they encounter along the way. If you are a student that studies by lists, be careful in this chapter because there are really three separate topics covered. The considerations are characteristics, solutions, and problems--but the "list" for each is similar.
2. The popular press, and even some academic disciplines, have trouble separating political systems from economic systems. The use of First, Second, and Third World classes is basically political; do not allow yourself to make generalizations about the Third World countries political and economic systems. The appropriate Third World generalization should be confined to their economic characteristics.

A LOOK AHEAD

The next chapter draws a comparison between socialist and capitalist economic systems. The discussion relies heavily upon the concepts taught in this chapter.

MULTIPLE-CHOICE QUESTIONS

1. One of the best criteria for determining the differences between developed and developing countries is:
   a. to visit the countries.
   b. the per capita GNP.
   c. to compare income distribution patterns.
   d. close observance of the rate of inflation.

2. Which of the following are characteristics of developing countries?
   a. large populations and low savings rates.
   b. low levels of human capital and low per capita GNP.
   c. high infant mortality and high pollution indices.
   d. low health standards and high literacy rates.

3. A common cause for the scarcity of capital in developing economies is:
   a. too many entrepreneurs each trying to strike it rich rather than working together.
   b. the lack of a pool of savings.
   c. too large a population.
   d. not a well-enough developed banking system.

4. Social overhead capital:
   a. includes a strong public health system that is free to the poor.
   b. is a necessary ingredient to economic development.
   c. is the same as human capital.
   d. does not exist in democracies.

5. Attaining economic development through industrialization may cause an economy to:
   a. suffer through high rates of inflation.
   b. lose export sales.
   c. become a net importer of food.
   d. default on international development loans.

6. Import substitution occurs when a country:
   a. strives to produce goods that they had previously imported.
   b. no longer has enough foreign exchange to purchase imports.
   c. erects trade barriers.
   d. becomes developed.

7. Generally speaking, Third World countries are:
   a. traditional economies.
   b. communists.
   c. not industrialized.
   d. all alike.

ESSAY QUESTIONS

1. Compare and contrast First, Second, and Third Worlds.

2. What are the major common characteristics of developed economies? of developing economies?

3. What strategy options are available to developing countries?

ANSWERS

Multiple-Choice

1) b,   2) b,   3) b,   4) b,   5) c,
6) a,   7) c.

40

Alternative Economies

LEARNING OBJECTIVES

After you have completed this chapter in the textbook, attended class lectures over this material, and completed this study guide chapter you should be able to answer the following questions.

1. What are the basic differences between socialism and capitalism?
2. What are the basic differences between Marxian and neoclassical economic theories?
3. Critically evaluate the structure and performance of the economy of the Soviet Union; of The People's Republic of China; of Japan.

CHAPTER REVIEW

As we have seen throughout the first thirty-nine chapters of the book and especially in the last few chapters, economic systems confront the basic economic questions in different ways; seeking different goals. In this chapter we look at the theoretical dichotomy between the two major economic systems: capitalism and socialism. These systems are classified on the basis of capital resource ownership.

Socialism is an economic system in which ownership of capital and land lies with the government, presumably on behalf of the people. There are no pure socialist economies extant; both the Soviet Union and The People's Republic of China have some limited private ownership. Because the government is the owner, most socialist economies follow a planning model, usually in five-year periods. Planning allows for ordered resource allocation but may not be as responsive to individual tastes and preferences as a market allocation. Yugoslavia is an exception to the above generalization; although the state owns productive resources, production and allocation decisions are left to market forces.

Socialism is based upon the criticisms of capitalism written by Karl Marx in DAS KAPITAL. Marxism is as much an historical theory of the evolution of economic systems as it is an economic theory. Marx believed that capitalism is morally wrong because of its ongoing dependence upon the exploitation of workers. Profits are created by the capitalists as the difference between the value of what a worker produced and the value of the worker's wage. Contrary to microeconomic theory of the wage, Marx believed that workers' wages were equal to the cost of subsistence for the worker rather than tied to production or productivity.

In order to increase output, the capitalist would substitute capital, which could not be directly exploited, for labor. In this evolution, Marx saw the seeds of the ultimate collapse of capitalism. As capital was substituted, the capitalist's profits shrank and as workers became aware of their exploitation or were laid-off, they would resort to armed revolution, overthrowing the capitalist system and instituting a socialist system.

The Soviet Union has practiced extensive planning since 1928. Initially, the economy was pure socialism, with complete state ownership. However, over the years, especially since 1965, there has been increased private ownership extending primarily to agriculture. The real GNP in the Soviet Union increased consistently over the first fifty years of planning; more rapidly than that of the United States. However, the relative standard of living and level of ownership of consumer goods in the Soviet Union is still behind that of the United States. Currently, under the leadership of Mikhail Gorbachev, The Soviet Union is going through another set of economic reforms.

The People's Republic of China is a newer socialist state, having been established in 1949. Through 1976, The People's Republic practiced extensive planning with the goal of maintaining full employment rather than increasing GNP. Since 1976, this economy has also experienced an increase in private ownership. Not only does most of the agricultural community experience private ownership, but there is a well-developed wage system in manufacturing in rural areas. Agricultural output has increased to a point where China is an exporter of food, in spite of a population of over one billion people.

Capitalism is an economic system in which private households and firms own the means of production, which includes both capital and land. Most capitalist economies rely upon the free market system. The theoretical base of capitalism is neoclassical economics. Neoclassical theory provides four basic criteria by which capitalist economies are evaluated: efficiency, equity, growth, and stability.

Efficiency in a capitalist economy suggests that production is concentrated in those efforts that consumers want. Additionally, capitalists are profit seekers so that efficiency implies cost minimizing production techniques. In those cases where the market does not operate efficiently, pure capitalism is relaxed into the more common mixed capitalism that we see in most of the First World countries.

Because capitalism is based on the acquisition of profits, through risk taking, there is wide room for inequity in the incomes of the participants. It is generally accepted that equity is provided in capitalism to the extent that the opportunity to accept risk is available to all of the economy's participants.

In a pure capitalist economy, growth is a function of the degree to which producers respond to market forces, providing the impetus to growth. Growth is another criteria where mixed capitalism may outperform pure capitalism.

Capitalist economies have the potential for instability. The business cycles that we observe, both when governments are laissez-faire and when they are active, exists in the face of market decision making.

Japan represents an example of an economy that has followed an industrial policy approach to growth. Since rebuilding after World War II, the real GNP growth rate has averaged slightly less than ten per cent. Although the government has taken an active role in assisting development, the economy is market-oriented. In general, four major factors are identified that have contributed to Japanese growth: high rates of domestic saving, a high quality stock of human capital, rapid absorption of new technology, and a pro-growth government.

GLOSSARY

CAPITALISM: An economy in which private firms and households own the means of production, which include both capital and land.

SOCIALISM: An economy where ownership of capital and land lies with the government, presumably on behalf of the people.

STUDY TIPS

1. Continue to pay attention to the differences between political and economic systems.
2. Use the examples of the Soviet Union, China, and Japan for illustration and illumination of the basic concepts and fundamental differences between economic systems.

A LOOK AHEAD

Within the confines of this book there is nothing more to look toward. However, as we suggested to you in the first chapter, the world of economics is a world of the social scientist. As a student of economics, the world is just opening up to you. We challenge you to continue studying our discipline and to use the economic way of thinking that you have been taught.

MULTIPLE-CHOICE QUESTIONS

1. Which of the following terms refer to economic systems?
   a. Socialism and democracy.
   b. Democracy and communism.
   c. Capitalism and communism.
   d. Capitalism and socialism.

2. The easiest way to identify the type of economic system that is used in an economy is to observe:
   a. the standard of living of the people.
   b. the level of industrialization.
   c. who owns the capital resources.
   d. how income is distributed.

3. Karl Marx wrote:
   a. Doctor Zhivago.
   b. Das Kapital.
   c. The Wealth of Nations.
   d. How To Profit In The Coming Depression.

4. For Marx, the source of profit for the capitalist was:
   a. exploitation of labor.
   b. substitution of capital for labor.
   c. in good planning.
   d. in serving the needs of society.

5. The subsistence wage is equal to:
   a. the labor theory of value.
   b. the profits earned from production.
   c. the marginal product of labor.
   d. an income sufficient for the worker to provide the basic necessities.

6. The best indication that market economies do not guarantee stability is:
   a. that socialist economies do.
   b. to overlook the shortcomings of democracy.
   c. the continued existence of the business cycle.
   d. simply not true.

ESSAY QUESTIONS

1. Compare and contrast socialism and capitalism.

2. What are the basic economic tenets of Marxism?

3. How might capitalist economic systems be evaluated according to the neoclassical theory?

4. Compare and contrast the economic development of the Soviet Union, The People's Republic of China, and Japan.

ANSWERS

MULTIPLE-CHOICE

1) d,   2) c,   3) b,   4) a,   5) d,
6) c.

471-5899

ASK A NURSE